AN EXCERPT FROM ROBER
"TEN-MINUTE FILM SCHOOL"

So you want to be a filmmaker? First step to being a film-maker is stop saying you want to be a filmmaker. It took me forever to be able to tell anyone I was a filmmaker and keep a straight face until I was well on my way. But the truth was, I had been a filmmaker ever since the day I had closed my eyes and pictured myself making movies. The rest was inevitable. So you don't want to be a filmmaker, you *are* a filmmaker. Go make yourself a business card.

Next.

Now, what about all that technical knowledge you actually need to make a film? I think some famous filmmaker once said that all the technical stuff you need to know in order to make movies can be learned in a few weeks. He was being generous.

You can learn it in ten minutes.

With the following information you can embark on making your own cool movies, all by yourself, without a film crew (and trust me, there are extreme benefits of being able to walk into business and be completely self-sufficient. It scares people. Be scary). . . .

ROBERT RODRIGUEZ was raised in Texas and has ten siblings. Since *El Mariachi* he has written and directed a sequel to the film, *Desperado,* participated in the collaborative film *Four Rooms*, and directed *From Dusk Till Dawn*, based on a screenplay by Quentin Tarantino. He lives with his wife, Elizabeth, in Austin, Texas.

REBEL WITHOUT A CREW

Or How a 23-Year-Old
Filmmaker with $7,000
Became a Hollywood Player

ROBERT RODRIGUEZ

A PLUME BOOK

PLUME
Published by the Penguin Group
Penguin Books USA Inc., 375 Hudson Street, New York, New York 10014, U.S.A.
Penguin Books Ltd, 27 Wrights Lane, London W8 5TZ, England
Penguin Books Australia Ltd, Ringwood, Victoria, Australia
Penguin Books Canada Ltd, 10 Alcorn Avenue, Toronto, Ontario, Canada M4V 3B2
Penguin Books (N.Z.) Ltd, 182–190 Wairau Road, Auckland 10, New Zealand

Penguin Books Ltd, Registered Offices: Harmondsworth, Middlesex, England

Published by Plume, an imprint of Dutton Signet,
a division of Penguin Books USA Inc.
Previously published in a Dutton edition.

First Plume Printing, September, 1996
10 9 8 7 6 5 4 3 2

℗ REGISTERED TRADEMARK—MARCA REGISTRADA

The Library of Congress has catalogued the Dutton edition as follows:
Rodriguez, Robert (Robert Anthony)
    Rebel without a crew, or, How a 23-year-old filmmaker with $7,000
became a Hollywood player / Robert Rodriguez.
        p.   cm.
    ISBN 0-525-93794-3 (hc.)
    ISBN 0-452-27187-8 (pbk.)
    1. Rodriguez, Robert (Robert Anthony)—Diaries.
2. Motion picture producers and directors—United States—Diaries.
3. Mariachi (Motion picture)   I. Title.
PN1998.3.R633A3   1995
791.43'0233'092—dc20
[B]   95–23424
                                                           CIP

Printed in the United States of America
Original hardcover design by Stanley S. Drate/Folio Graphics Co., Inc.

BOOKS ARE AVAILABLE AT QUANTITY DISCOUNTS WHEN USED TO PROMOTE PRODUCTS
OR SERVICES. FOR INFORMATION PLEASE WRITE TO PREMIUM MARKETING DIVISION,
PENGUIN BOOKS USA INC., 375 HUDSON STREET, NEW YORK, NY 10014.

CONTENTS

INTRODUCTION

I associate my earliest memories with the movie theater. Being third oldest in a family that eventually grew to ten children, my mother would take us all to a San Antonio neighborhood revival house, The Olmos Theater, for our weekly dose of double and triple features of classic films.

My mother, who was always wary and suspicious of the current slew of movies out at that time, trusted our young eyes and minds only to the kind of cinema she grew up on. So our big screen diet consisted of heavy doses of MGM musicals, Marx Brothers comedies, and the occasional Hitchcock double bill. I still remember that strong dose double feature of *Rebecca* and *Spellbound*. My mother's name was Rebecca, so I figure that must be the reason why she took her young children to see such powerful imagery as the Salvador Dalí dream sequence and the kid falling onto the spikes in *Spellbound*, or the burning Manderley crashing down on the possessed Mrs. Danvers in *Rebecca*.

In fifth grade I remember sitting in the back of the class with a paperback dictionary in my hands and using the side margins, where there is no writing, to draw in little stick figures on each page, creating my own little flip cartoon movies. Since I wasn't paying attention to the teacher, I had the entire day to draw my movies, giving me the patience and attention to detail I could never have now. The elaborate cartoons featured invincible characters bouncing around and off the pages, battling evil, and blowing up everything in sight.

I wasn't very good in math, science, history . . . in anything really. But I would get approval from the other kids through my flip cartoon movies. I remember how good it felt when someone would see my paper movies and laugh. It was addictive. I drew all the time. In eighth grade a few of my friends and I, after seeing John Carpenter's *Escape from New York*, decided we wanted to start making our own real movies. Even if they were stop-motion. But we had no equipment. I'd read books about Ray Harryhausen and they said you needed at least a 16 millimeter camera with stop-motion capabilities to do animated movies or claymation movies. Clay animation is the best kind of movie to make when you're younger because you can shoot for hours and hours and your clay actors never complain, they don't ask for food, and they don't need stunt doubles. My father did have an old super 8 film camera but it couldn't do stop-motion. So I improvised. I'd tap the shutter and move my clay guy around, but the camera produced an annoying flashing effect. I needed the proper equipment.

I tried to shoot a regular movie with my friends using the super 8 camera but it was completely discouraging. We'd shoot a $5 roll of super 8 film that lasted 2½ minutes, wait several days for it to get developed, spend another $7 on developing, and then when I'd view it, I was always disappointed. The footage was too rough looking, the automatic exposure was usually off, the footage looked primitve, and it upset me. Waste of money. I did it only a half dozen times more before hanging it up. It seemed that making movies required too much money. Money I didn't have. Then a miracle arrived.

In 1979 my father, who makes his living selling cookware, fine china, crystal and all that kind of stuff, bought yet another one of the latest gadgets out on the electronic market (he'd buy anything he thought would help him with his sales). It was a four-head JVC video cassette recorder that he figured he could use to make sales presentations with. It was an expensive machine at the time, so the store where he bought it threw in a video camera for free. The camera was an old Quasar camera that connected to the VCR with a twelve-foot cable. It had no viewfinder and was completely manual, so I had to look at the TV set to see where I was pointing the camera. My father gave me the instructions to figure it out and before he knew it, I was using the machine to make my claymation movies and little action comedies with my brothers and sisters. The nice thing about being a budding filmmaker and growing up in a family of ten is the endless supply of cast and crew. The stop-motion movies didn't look very good because of the glitches every time you hit the pause button, but the live action movies came out great. The VCRs in those days had more extra features than the newer models today. This one had an audio dub feature which allowed me to erase the sound track and add a new one without erasing the picture. So I'd make short movies, edit in the camera, and lay music over it later. This new toy kept my interest for about a whole year. I shot everything. My newborn sister (the tenth), family gatherings, my own mini sci fi comedy kung fu action movies, anything I could think of that I could shoot within a twelve-foot radius (I was still limited by the attached cord). The nice thing about this machine was that whereas before I'd spend over ten bucks for a two-minute super 8 movie with no sound, now I was getting two hours of erasable color picture and sound for the same price. The video age had arrived. Things really took off when my father decided to buy another VCR, since I had taken over the first one. To his surprise (or maybe not) I took over that one as well. I had realized that with two VCRs hooked together I could edit by playing my movie on one VCR and recording on the other VCR, using the pause button on the recorder to edit out unwanted material. My editing system was born. From then on I shot my movies, edited them between the VCRs, and then laid sound effects and music over them. I did this from the age of thirteen to twenty-three. What I didn't realize was that by making movies in this homemade, extremely crude and time-consuming manner, I was actually training myself for my future filmmaking challenges.

When you edit between two VCRs, you are playing your raw footage on one VCR and recording on the other while pressing pause. The pause button made nice clean edits but if I stopped the VCR to check my work and then restarted the machine in the place I left off, it would make a huge glitch, ruining the flow of the film. So I had to edit the entire film without being able to check my edits until I finished the entire movie. And I had to do it all in one sitting because the VCR would only stay in the pause mode for five minutes before shutting off, meaning that I'd have to restart the machine and get the dreaded glitch. So I'd edit a shot then I'd have to find the next shot before the five minutes were up.

This taught me to shoot as little footage as possible and as few takes as possible, because the more raw footage I had, the longer it would take to find the take I wanted and the greater chance I had of the recorder turning off and giving me the dreaded glitch. Learning how to make films this way for ten years trained me to see the movie edited in my head beforehand, I *had* to see it edited beforehand. When I made a cut it had to be right because there was no going back. That kind of previsualization skill came in extremely useful on my later films. These are skills they could never teach you in any film school but that proved invaluable to me later.

I attended a private boarding school, actually a junior seminary, during my high school years. I practiced making my movies all through school and I found that the movies consistently got better the more of them I made. I'd pour all of my weekends and after-school hours into my movies and my cartoons. My short movies were getting so famous that my teachers would let me turn in term movies instead of term papers. No one complained because they knew I was pouring more work, time, dedication, and hours into my movies than if I were writing a hundred term papers. Besides, they were entertaining, they starred my schoolmates, and we'd screen them in class. I never learned to write very well but I did learn to visualize.

I met another young filmmaker there, named Carlos Gallardo, and he eventually was the star of many of my short movies. He was a boarding student from Mexico, and since I lived across the street from the school, he'd come over on weekends and help make short action comedies in the backyard. I kept all my movies under fifteen minutes because I wanted captive audiences and I found the faster and shorter I made my movies, the more people liked them. It would leave them wanting to see them again, which is the best compliment you can get on a home movie.

During summer vacations I would go to visit Carlos in Ciudad Acuña, Mexico, and we'd make an action comedy of some sort. The town was a beautiful, natural location, and the townspeople were used to seeing us running around with Carlos's video camera. So we'd get away with staging elaborate stunts in the middle of a busy street. After I'd shoot the movie, I would return home and edit between my two trusty VCRs, add music and sound effects, and then send Carlos a copy to air on the local television station. He would also lend the tape to the dance clubs who would play the movies on their video monitors.

I graduated from high school and miraculously got a scholarship to the University of Texas at Austin. My grades were never very good in school but I found myself making the honor roll and getting straight As by my junior year in high school. I attribute my sudden boost in scholastic achievement to the fact that I had finally become comfortable with myself through my movies and cartoons. I found so much validation from peers and faculty who all appreciated my hobbies that I became more positive. I had a better self-image and my grades went up.

Because of the scholarship I decided to attend UT–Austin. They had a film program there. I knew that my parents expected all of us to go to college and get our degrees. I figured the only degree I could possibly get would be a film degree since there wasn't anything else I'd work harder at. I thought it was a good plan.

Then trouble struck. You can't apply to the film department until you've first completed two years of all the math, science, history, and English classes. These were called "weed out" classes. Those are the kind of academics I'm worst at, the monkey drills designed to teach nothing except how to cram as much information into your short-term memory as possible. My grade point average at the university started out bad and got worse. By the time I finished my two years of weed out, I couldn't get into the Film Department because my GPA was too low. The film classes are so small (fewer than thirty seats) and so many people are trying to get into them (more than 200) that the school chooses their film students by their GPA. If you've got a high average, you've got a good chance. If you don't, forget it.

There were a lot of academic types who got into the film classes but made horrible movies. I was one of the many creative types with low GPAs stuck on the outside looking in.

While I was taking art classes trying to get my grades back up, I applied for a job as a cartoonist at *The Daily Texan*, our school newspaper. I got the job and started up "Los Hooligans," a daily comic strip based on my youngest sister Maricarmen. It became popular and it allowed me to exercise my creativity. Meanwhile, I had continued making my short video home movies and a couple of them—"David and his Sisters" and "Waterlogged"—both starring my own siblings, won a few video festivals. I also made "Austin Stories," a trilogy of short movies shot on video and again starring my siblings, and entered in the National Third Coast Film and Video Festival based in Austin. I won first place, beating out movies made in the UT–Austin Film Department. I took my award-winning video to Steve Mims, the film professor who taught Production I, and asked if he would admit me to his class since, in spite of my GPA, I beat his students and I hadn't even taken his class yet. He saw my movie and let me in the class.

Before school began, I knew this was my big chance to shoot on 16mm and make an award-winning film to get myself some recognition. The problem with my video movies, although they were good, was that most festivals at that time only accepted movies shot on film. I knew that in the school environment I would get free 16mm equipment and could make a great movie with very little money. I cast my movie with my younger siblings once again, storyboarded heavily, and I even shot a home video version first, cut it together, and showed it to the children so that we'd all have a better idea of what to do.

I shot my movie, pouring every idea and camera trick I could think of into it, and my eight-minute film "Bedhead" was born. It won several first places among the fourteen film festivals I sent it out to. The nice thing was that a lot of festivals were starting to allow videotapes into competition. I shot my movie on 16mm but I transferred the film to video and edited on video. I sent VHS copies to the festivals and the tapes were treated as films since they were shot on film. This provided me with an extremely low-cost way to make films and get recognition in film festivals without the huge cost of a final film print.

"Bedhead" cost me around $800 to make and it was eight minutes long. I had written the script around production values I already had available to me: my siblings, my parents' house, my sister's bike, and my brother's skateboard. All of these things are featured prominently in the movie, along with a lot of creativity and lightning-fast storytelling techniques I had learned through all those little home video movies I had made over the years. All that experience plus the experience I had gotten drawing my comic strip for three years helped me to make that movie what it is.

With the awards and recognition I was getting at festivals, I realized that it was time to venture into feature films, because if someone offered me a film project to direct, it would not be a short film, it would be a feature. So I decided what I needed was as much practice making features as I had gotten making short films. I realized it was the experience that had gotten me where I was. If you want to learn the guitar, you don't take a couple of guitar classes and expect to do anything innovative. You practice in your garage until your fingers bleed. I had done that with my home movies. I made over thirty short narrative movies, edited, with opening and closing credits, sound effects, and music.

I had realized when I got into the film class that a lot of the other students had never touched even a video camera, yet they wanted to be filmmakers. They spent almost $1,000 on films that didn't turn out as good as they expected, so they figured they weren't cut out for movies and would go into something else. I remember my first movies on video. I never would have wanted to spend $1,000 on those terrible experiments. Since it was video, it was no great expense; and since I loved to make movies, I just kept at it until I got better. So, if you're noodling around with a video camera, keep it up. Don't listen to film snobs who tell you that you're wasting your time, either. I started on video and used the less expensive format to learn storytelling, and later found the tiny jump to film was no big deal at all. It's all the same thing.

If you want to be a filmmaker and you can't afford film school, know that you don't really learn anything in film school anyway. They can never teach you how to tell a story.

You don't want to learn that from them anyway, or all you'll do is tell stories like everyone else. You learn to tell stories by telling stories. And you want to discover your own way of doing things.

In school they also don't teach you how to make a movie when you have no money and no crew. They teach you how to make a big movie with a big crew so that when you graduate you can go to Hollywood and get a job pulling cables on someone else's movie.

Or they teach you how to make contacts. They say that the only way into the business is by knowing people. It's not what you can do, it's who you know. That might get you through the door but it won't keep you there. When it comes down to it, sooner or later someone figures out you can't make them any money and you're out. Flavor of the Month. Adios.

So how do you get in? We're getting to that . . .

I was never big on writing scripts. I have read many times that the best way to learn to write scripts is to actually sit down and write two full scripts and after you're done you should throw them away. You'll learn a lot by doing those first two but they'll be awful, so after you write them you should throw them away and *then* start writing your real script. *What?!* Whoever thought of that game is whacked. In a way it makes sense. I mean, I think everyone has a few bad movies in them, the sooner you get them out the better off you are. I just know I could never bring myself to create two complete, time-consuming scripts only to throw them away afterwards. It is hard enough to try and find the motivation to write *anything*, much less something that you know you will throw out because it will be awful. I knew that in all honesty, I could never bring myself to actually write a script not knowing what was going to happen to it before I started. Will I sell it? Will I burn it? Will I write it over a three-year period and hope it makes me rich someday? In that kind of a situation, motivation is practically nonexistent. You need motivation in order to take on something like writing a script.

My motivation to write *El Mariachi* was very simple and it really opened my eyes. It suddenly hit me: Instead of writing two scripts and throwing them away afterwards, why not just take the scripts and make them for really low budgets? That way while you're practicing your writing skills you can also practice your filmmaking skills. That's what I decided to do with *El Mariachi*. I would write two scripts, both about the same character, but I would film them on a low, low budget all by myself. Then I would sell them to the Spanish video market where no one in the movie business would see them if they were no good, so it was almost like throwing them away, only I would get paid for them. That's a better motivator. Then I would write and film my third script. The third installment in the Mariachi series. I would sell that to the Spanish video market as well, but if it came out as good as I thought it would . . . Writing and directing three movies in a row like that would give me so much experience and confidence that I could use the best scenes from the trilogy or all of Part III as a demo tape and get financing for a *real* movie—say a *sex, lies, and videotape* or *Reservoir Dogs* times *ten*—and explode onto the American independent scene and pretend like I had never made anything before in my life. My brainstorm came so strongly it almost knocked me out. I remember thinking, why hasn't anyone else done this? Could it be that no one else has ever done this? Could it be that I may be on to something? Even if Part III is awful, if I can sell my movies to the Spanish video market and make a profit, I'll be in heaven. I love to make movies. But to make movies and make some money to live on so I could make movies full time would be the greatest thing in the world. I was excited beyond belief with the idea.

We've all heard of independent filmmakers that make one great film, are pushed into the limelight, then are so scrutinized on their second movie they are never heard from again. I think part of the reason is that their success came unexpectedly, before they ever got the chance to experiment and hone their style and talents. I was only twenty-three and in no hurry to rush into the film business ill-prepared, and I was already winning festivals with some short films. I realized that by making my first, second, and third feature film in complete obscurity, I could make mistakes quietly, experiment freely, hone my talents in every department because I would make this Mariachi Trilogy with no crew whatsoever. I was inventing my own film school where I would be the only student and where experiences, mistakes, problems, and solutions would be my teachers. And the best part was that even if my movies were no good, no one would ever see them and I'd still be able to get my money back.

Now *that* was motivation. I went on to write the first Mariachi in three weeks. It's amazing how quickly ideas come to you for a script when you know you're going to be actually making the movie in a few months, not just writing for writing's sake. How did I get the idea about the Spanish video market? I guess it all started for me in March of 1991. "Bedhead" was on the festival circuit and doing well. I got a call from Carlos Gallardo. He told me to come back to his hometown in Mexico.

"To make another movie?" I asked.

"No," he said, "to see a movie being made." He filled me in on the movie that was being shot in his own hometown. He was amazed because it was the biggest budget movie ever to be produced in Mexico. It was the film version of the bestselling Mexican novel, *Like Water for Chocolate*. And it was being shot in Ciudad Acuña, Carlos's hometown. Carlos said the director, Alfonso Arau, had chosen Carlos to help with the production since he was from the town and had some movie experience. I decided to come down and shoot some behind-the-scenes footage of what was to become one of the most popular Mexican movies of recent years. I wanted to see the lighting and the camera setups. I thought it would be an interesting and very productive spring break vacation. So I went.

AUTHOR'S NOTE

The following are excerpts from the journal I kept during the making of my first feature film *El Mariachi* in which I recount the heaping amounts of luck and good fortune that accompanied almost everything I attempted. It's also interesting to see the consequences of what originally started out as a quick money-making scheme and a chance to get a little practice making a feature-length movie.

The book has a natural and interesting trajectory. From the idea of *El Mariachi;* to the raising of the money and writing of the script, which in my case went hand in hand; to the shooting of the film; the video editing; the trip to Los Angeles to find a distributor; also how I got an agent at one of the biggest talent agencies in the world while I was in Los Angeles, and what you can expect to happen after you get a big agent like that; then what happened when I got calls from the studios to pitch my ideas for future projects; to the sale of *El Mariachi* to Columbia Pictures; the reediting of the movie to produce a final film print and 35mm blow-up; the festival circuit including Telluride, Toronto, and Sundance; up to the theatrical release of my home movie by a major Hollywood studio. Enjoy . . .

THE IDEA

Friday, March 8, 1991

I'm feeling sick. I tried to escape Austin without catching my wife Elizabeth's stomach virus. I didn't make it.

I drove to Ciudad Acuña, Mexico and arrived at Carlos Gallardo's empty house. HB, Carlos's pit bull, didn't even recognize me. He tried to jump the fence and kill me. I threw him a few leftover fried chicken bones I had scattered in my car, and that seemed to quiet him down. My pal.

Carlos's sister arrived and let me inside the house. I love this place. The whole house is dark and the air is always cool, the guest room is comfortable, and the refrigerator is always stocked. I slept. Carlos had arrived by the time I woke up. We talked until 1:30 A.M. He told me about *Like Water for Chocolate* and its director Alfonso Arau. He told me how complicated the shoot is. I've brought my video camera so that I can document the film while I'm here. It's my spring break. When I return to Austin I will begin a student short film, "Pretty Good Man" with fellow film students Tommy Nix and Edison Jackson. Carlos told me that I'll meet Alfonso Arau tomorrow.

Saturday, March 9, 1991

We woke up at 7:30 A.M. and drove to the Mirador, where the cast and crew were eating cafeteria-style breakfast. It smelled like menudo. Carlos introduced me to Emmanuel "El Chivo" Lubezki, the cinematographer, a real nice guy who looks like Kenny G. I was taken to another table where Alfonso Arau was eating alongside his star, Lumi Cavazos, and a few other crew members. Alfonso stood up to greet me, welcoming me to the set, and encouraging me to videotape as much as I wanted. Carlos introduced me to Alfonso's wife, Laura Esquivel, the novelist who's responsible for all this. She also wrote the screenplay. We went to the set and I taped the action until 3:00 P.M. Saturdays are half days. They stopped for the weekend. I went back to the house and tried to sleep off whatever bug I have.

Monday, March 11, 1991

I am still feeling so sick that Carmen, Carlos's mother, took me to the doctor next door. The nurse gave me a shot in the ass. Haven't had one of those since I was a kid.

Tuesday, March 12, 1991

Since I was locked up in the hosue recuperating, I watched cable. This town is movie-making paradise. The local Mexican TV station gets the cable signal from the US with their satellite dish and pumps it through their cable so that everyone in town has free HBO, Cinemax, even free pay per view.

I'm feeling better so at 4:00 P.M. I went to the location. They are on a night schedule now. I had told Laura Esquivel about "Bedhead" so I gave her a copy to watch since I know Alfonso's too busy. If she likes it, she'll probably get him to watch it. That's the plan, anyway.

Wednesday, March 13, 1991

I went to the location. Laura and Alfonso arrived. Laura saw me and exclaimed, "Bellisima, Roberto. I saw your movie three times." She told me that she saw it alone, woke her husband and they watched it, then she woke their daughter and they all watched it again. She gave me their address to send them a copy of my next movie. Alfonso came over and shook my hand. "Excellent work, I enjoyed your work very much— very creative, very funny." Laura said how much she liked the pacing, the story, the camera, the kids, everything, and how Alfonso said, "Now this is a muchacho who can direct."

Thursday, March 14, 1991

While I was taping behind-the-scenes interviews, I taped one conversation between Poncho, the production manager, and Carlos. Poncho was saying that he produces Mexican video action movies and that he wants us to make a film for him. He says he shoots on film and releases on video. The budget would be around $30,000. He said he can't pay us anything (?) but we'd get to make a feature film. I told Carlos we should look into this some more, because if it's true we could make a cool movie on our own for much less. Carlos agreed. Why work ourselves to death for this guy for free, and not own the movie?

I began thinking about an old story idea I've had for a few years of a man with a guitar case full of weapons and gadgets called "The Mariachi."

I'm ready to go home. I got some great footage, wonderful compliments on my movie, so now I'm charged up to make another one.

March through May, 1991

During this period, I came back with a renewed charge for filmmaking. "Bedhead" was off to film festivals, and I was back at school making a short film. This was my first 16mm color film with sync sound. What a pain in the ass. I worked hard on it along with Tommy Nix and Edison Jackson. I even took the extra time to draw a color animated title sequence. I did that for "Bedhead" as well. Three hundred drawings on typing paper by hand for a thirty-second opening sequence.

We finished the short, fifteen-minute film entitled "Pretty Good Man," and it came out . . . pretty good. We showed it at the student film screening and it got a huge response. I'm charged up to pursue my feature film idea this summer.

My first job in high school was at a photo lab and I remember what my first boss, Mr. Riojas, told me one day after he saw some of my cartoons and photographs. He said that I had creative talent, but what I really needed to do if I wanted to be successful was to become technical. He said that just about anyone can become technical, but not everyone can be creative. And there are a lot of creative people who never get anywhere because they don't have technical skills. Part of what makes a person creative is his lack of emphasis on things technical. My boss said that if you are someone who is *already* creative, and then you become technical, then you are unstoppable. I like that. Creative and technical. I've made some crazy movies, but as long as I have to rely on a crew for the technical demands of making a movie, I will always be at the mercy of having to spend a lot of money to make a feature film. But, if I learn all there is to know about making a movie myself, and do it all myself, I will be light years ahead of other people still trying to tackle the basics. What I need to do is learn everything at the same time on a movie that I can quietly fail on, and learn from my mistakes. By making a movie for the Spanish video market on my own, I can do that. I will learn sound, camera, lighting, effects, and then I'll be more prepared to make real films later.

Carlos has been looking into it and he thinks that if we make a movie on film and transfer to and edit on video we could sell the final tape to the Spanish video market for at least $20,000. I told him that to be conservative, we have to imagine getting half of that. So let's figure we can only get $10,000 for it. So we obviously can't spend more than $10,000 on our movie unless we want to risk never seeing that money back. But I told him that since "Bedhead" cost about $800 and was eight minutes long, and if we shot *Mariachi* the same way (with no crew so that we don't have to feed anybody), with an old bought or borrowed camera (so we don't need insurance or rental fees), one or two takes of each shot, then it's conceivable we can make an eighty-minute movie for $8,000. We can edit on ¾″ video like I did with "Bedhead" since we are selling the movie to the video market. That way we can avoid the outrageous cost of a 16mm film print, the way I avoided it on "Bedhead." I told Carlos to call the Spanish video distributors and find out what format they want their master tapes to be on. If we can get away with selling them a ¾″ master, then we have a good chance of pulling it off for about $8,000.

It would be cool to come back to school after summer with a feature film under my belt. When people ask what I did over the summer I can say, "I made a foreign film. I have a lot of friends who like foreign films so I figured I'd make one."

Tuesday, May 14, 1991

I saw one of my film school teachers today, Nick Cominos. We talked about "Pretty Good Man" and the great response at the student film screening. He asked what I was doing this summer and I said, *El Mariachi*. He asked me, "Who's your director of photography?" I paused. I know he'll shit all over me if I tell him the truth—that I'm planning on shooting it all by myself, without a crew. So I told him, "I'm going to be the director of photography but I'll probably have a small crew around to help out." He shook his head. "No, no, no, no . . . You're going to fail! Your actors are going to hate you! They're going to be sitting there waiting for you while you light the set! Don't be an idiot! Get a director of photography. You have to learn how to delegate. You can't be doing everything yourself anymore!" I told him I hate having someone else operate the camera. Half the effect of the movie has to do with the camera. I can't stand not being able to look through the lens as the action rolls. I told him he'd seen all my other short films; I did all those myself. I told him more about my plan and before long he was changing his tune. Within fifteen minutes he was enthusiastic. He started warning me about getting robbed blind, asked me if I was going to have a joint account so that no one person can run off with the production money, asked how much per diem (?) I would get, who was keeping the master edits, contracts, negatives, etc. He started confusing me with terms and jargon I knew nothing about. I figured I'd learn what he was talking about as the movie got going. That's the main reason I want to do this myself, my way, so that I can see for myself what is actually necessary and how much of it is just the traditional way of doing things. He got so excited he said that if the producer fell through he would put up some money and go in it with me. He asked where I was getting the camera from, and I told him Carlos was bringing a few cameras up for me to look at that a guy he knows is selling. If not those, we will try and borrow an Arriflex that a couple of friends, Keith Kritselis and Ben Davis, have on loan from a friend of theirs who owns a local commercial production company. The production company shoots all their ads on video now, but they used to shoot on film. So they have a bunch of old Arriflex 16s cameras lying around. They're not sure if they work, but I'll be glad to get one fixed. One of those used runs about $1,800. If we can save on a camera, we can shoot the movie for less than $10,000 easily.

Wednesday, May 15, 1991

Carlos arrived with a 35mm Bell and Howell 71-QM and a Bolex Paillard. Beautiful but too expensive. I'll call Pharmaco, the local drug research center, tomorrow. They have a $3,000 drug study coming up. I'd have to be locked up for a month but I'd make good money and have time to write the script. Pharmaco is a drug research facility that pays healthy male specimens to be guinea pigs to test their latest medical break-throughs. These places are all over the country, usually in college towns where there's no shortage of healthy young men to test their drugs on. Pharmaco has been my second home.

I've been working so hard these last two semesters, I really need a vacation. I made two short films and held on to two jobs while going to school full time. So I have no time to write a feature-length script. But I need to get cracking if we plan to shoot the movie this summer. If we plan to come in under budget on this, we have to have the script completely worked out beforehand.

I can't just quit my two jobs to go and write. I need to go somewhere quiet to write, plus earn money for the movie. Pharmaco. The ideal place. I can leave work for a month, make more money there than I'll make at my two part-time jobs put together, have my room and board paid for, and yet I'll have plenty of free time to write my script. Since they don't let you leave the facility for a full month, I'll have nothing to do but watch movies and write. Perfect. Vacation and a writing sanctuary all in one. If only I can qualify. The competition is pretty stiff. You're going up against forty other guys for a drug study that only accepts about twenty.

Thursday, May 16, 1991

Carlos and I do our homework by going to the local video store that carries Spanish videos and we rented the most recent Mexican action movie, *Escape Nocturnal*. It sucked. These straight-to-video movies are done for the quick buck. It's obvious whoever made it concentrated on putting a good cover on the video, getting a name actor on the sleeve, and then filling the tape with a crappy movie. I know we can make a better movie for a lot less, because we'll actually be trying to make a good movie so that we can learn from it. On these other movies, they don't even try to make the movie look like it has any kind of production value. No one running in the streets, no action. Everything is shot in someone's apartment. That's what we can do in Acuña. We can run around in the streets and make the movie look expensive. One thing they did have was a famous Mexican soap opera actress in the starring role. That's the key. We need some kind of name actor in the movie somewhere, even if he gets shot in the first five minutes. Unfortunately, we have no contacts or any money to pay them. Carlos told me his family is good friends with Lina Santos's family. She's a known actress in Mexico, and she's from a town near Acuña. Carlos thinks he can get her to do us a favor and film for one day.

Elizabeth cooks us spaghetti. Carlos and I eat and talk about the story I'm trying to write. So far I have a scene where Azul (the bad guy) and the Mariachi walk into the same restaurant at different times. The Mariachi arrives at the restaurant to find work playing his guitar. He asks why there's no music and the bartender points to a keyboard player who plays some awful synthesized music. The Mariachi takes the hint and leaves. Afterwards Azul, also carrying a guitar case, walks into the restaurant, orders a beer, and then walks up to a table with some bad guys. He opens his guitar case and shoots them dead. Azul leaves. As the bartender tries to call the cops, Azul reenters the restaurant and walks straight up to the bartender, who thinks he's going to be killed. Instead he hears the sound of a bottle opening and it turns out Azul is drinking and then paying for his beer. Azul leaves. The bartender calls the boss on the phone and describes the bad guy as a man dressed in black carrying a guitar case. Maybe this is the opening scene. I acted out the scene for Carlos. He liked it.

Tuesday, May 21, 1991

I had a screening at Pharmaco for the $3,000 study. A screening is where they run tests on you to make sure you are a good specimen. You're supposed to eat really healthy for a few days beforehand so that your blood is clean. Drink a lot of water to flush out all the pizza. We all sit in a room with a nurse asking all kinds of "weed out" questions before taking our blood for tests. One guy raised his hand and asked if it mattered if he ate a couple of Eskimo Pies last night. The nurse told him to go home. He has no chance of having competitive blood with arteries full of ice cream. There are some real pros here. You can tell by the holes in their arms and the familiarity they have with all the staff. Scary. I met a few people who do this full time. It's good money but I'm sure after a while the drugs start building up.

Wednesday, May 22, 1991

I sent off "Bedhead" to the Marin County Film Festival and to the Melbourne Film Festival in Australia.

I went to the movies to see John Woo's *The Killer.* Damn. I wish we had more money for squib effects (bullet hits).

Tuesday, May 28, 1991

"Bedhead" won another contest! This one was The University of Missouri Fine Arts Competition. So far "Bedhead" has aired on Night Flight, won the Carolina Film Festival, the Third Coast Film Festival, and now this one.

The more I've looked into this feature film for $8,000, the more I think we can pull it off. No one else at the film school thinks we can, but I really can't see how we could screw it up unless it's a technical thing, like a huge film scratch across all the footage or constant equipment breakdowns. Otherwise, if we plan it carefully, which I intend to do as always, I just see it working all right. If it doesn't come out perfect, so what? Our movie will still have more action, hard work, and passion packed into it than a dozen of the regular cheapies cranked out for a quick buck. We shouldn't have too much trouble selling it, and with the profit we'll make Part II and just work harder on the sequel. What I think about most is . . . Why hasn't anyone else done this?

Some shark of a producer in Mexico heard that we were getting into the straight-to-Spanish-video market and wanted to come aboard as a producer. He said he'd equip us with a crew, oversee the production to make sure we do it right, blah blah blah. Yeah right. I told him we didn't need him.

I told him we didn't need *anybody*.

Wednesday, May 29, 1991

I went to Pharmaco for my physical. I better make it into this study or the project is dead before it's begun. There's no one we can borrow the money from and I really don't want to borrow it. The money we make back once we sell the movie is what we'll use to finance future films. We don't want to have to pay someone back with that money. We've decided this project has to be our own risk. Besides, it's been my experience that you're a lot more careful where the money goes when you are using your *own* money.

I WAS A HUMAN LAB RAT

I've been a lab rat about four times. The first was back in 1989. My college roommate had been checking into these research hospitals to make some extra cash to pay for his stereo. I told him he was an idiot to participate in medical experiments. I warned him that the drugs would eventually accumulate and make him sterile, screw up his blood, burn his brain cells, who knows? Whatever they'd do to him wouldn't be worth the money. So I thought at the time.

After a few months of being broke myself, I didn't have much choice but to follow in his footsteps. He called me a hypocrite back then and he calls me one now, especially after he saw me on television talking about how I sold my body to science and made *El Mariachi* with the proceeds. At the time I felt selling my body to science was my *only* option, which is a terrible feeling to have.

I had finally been accepted into the Film Department at the university and I wanted to go into the class with enough money to make an award-winning film. Since it would be my first 16mm film after years of video movies, I knew I was going to be pouring a lot of time and hard work into it so that I could send it to the bigger film festivals. I didn't want money to stand in the way of doing it right.

So I called the Pharmaco Research Hospital Hotline and got information on the upcoming drug studies. After listing several different studies, some lasting a few days, others several weeks, they mentioned one that paid $2,000 for a seven-day stay in their facility. That one sounded the best. It was certainly the most money offered for such a short time period. I thought I had struck gold.

It turns out that the drug they were testing was a speed healing drug. Meaning that in order to test it, *they had to wound you*. They took a punch biopsy out of the back of each arm, then applied placebo on one arm and the speed healer on the other. Then they slapped clear tape over the holes and let me wander around the hospital. Seven days later, I was paid $2,000 and let go. The only catch was that they wanted my arms for further testing. So they cut out the section of the biopsy on both arms then sewed me back up. Now I've got two tiny football-shaped scars to remind me of how I used to finance my films. The happy ending to that episode is that I put the money to really good use by making the award-winning short film, "Bedhead." So it follows, if you bleed for your money, I mean really bleed for it, you're very careful on how you spend that money.

The money went fast. Some to the movie, most to paying tuition, bills, etc. Six months later I was back in Pharmaco for the second time doing a nine-day drug study that paid $1,000. It was less money for a longer stay, but the pain factor was less as well. This time they were testing an antidepressant. I guess it worked. By the end of the nine days everyone in our group was ready to beat each other up.

The main reason I did that study was because I wanted to finally buy myself a camcorder. I'd been making movies on video for years but always with borrowed equipment. So with my drug money, I bought my camcorder and have gotten a lot of use out of it since. In a way, the medical studies allowed me to make my dreams come true. They allowed me to have access to instant capital.

When it came time for me to make *El Mariachi*, I needed someplace quiet to write and earn money at the same time.

Naturally, the research hospital fit the bill. I knew that if I checked in for a monthlong drug study I could clear about $3,000, with room and board paid for, and have plenty of time to kick back and write my script. Also, I found that the longer studies were less painful than the short-term studies. That's why I got $2,000 for getting my arms cut open in seven days: the pain factor. Whereas a monthlong study, where they're basically paying me for my time, would earn me $3,000 with mild procedures and less radical medication. Maximum writing time, top dollar, and less pain. Sign me up.

In my mind I simply imagined that I was getting paid to write a script, which made the whole thing easier to swallow. With that attitude I would be able to write comfortably and enjoy the experience as a pseudo-vacation. I had just come off a rough ten months of nonstop work, having completed two short films, plus school and my two part-time jobs, so I was ready to get locked up somewhere and simply relax, watch rented movies, and write my action film. Upon reflection, and only upon reflection, do I realize that it was a crazy time.

Friday, May 31, 1991

I checked into the research hospital at 1:00 P.M., carrying a bag with my daily planner, several packs of ruled index cards, personal items, a Stephen King paperback, blank legal note-pads, drawing pens and pad, and my oscillating fan. (I can't sleep unless I have the sound of a fan running right by my head constantly, even in the winter. A source for constant ribbing by fellow lab rats.)

How these studies work is that even though the hospital may only need fifteen subjects to run tests on, they'll bring in nineteen of us on the first day. Those four extra guys are the backups. The researchers run the tests that they held during the screenings all over again as soon as you get there: blood tests, piss tests, heart tests, the works.

If for some reason you don't check out perfect, because you drank a beer a few days ago, smoked a cigarette, or for some reason you have an enzyme level or triglycerides that are just a wee bit away from where they were the first time you tested, they'll send you home and use the backup guy in your place. The backups help cover the few guys that inevitably won't make it in because they went on an unexpected joyride a few days before and screwed up their systems. On this occasion, though, one of those unlucky fellas was a guy who during the routine baggage check and strip search that happens when you enter the hospital, was found to be in possession of an experimental toothpaste. The researchers felt that this experi-mental toothpaste he'd been using might throw off the results of the drug they were going to test. The poor guy started beg-ging and pleading with the researchers that the toothpaste, which he had never even used and was indeed unopened, had been unwittingly packed by his unsuspecting girlfriend who got the toothpaste at school as a sample. The researchers told him that they'd have to call the sponsor of the study for their approval.

We all sat and awaited the fate of the toothpaste guy. The sponsor was paged. While awaiting authorization, toothpaste guy was begging them to let him into the study. He'd already planned to be away for a month and had been taken off the payroll at work, he had a part-time substitute taking his place, he needed the $3,000 this study would bring him. The call came back from the sponsor. They didn't want to take the chance, so they discharged toothpaste guy.

This sort of thing struck an uncomfortable chord with everyone there. I knew that I too had planned on being locked away for a month, had been taken off the payroll at work, had a substitute taking my place, was counting 100% on this opportunity to write my script in peace and earn a quick $3,000 to finance my movie. So I was quietly praying that my tests would check out normal, for already I could feel my pulse rising at the thought of having to go home tonight, empty-handed, after mentally preparing to drop off the Earth for four weeks.

By far the scariest thing about this place isn't the experimental pharmaceuticals they're testing, the strip searches, the heart monitor hookups, the piss jars and crap buckets, but the thought that you might actually have to turn right back around and go home the first day because of a funky enzyme, twitchy triglyceride, blood in your urine, or maybe even something as silly as a pulse rate that's higher than normal, something that was happening to me just thinking about it.

We went through our tests and awaited results in the television room. After an hour the intercom kicked up. Four names were called and asked to go to the lobby. My name was one of them. The scariest feeling I was to have the entire time was the feeling of maybe getting thrown out before my stay had begun. What a failure you are if you can't even qualify to be a lab rat of all things!

I got to the lobby to find out there was a problem with our EKG readings. Supposedly they weren't hooked up correctly when they were taken the first time and we'd have to redo them. I went into the EKG room where they have you lay on a table and hook up about twelve leads to different points on your chest, arms, and legs. You are asked to breathe normally, stare at a singular point on the ceiling, and not move a muscle, not even your eyes. The test was taken and I came out normal. All my other tests cleared as well.

At 7:00 P.M. I was approved to stay in the hospital as a subject for the rest of the month. I made it! I'm a lab rat! The whole group was excited that they made the team. They could pay off that loan, that credit card bill, that tuition, whatever. The coast was clear. Now all we had to do was make sure we *stayed in.* You only get the full amount if you complete the program. But for now we were happy. Imagine a voluntary prison system where all the prisoners are glad to be locked up. That's what this was. I even called my wife to tell her the good news. There are about five pay phones for the patients to use. They were filled with other patients telling their girlfriends the good news as well. I heard one guy on the phone next to me, near tears, saying, "Aw come on baby. I'm doing this for us . . . let me do this . . ."

We have the rest of the night to go about our own business trying to settle in for the month ahead of us. The dorms are set up so we each have a bunk bed with a drawer under the mattress for personal belongings. You don't need a wardrobe, since you're provided with a uniform.

I set up my fan, and like others in the group, I placed the calendar they provided for us on the mattress above, so I could wake up every morning and see how many days I had left. We all crossed off the first day.

We were issued our uniforms: green scrub pants and red T-shirts with the research hospital's logo emblazoned on the front. We have to wear our red T-shirts at all times so that the coordinators and paramedics know what drug we're on. Every group has a different color T-shirt to represent their drug study. When you are being paged over the intercom for a call at the pay phone or because you're late to a procedure, you are referred to by number and T-shirt color. No names. So you'll hear Teal Blue 15, Wild Orchid 5 (for real), Canary Yellow 4.

I'm Red 11.

I went back into the television room, where a movie was being played on the big screen TV. "I've seen this movie already," I thought. I was about to get up and find something more productive to do but then realized that there was nothing else to do right now. Nothing to do but relax and get used to the idea of being on vacation. It had been such an insane, nonstop ten months that it was strange realizing that I had plenty of time to sit back, relax, and watch a movie that I'd already seen. So I did. I like this.

I'll start my script next week, this first week I'll just relax.

Saturday, June 1, 1991

Our first real day here. Life as a lab rat has begun. For breakfast: two bowls of raisin bran cereal, juice, two milks, banana, bagel, and butter. This is much more than I eat at home. That's another reason I like this place. Four meals a day.

They're taking ten blood draws today. But on regular days there will only be one blood draw. That's not bad at all. Some studies have as many as twenty-four blood draws in one day. Every hour on the hour. By the end of the study the subjects have pincushion arms. One technician told me that once she had to work one of those twenty-four-draws-in-one-day studies, and she would even have to draw blood from subjects while they slept. She said that some of the other technicians would get lazy and instead of finding a part of the vein that hadn't been punctured yet, they would just use the same puncture holes. She said that the punctures would get so stretched out that a tech would barely get the tourniquet on and the arm would start spurting blood. Ouch.

The guy bunking next to me, Peter Marquardt, was a little freaked by all of this. This was his first study. Most people who come to these research studies start off with a shorter stay, maybe a weekend or a weeklong study, and then work up to the monthlong studies. Peter, though, jumped right into a one-month study his first time out so he doesn't know his way around just yet. I tried to tell him that the studies are painless, a breeze, but so far it hasn't been. For some reason we've been stuck with the worst blood draw technicians around. I'm only on number five with the blood draws and I've had two different techs miss my vein completely. I'm going to be all bruised up and it's only the first day. Peter doesn't think he's going to make it.

One guy in our group, Hernan, came out of the blood room with an ice block on his arm as he dabbed the dripping blood with a cotton pad. He looked awful. Peter was next. Hernan had bruises already showing up on his arm. He said that the tech who was drawing his blood pushed the needle in too far. The needle went through the vein, making another hole on the other side of the vein, seeping blood under his skin, and that's why it was bruising. Nasty. I went in first. The tech looked incompetent enough so I sat there and pumped my arm to make my veins stick out as much as possible, so he'd be sure not to miss. He tapped at the vein and said, "Monster veins, hit in the dark veins." Fortunately, I got out all right. So did Peter.

Monday, June 3, 1991

We are into our normal routines now. Only one blood draw a day. Most of my bruises have already healed. We have to take our daily dose of horse pills.

You have a clipboard with you at all times that has your daily schedule down to the minute. There are synchronized electronic clocks all around the facility, so that you show up where you are supposed to go at the designated time. Everyone is a few minutes apart, so that if the guy next to me starts eating breakfast at 9:00 A.M., my clipboard tells me I start at 9:10 A.M. Everyone performs at three- to ten-minute intervals. If you are late to a procedure, a meal, a blood draw, a medication session, you are docked twenty-five bucks. They are paying you for your inconvenience and proper performance of all procedures, so they dock your pay if you screw up. This is a big business. It costs a sponsor more than 70 million dollars to test a new drug and takes more than seven years. They don't want mistakes.

In this study, you have thirty seconds to swallow your five horse pills, and you have a tech sitting there timing you, watching you swallow them, and then checking your mouth with a flashlight to make sure you didn't hide them to spit out later.

Tuesday, June 4, 1991

We cross off the days on the calendar like inmates. So far everything has gone by at a snail's pace. It seems like I've been here three weeks, it's barely been five days. Peter, the first-timer bunking next to me, just happened to have brought in the same book I did: Stephen King's *The Dead Zone*. I've noticed that an unusual amount of people in here are reading Stephen King books. It's really funny. People have asked me, "What kind of person would sell his body to medical experiments for extra cash?" The kind of people that read Stephen King books, that's who.

Wednesday, June 5, 1991

Just when we thought this study was going to be an easy ride, they start up a new procedure today. We are all issued a clear plastic jug that we carry to the bathroom every morning to fill with urine. But you have to urinate at a certain time designated on your clipboard.

If that isn't enough, whenever you feel the urge to defecate, you take what looks like an empty Cool Whip bucket in with you and fill that up. When you finish you write the time of birth on the lid and place it in the refrigerator with all the other buckets belonging to your fellow lab rats. The refrigerator was full by the time I made my contribution.

Now if that wasn't humiliating enough, how about discussing the quality of your dung with your study coordinator? That's what we have to do. At a designated time, we all sit down and have the study coordinator hand us two sheets of questions to fill out about the consistency of the stool, how long it took to deliver it, all kinds of stuff. The coordinator then sits down and discusses it with you. "What was it like? Hard, soft, jagged?"

Someone in the group said, "We're earning our pay now."

Thursday, June 6, 1991

There was another one-month study going on in the next dorm. These guys were getting $3,500 for a one-month stay, but the drug they were testing was a narcotic painkiller. They all got sick after being on the medication five days. They were all throwing up and everything. All except one. He was probably on placebo. But the others were taken to a hospital and then released the next day with *full pay*. The guy who was left behind kept trying to make himself sick so that he could also go home with full pay, but the sponsors weren't buying it. We all started hoping our medication would make us sick. I wouldn't mind tossing my cookies for an early discharge with full pay.

Friday, June 7, 1991

I've had a week of relaxation, and now I've got to start putting the movie together and continue to work out the logistics of how we're going to shoot this thing and get it in at a certain budget. I called a film teacher of mine at the university, Steve Mims, and asked him for some advice. He said I could probably *shoot* the movie for $10,000 if I was really careful. I told him that I wanted to shoot 16mm film but then edit on video. Since I was going to sell it to the video market, I would never need to make a film print. I asked if I should shoot on reversal film, which would be a positive film image when developed and then transfer that straight to video, or shoot negative. I'd have more exposure leeway with a negative image, but then I'd have to take on the extra cost of printing dailies on film before I could transfer it to video. He told me I should shoot negative because a post lab then transfers the negative straight to video making a *positive* image on video without the extra cost of having to make a positive film print first. I didn't know any of this could be done, but then again, that's the whole reason I'm making this movie, to learn as much as possible in a short amount of time about making a low-budget movie.

I knew that this would be a great way to learn filmmaking. By throwing myself right into the fire.

Saturday, June 8, 1991

The group rented and enjoyed immensely the Steven Soderbergh film *sex, lies, and videotape*. Everyone was saying that Peter looked like James Spader.

The fun thing about being locked in here so long is that you get to observe the other lab rats from other drug studies as they go stir-crazy. There is another group, the Teal Blues (wearing the teal blue T-shirts) and they're on some low-fat/low-calorie diet. So while every other group gets to eat real food, the Teal Blues have to eat rabbit food. And they're starving. For example, our lunch consists of a ham and cheese sandwich, potato chips, an apple, an orange, a dessert, and lemonade. The Teal Blues get a huge chunk of cauliflower, a big chunk of broccoli, carrots, and lemonade. It wouldn't be so bad if they didn't have to watch us eat our food while sitting at the next table. Worst part is that you've got the cafeteria servers watching you to make sure you eat everything. Everybody has to eat the same thing as the others in their group and the same amount.

Some of the Teal Blues are starting to lose it. They're trying to bribe some of us to pass them some sandwiches and chips.

Monday, June 10, 1991

It didn't take long to figure out that there's not much to do in here. Besides playing pool, watching rented movies on the big-screen TV, or scanning bad programming on the two other TVs with cable hookups, life in The Hole, as they call it now, is pretty stale. I write as much as I can, but every once in a while I need a break. I can either go to the TV room and get sucked into a meaningless debate with one of the Debaters, a couple of guys who do nothing all month but argue their point of view, or visit a room where you can check out board games. Peter and I checked out that old Milton Bradley game Battleship that I used to see ads for during Saturday morning cartoons growing up. The game was actually fun to play. I guess we're dying in here.

We rented Paul Verhoeven's classic *Flesh and Blood* and I pointed out that in addition to James Spader, Peter also resembled Rutger Hauer.

The Teal Blues keep getting in trouble. First, the cafeteria was broken into last night. Someone stole several boxes of breakfast cereal and a couple of pies. There's only one group to suspect. The Teal Blues. They're the only ones on a low-cal/ low-fat diet. They're the hungriest around here. The rest of us eat like kings. So the paramedics are taking blood samples and checking enzyme levels to see who ate the extra goodies. Since it will show up in their blood, whoever gets caught will be docked money or hopefully thrown out. If they're thrown out, there's less competition for the best seats in the TV room.

If that wasn't enough bad news for these guys, the sponsor gave the Red Shirts and the Red Shirts only, the option to go outside for a supervised breath of fresh air, since it won't affect our experiment. On our way outside, a couple of Teal Blues tried to sneak out with us. They had taken a couple of red T-shirts from the laundry room, put them on, and tried to pass themselves off as Red Shirts so that they could get some fresh air, too.

They didn't realize that we'd rat them out. We've been locked in here long enough to know who's in our group. They got docked $50 each.

Wednesday, June 12, 1991

Having finished reading our books, Peter and I rented *Dead Zone*, the movie, and the first thing we all noticed was how much Peter resembled Christopher Walken.

That clinched it for me. Anybody who can manage to have the menace of a Rutger Hauer, the icy coolness of a Christopher Walken, and the playboy air of James Spader had to be in my movie. As it was, I was having difficulty figuring out

who I could get to play the bad guy in *Mariachi*. I didn't want
the character to be Mexican; there's enough bad guy Mexicans
in movies. I wanted the bad guy to be an American drug lord
who had fled the states, set up shop in a small Mexican town,
and took it over, barely speaking the language. Peter Marquardt fit the bill.

Thursday, June 13, 1991

Elizabeth brought me some mail to read, a few letters, some
magazines, and some copies of my short films. The coordinators searched the package to make sure Elizabeth wasn't slip-
ping me any booze, chocolate, cigarettes, anything that could
mess up their results. It's not that they're being overly cautious, they actually have guys in here breaking the rules all the
time. It's stupid because you'll always get caught, whatever
you consume shows up in your blood and you get docked.

I showed my short movies to the Red Shirts. We had a good
time and talked about low-budget filmmaking for, literally, the
rest of the day. It's funny how long a few people can hold a
conversation when there's nothing else to do for a whole
month.

Peter is excited about the short films and said that he wants
to be in a movie. I told him about the Mexico movie I'm getting ready to go make and told him that he could play the bad
guy if he wants to. He wants to. Had he acted before? No.
Good. He'll be just like everyone else who'll star in this movie.

Saturday, June 15, 1991

I've written out most of the scenes on the index cards. The
first scene I wrote out is the one where the Mariachi comes
into the bar looking for work, but the bar already has a key-
boardist, so Mariachi leaves. Then Azul, the man in black,
comes into the bar, and the bartender thinks he's another mariachi looking for work. Instead, Azul just shoots up the bad
guys and leaves. That's the clearest scene I have so far. I knew
I couldn't open the movie with that so I stuck a couple of blank
index cards in front of it, knowing that at least two scenes

would precede it, but I don't know what those scenes will be as of yet.

I then titled some other cards with a logical progression of scenes: Mariachi goes to find work in another bar and meets the girl, he then goes to the hotel to wash up. That's where the bad guys attack him, thinking he's the man in black who shot up the bar. All I have are the names of the scenes and a brief description of what happens on the back of the index card. When there's two scenes with the girl back to back, I shove another card between those and title it Bad Guy Scene, knowing that later I can include a scene showing what the bad guys are up to in order to jigsaw the scenes a little. So far so good. All I have to do later is take each card and flesh out the scenes by writing them out on the legal pad, based on the descriptions on the cards.

Monday, June 17, 1991

This morning after using the jug, Peter said, "Can't wait to get out of here so I can finally have a real piss in the morning again."

We found out what happens to the Cool Whip buckets after we fill them up and put them in the refrigerator. Someone downstairs, a lowly technician, no doubt, has to scrape samples of the droppings using a popsicle stick and put them on glass slides for someone to inspect. What a shit job, we thought. So we came up with a few ways to cheer up the guy that had to scrape our poop. Peter suggested someone should have a Mr. Potato Head delivered to the dorm. Then we'd place the eyes, ears, and pipe onto the pile, so when the lowly technician opens the Cool Whip jar to scrape samples, he or she would find a surprise. After that suggestion we all realized that boredom was really kicking in around here.

Tuesday, June 18, 1991

One thing you notice after a while is that the different color groups don't hang out together. Reds hang out with Reds. Wild Orchids hang out with other Wild Orchids. No one even talks to the Teal Blues. It's this guy thing; you only hang out with the members of your own group and you instantly don't care for the guys in the other groups. If you're edgy and you want to pick a fight it'll be with a guy in another T-shirt color. That's just the way it is and it's funny because we're all desperadoes locked in the same shithole together, but somehow we all have that basic need to feel different than the next guy.

Thursday, June 20, 1991

It's my birthday today! My wife sings happy birthday to me over the pay phone. I asked our study coordinator if they could serve cake for dessert today. They said that it would have to be cleared with the sponsor and it takes so long to get a meal change that I would have had to ask for it months ago. It's fairly depressing having your birthday in a place like this. It really makes you think about where you're going with your life.

I'm twenty-three years old. Orson Welles made *Citizen Kane* when he was twenty-five. Spielberg made *Jaws* at twenty-six. So I've only got about two or three years to make my breakthrough film. I've got to get moving.

This trilogy of quickie Mariachi movies should give me the confidence and experience I need to make my breakout film, whatever that will be. I'll worry about that one later. For now, experience. Gotta have experience. Learn by doing.

Peter and I played Battleship. I won, mainly because I cheated. To think I have to cheat in order to win on my birthday. This place bites.

There were guys in another group playing poker for money who were told to stop. They've banned any gambling in here because too many people were betting money they hadn't earned yet, and then losing their paychecks to card sharks. I couldn't imagine finally getting out of here a month later and having to hand my paycheck over to some lucky fool I played poker with three weeks earlier. But it happens.

Elizabeth calls later to tell me the good news: "Bedhead" won First Place at the Marin County Film and Video Festival. $700! More Mariachi money.

Sunday, June 23, 1991

Carlos Gallardo, the Mariachi, sent me a videotape of the locations I asked for. He videotaped several bars, his ranch, and a few hotels so that it'll be easier for me to plan out the scenes. It's also easier to write a script if you already have seen all the locations and elements you can work with. I tend to work the few assets we have into the script to feature our production values more.

I told him to contact a real mariachi so he could start taking guitar lessons. Or, if nothing else, to hang out and get a sense of what they do. I also asked if he had found an actress for the female lead. It's a tough part so I asked him to find me at least five women to choose from; we'll do a screen test and pick the best one. I also told him to start contacting the Spanish home video distributors in Los Angeles and find out what video format our master has to be on. 1"? ¾"? If they need a 1" master, we're screwed. If they'll accept a ¾" master, I know people that have old ¾" editing systems—not the SP decks, but the earlier models that work just fine. They make only straight cuts but that would be sufficient. If this were for the American home video market, it wouldn't work. I'm sure they'd only accept 1" or digital tape. So Spanish home video is our best bet, since they're more likely to be lenient. I also told Carlos to look into getting discount squibs and movie blanks through his contact Falomir, the special effects man who we met on the set of *Like Water for Chocolate*.

Monday, June 24, 1991

I've been trying to order long movies so that we can pass the time easier. Today I rented *Raging Bull* and *Scarface*. It's surprising how many of the guys in here have never seen these movies. They loved *Raging Bull*, then after dinner we watched *Scarface*.

I was sitting around talking to Peter about his character. I told him I was going to be giving all the bad guys stupid names. In this town where we are going to shoot, a kid will grow up with a nickname that a lot of times follows him into manhood. I know some guys down here named La Palma (palm), Pepino (cucumber), Azul (blue), so I thought we'd name all the bad guys after fruits and colors, as if they grew up in that town and never shed their childhood nicknames. So Peter would be named Mauricio in the film, but all his henchmen would refer to him as Moco (booger). After saying it a few times it started to sound like a good bad guy name.

The study coordinators found out which of the Teal Blues ate the pies and extra cereal because their blood level went way up. They got docked heavily. Today in the cafeteria they had two supervisors watching them eat because it was discovered that they were also paying people in other groups to slip them desserts or pieces of sandwich. Peter called over to their table and said, "I bet you guys can't wait to get out of here ... with your twenty-five-cent checks." Everybody but the Teal Blues laughed.

Thursday, June 27, 1991

I've switched over to a night schedule. Last weekend was so crowded that you couldn't leave your dorm. The television room was packed, the pool room was packed, even the usually empty study rooms were packed. What happens is that there are a lot of weekend studies, they pay about $300 to $400 for a weekend. Those are the studies that usually have twenty-four blood draws in one day. They're painful but it's quick money for those who are in school full time or working full time and can only take off for a weekend to participate in a study. The Red Shirts have got the run of the place during the week since there are only a few long-term studies going on at one time, but the weekends are so flooded that you can't watch television, you can't play pool, you can't even get a game of Battleship since all the games are checked out. So now I'm sleeping during the day so I can switch to a night schedule. I wake up for meals and then go right back to sleep. At night everyone has to go to bed at 2:00 A.M., but you can get back up at 3:00 A.M. So by 3:00 A.M. I'm up, roaming the halls, pacing, writing, watching movies. It's the "bat" schedule and it's a lot more relaxing and productive as far as writing goes.

Friday, June 28, 1991

I'm so used to making short films, I'm having trouble writing something that can sustain ninety minutes. So what I decided to do is write a short film structure and then repeat it three times. So now I've got Azul asking for a beer three times throughout the movie, but on the third time he actually gets the beer served the way he wants. The Mariachi jumps into a truck three times to escape the bad guy. The third time, though, he jumps into the bad guy's truck. Then, Moco lights a match across the chin of his henchman three times. On the third time the match is lit on Moco's dead face by his henchman. So I'll repeat everything three times but add a twist to the last one. I call this the kindergarten approach to screenwriting. I'll try it out, and see if it works.

Our sponsor actually showed up today making an unannounced visit. Our study coordinator told us all to be on our best behavior. So we all behaved like good little lab rats as the suits came in and looked us over. They nodded and went on their way. Rather humiliating to be looked at like livestock, most of us unbathed and unshaven, with the bedhead sticking up and the sleep rocks in our eyes. Not too cool.

Saturday, June 29, 1991

Peter and a few others in the group have joined me on the "bat" schedule. We can actually have a pool tournament without having to wait for a table to open up.

Most of the time everyone just talks about food. We've all grown tired of eating the same thing every day. The food here is too healthy. We need grease and lots of it. Peter spoke of his favorite seafood restaurant where the beers are "Soooo cold." He looks like he's in pain. We all are. Every time you turn on the TV they have all these ads for different restaurants. They had one of those Pizza Hut ads that nearly killed us. We're jotting down all the restaurants we want to hit as soon as we get out of here.

Monday, July 1, 1991

Two more days and we're out of here. By far the hardest part of this study is the last few days. In fact the whole last week has just been crawling by. I try to work as much as I can to pass the time faster. The anticipation of finally getting the hell out of here gets unbearable the closer you get to the release date.

I haven't done much drawing in here. I had planned on drawing storyboards like I did for all my short films, but this movie is ten times longer than my short films. It'll take forever. I'd need over 1,000 drawings. The reason you draw out storyboards is so that as the director you can show your crew what you have in mind. Since I won't have a crew, there's no point in my drawing out something I already have in my head just to show back to myself later on. So forget it.

Tuesday, July 2, 1991

Today is Peter's birthday. At least I wasn't the only one stuck in here on my birthday. Someone sent him black balloons. It's depressing. He's trying to make some extra money for school, but there are others in here that don't have a real job, can't get a real job, or are in so much debt they're trying to get some fast capital to pull themselves out of the hole. A lot of the guys in here are students who are paying off outstanding debts on credit cards.

Talk about a scam. All these credit card companies have started to saturate the college campuses by offering credit cards to college sophomores so that when they finally get out of college, they'll be in debt and have a job so they can continue paying until their dying day. You hand college kids a credit card, the first thing they do is use it as if it's cash. In a few months time they have run the limit buying books, tuition, a stereo, whatever. The only way they can pay it off completely is by hitting up their parents or checking into one of these places where in one month they can pay off the card completely. Then run right out and fill it up again. If I ever find out that these research hospitals, which are usually located in college towns, and these credit card companies are in business together . . .

I brought this up one night here and the debaters jumped all over it and were talking conspiracy the rest of the night.

Whenever you lock a bunch of guys up together it's inevitable that a few will be heavy debaters and conspiracy theorists. The rest of us just try and stay away, because if you're not careful, you can get sucked into a marathon debate that lasts three days.

Wednesday, July 3, 1991

It's 9:00 A.M. and I'm finally checking out of this place. I've got a stack of index cards representing *El Mariachi*. Most of the scenes are written up on legal pads, the unfinished scenes on index cards. All I have to do now is punch it into a computer and print it out.

It's funny, you've got a new lease on life by the time you get out of this place. You really get the chance to think about what you've been missing or overlooking in your life. As corny as it sounds, it makes you appreciate what you have: your health, your family, your social life or lack thereof, whatever. As soon as that door opened up people couldn't get back out into the world fast enough. Like opening the floodgates. Everyone had someone picking them up or they had their own car out in the parking lot and they drove off so fast, as if they had a million things to catch up with. Sadly, many of us leaving will be back again next month.

I laid out in the sun until Elizabeth got back from work. I've been under fluorescents all month and I look green. I want to get my color back before going back to work and especially before my family sees me, or they'll freak out. Elizabeth got home and we went to see *Terminator 2*, which opened today.

PREPRODUCTION

Monday, July 8, 1991

I've finished the script except for some of the scenes with the female lead, Domino. I'm afraid to write too much dialogue, since I haven't seen who's going to play the girl. If she can't act I'll have to give her fewer lines.

Carlos came up from Mexico with some clothes he thinks will work for his costume. He has one short-cut jacket I like but it doesn't match his black pants. I guess this will have to do.

Later we went to Keith's so he could borrow my video camera. We checked out the Arriflex 16s camera he has. Keith said that they're still working on a script for a short film that they plan to film with the Arriflex. Carlos and I were drooling over the Arri. If we could borrow it, we could make a great-looking film. It's a 16mm, it's got a 5.7 Kinoptic wide-angle lens that is so wide it doesn't need focusing. Point and shoot. That would really come in handy in action scenes and general running around handheld, because the wider the lens the smoother the shots. It also has a good zoom lens on it (a 12-120 Angeniuex zoom lens). I told Carlos we can't go over $10,000 or we'll risk losing money when we sell the movie. I asked him if he had called the Mexican video distributors in Los Angeles to try and find out how much they'd buy the movie for. He said that they have to see it first, that it depends on the quality, what Mexican name actors we have, etc.

What we'll have to do is jam pack this movie with action and a lot of movement and camera angles to make it look as expensive as possible, that way we can get a good price even if we can't get a name actor to star in it. We still haven't heard from Lina Santos yet, so we've got to move forward as if we don't have her.

Carlos left me $100 to buy a few lights and things.

Friday, July 12, 1991

On my way to Mexico, I stopped off in San Antonio so that my friend Mario at the photo lab I worked at in high school could check out my Sekonic light meter. I banged it up quite a bit on the last short film I shot. I told him that I was trying to shoot this low-budget action movie and he thought I was crazy. I asked Mario about lighting. He said that at his old store in Eagle Pass they used to sell a starter's lighting kit for 16mm film. They even sold a simple 16mm camera. Not anymore. Everything's video now.

I realized that I was not going to find someone with a decent lighting setup for me to borrow, plus I'm afraid that if I have big lights, I might not have any place to plug them in. I'll be shooting in a small Mexican border town, I don't know what the electrical conditions will be in places like the jail, the bar, etc.

I've decided to light with 250-watt photoflood lights, also known as practicals, and to use a faster speed film. These are regular size light bulbs that fit in regular lamp sockets, but that give off light at 3200° Kelvin, so they're color balanced for indoor film. With indoor film, a regular light bulb registers red on film. But the 250-watt bulb registers as white light. Maybe I can use that as my light source and shoot all my indoor scenes in tight medium shots or close-ups so that I can bring the light in close and set it up right out of frame. So what if the movie looks a little grainy? It's what happens on the screen that counts not the little grainy things floating around the frame.

I bought a couple of bulbs at another photo shop since they didn't have any at Mario's store. My light meter checked out fine, so I'll run some tests with the lights in Mexico.

I arrived in Mexico to scout locations with Carlos. I looked at the two hotels Carlos had sent to me in the research hospital on videotape. They look completely different in person. The one I like is actually the one right across the street from Carlos's house. He hadn't videotaped the back portion. It's amazing. It looks like an Escher drawing. The color is a weird, peeling aqua, and the stairs are narrow and perilous-looking. We can easily stage a great escape/shootout here.

I looked at the several bars he had videotaped for me. None of them really look right, but I chose our friend Samuel's bar, Amadeus, for Domino's bar. It's a little too fancy, but it's dark, air-conditioned, and less than a block away from Carlos's house, our base camp. We're calling this section of town our backlot, since everything we need is within a two- or three-block radius.

We still can't find a place for Domino's upstairs bedroom. In the movie it will appear as if it's upstairs from her bar. I checked out the unused upstairs of Carlos's house. It's full of weird, slanted green furniture from the '60s, but we have no choice. It's big enough to put in the freestanding antique bathtub I have in the script for the scene where she holds a knife to his balls as he takes a bath.

I don't usually like to write in props we don't already have access to or can get easily, because it just causes a lot of headaches trying to find things at the last minute. It's better to figure out all the things you own or can borrow that will add production value, and then include those in the script. But I like the tub scene. I couldn't resist. It'll be worth the trouble. I asked Carlos if he can look around town for an antique bathtub. He said it would be impossible. He knew because Alfonso Arau wanted a bathtub like that for *Like Water for Chocolate* and they had to go to San Antonio to get it.

"Well, where's the one you got for him?" I asked him. Carlos thought it might still be at the set, since they're preserving the set as a tourist attraction. "Well, call Alfonso and ask him if we can borrow it; they're not using it anymore." Carlos took care of it.

We've run into a problem. The whole time I was in the research hospital Carlos was interviewing girls to play the part of Domino in case we couldn't get Lina Santos. We decided I should have at least five finalists to choose from, since it'll be a difficult role. It would be next-to-impossible to find someone with prior acting experience; this is a small border town. Well, Carlos couldn't find *anyone*. No one wanted to do it. Everyone was working, or busy, or too young, or too old, or just not right. We're doomed. My sister is an actress. She could do it. But she's in New York. We can't afford to fly her down. That would be the last resort. Plus I wouldn't want her to waste her time on something no one will see. I'll save her for Part II or III.

Saturday, July 13, 1991

Carlos told me about a great jail he just found. It's right outside of town and it's fairly new. He didn't even know it existed until his ranch hand, Roberto, got picked up for being drunk and unruly one Saturday night. Carlos had to go bail him out at this funny-looking little blue-colored jail. Mainly weekend wackos spend the night here. It's a little too small and cutesy for our big bad guy to be locked up in, but what the hell. It's all we got.

I got videotape of it so I could start planning the shots. The jail consists of three fairly good sized cells and a front area with two desks. Best of all, there are porcelain light sockets all around on the ceilings. I can screw in some of my photoflood light bulbs and we'll have plenty of light. Some sunlight streams through the bars.

I took some readings with my light meter. They're low. It'll be close, but we should do fine with some high-speed film and the natural light streaming in.

Carlos asked the Chief there at the jail if they have any machine guns. The Chief opened the drawer to his desk and there was a Mac-10. In another drawer was the extension barrel. We asked if we could shoot it outside with our blanks. They came outside with us and we shot a few blanks. Carlos said that we can get permission from the mayor to borrow a few guns, as long as the cops are around when we use them. Cool.

We have two ranches. One is Carlos's mother's ranch. It's the same ranch we've used in all our other Mexico short films. It's about five miles from base camp and it has a nice rusted swinging metal door attached to a containment wall. It's small, but if we combine it with another ranch belonging to some friends some thirty minutes away, it will give the illusion that Moco lives in a big fortress. The bigger ranch has a swimming pool that circles part of the house like a moat. We can have one of the scenes of Moco on the phone as he floats around in the pool for a change of scenery.

Carlos and I went shopping for a heftier guitar case. The one I got is made of cardboard. It looks stupid.

All the cases we saw cost about fifty bucks. Damn. I guess we'll just use the shitty cardboard one we have. Since you never see the two cases in one shot together, we can probably get away with using the same case for both Mariachi and Azul.

I'm happy now. The 250-watt practical photoflood bulbs worked in the Amadeus bar. (For some reason I was afraid they'd blow out or something, since the wiring looked a little faulty.) Now we'll be able to get all our indoor shots and have plenty of light. I'll just hold the reflector light right out of frame to light the subject's face and shoot medium close shots and close-ups. I won't be able to get wide establishing shots, but that's alright. We don't have extras to fill the wide shots anyway.

Monday, July 15, 1991

As I left for Austin, I told Carlos to find a local musician who can be our music man, since we'll need to prerecord at least two songs to play back on the set so Carlos can have something to lip-synch to when he's playing the guitar in the bathtub and when he sings in the bar. Carlos said that he has someone in mind, but the guy is hard to get a hold of since he has two jobs and is always working.

Friday, July 19, 1991

After looking through *American Cinematographer*'s want ads and eyeballing the prices on used Arriflex 16s cameras (about $1,800), I finally broke down and asked Keith if we can borrow his Arriflex for a couple of weeks. He said he's leaving town and going on a road trip with his roommates. They're going to shoot a movie on the road with a video camera, but they planned on also shooting some old 16mm film that someone had sitting in a fridge for five years.

I told him I couldn't get a camera anywhere else and that

we're all set to shoot. He's been a fan of my work for a long while, and he told me that I can borrow it because he's sure I'll put it to good use. Hallelujah.

Monday, July 23, 1991

Now I have my borrowed Arriflex camera, which I know nothing about. I called Pro Film and Video, a company that advertises in *American Cinematographer* that sells used camera equipment. They're based in Texas, so I figure if anyone knows this equipment and can tell me what I need, they'll be able to.

I called them up and asked one of the helpful knowledgeable salespersons for information. He happened to be the co-owner of the company so he really knew his stuff. I told him I had an old Arriflex 16s camera in front of me. As far as I could tell it had a 400-foot magazine on it, a couple of different shaped battery packs, two motor looking things—one that had a dial, the other which said 24—and then there were two lenses, an Angenuiex 12-120mm zoom and a Kinoptic 5.7mm lens. (You get this info by reading it off the top of the lenses.) I asked him if it was ready to run as is. He asked me if I had a torque motor.

"What's that?" I asked.

He told me it runs the 400-foot magazine from the camera.

"How much do those cost?"

"About $800," he told me. Hmmm.

"What would it look like if I already had one?" I asked.

"It would be attached to the side of the magazine," he told me.

I've got it. Thank God. I told him I needed a battery cable. He asked what the battery receptacles looked like. I described them and he told me he'd dig one up for me. I needed a neutral density filter for the zoom. He said he'd dig one up for that as well. The 5.7mm lens already came with a filter. He told me how to install them.

"Wait, what are these motor looking things I've got?" I asked. "One has a dial that goes from 8 to 64 and the other just says 24."

He said the dial one is a variable speed motor. He said that by turning the dial I can set the camera to shoot fast-motion or slow-motion. I asked him if the motor that said 24 was a sync motor (meaning it would run at a constant speed to sync up with a crystal sync tape deck for sound). He said it was a constant speed motor but it probably wasn't crystal sync. That's alright; I don't have a crystal sync tape recorder anyway. I'm recording all the sound wild (no reference back to the film at all. Everything will have to be synced to picture by hand).

Wednesday, July 24, 1991

I got my battery cable. I loaded a roll of black and white film into the camera for a test run. The camera seemed to be working. It was loud, but it didn't sound like it was eating any film. I shot some footage of my wife running around the apartment complex while aiming a shotgun at me. I shot fast motion and slow motion and swapped lenses.

I was being very conservative with the film. I planned each shot quickly, rehearsed it once, then shot it, making sure to start the camera only just before my wife entered the frame and then cutting the camera as soon as I thought I got enough footage.

Before I knew it I had shot everything I wanted to test and still had half the roll left. And this was only a 100-foot roll! When we film the movie we'll be using 400-foot rolls. I figure if I shoot the whole movie this way, planning and cutting quickly, I can save a lot of film. Also, I found that the camera is so noisy that psychologically it seems like you're shooting all your film away very quickly, so you tend to shoot faster and use less film. That will help me a lot. Providing nothing technical goes wrong, the footage should come out good enough to work with. Even if it doesn't, the movie is an action picture and will have so many cuts and move so quickly there won't be time to see the inconsistencies and errors. Hopefully.

I developed the black and white roll locally. I took it over to the university and viewed it on a Steenbeck that was sitting idle in the Film Department. My test footage came out fine.

There were no scratches on the film so I knew the camera was OK. Everything seemed to be running at a normal speed. The slow-motion sutff looked fantastic, almost like a real movie, I thought to myself. There were no annoying hairs flickering across the screen even though I forgot to check the film gate.

I was excited. I had a working camera, a decent script, almost all the props, the locations, maybe an effects man. All I needed now were a couple of reflectors for my lightbulbs and we'd be ready.

Tommy Nix, a fellow film school reject who worked on "Pretty Good Man" with me, wants to come along to help out on the "crew." I've been thinking about bringing an extra guy to help haul equipment around and pull the wheelchair dolly but I'm afraid I'll be jinxed by bringing anyone down. I'd hate to take someone down all excited to make a movie, and then have this old camera break down on the second day of filming and have to come all the way back home defeated.

It's not that I fear failure. I just fear failure in front of other people. I told him that I'd shoot for a while and if it's working out and I feel I need someone, I'll have him come down and help out. If nothing else he can film a behind-the-scenes video for me. I'd like to document this, so if things don't work out, I can study the behind-the-scenes footage to see what I did wrong. For now, I told him to sit tight.

Saturday, July 27, 1991

Good Morning. I'm leaving for Mexico. I have my newly borrowed Arriflex 16s camera, lenses, one 400-foot magazine, three batteries, practicals, gaffer tape, audiotape, film, my Nikon with a 28mm lens for publicity photos, and a crappy stand. We still need a few props from Del Rio, but so far things look good.

I bought two Acme lights, the kind of aluminum dome reflector clip-on lamps you find in hardware stores. I bought both my lamps and seven 250-watt bulbs at a photo shop. I ended up buying the lamps at full price: thirty bucks each. I could have gotten them for less at a flea market or borrowed them from somebody, but when you rush, you overspend. I got ripped off.

When I got to Mexico, Carlos and I celebrated the beginning of our film at our hangout—La Posta. Great fajitas, charro beans, the works. As we ate, I explained the movie and pointed out scenes I like. He said one word to me: "Genius." They say genius is 10% inspiration, and 90% perspiration. This script represents our inspiration. Now it's time to sweat.

Sunday, July 28, 1991

We visited Reinol Martinez. He's an old friend who had starred in some of our earlier home movies. We want him to play the bad guy with the guitar case of guns named Azul, so we're here to choose his Azul costume. We choose costumes for each actor by raiding their closet and giving them one of their own outfits to wear every day. The script calls for Azul to wear black so that he can get confused with the black-clad Mariachi. But Reinol doesn't own any black shirts. *Not even a black T-shirt.* Doesn't anyone wear black around here? I don't have a black shirt either, and I'm too cheap to buy him one, so I let him wear my dark navy blue T-shirt. That will have to do. He put his black leather vest over the navy blue T-shirt. Costume complete, I guess. El cheapo productions.

We have to shoot his scenes first since he begins school in a few days. Carlos and I went to the town church to start our movie off with a Divine Blessing. We heard a piercing voice belting out *Ave Maria.* I told Carlos to find that person and if he plays guitar, he's our music man. We couldn't find him. The voice seemed to be coming from the walls. Someone showed us to the outdoor stairwell that leads to the balcony and the singer emerged. It's Juan Suarez. He's the guy Carlos had been telling me about. I'm convinced he's our music man. He agreed to come over Monday during his lunch break to write us a song or two. Things are really starting to fall into place now. It's amazing how many small details have to be addressed in order for it all to come together.

Carlos decided to push our luck by asking Lina Santos, who is in Del Rio for a few days, to play the part of Domino. We

called her and set a time to meet with her on Monday since
we'll already be in town to pick up the squibs Carlos ordered
from LA.

Monday, July 29, 1991

We crossed the border into Del Rio and sent a check for
$2,000 to Allied Film Labs where we'll be getting our film de-
veloped and transferred to video for our future services account. We went to Lina's house. She was swimming outside,
looking like a real star. We sat down and nervously asked her
if she'd do us a favor. I told her about our plan, our good
script, and how we needed to sell this movie in order to make
some money to make additional movies, each time moving up
the ladder a little more.

I told her we were already going to jam-pack this movie
with the kind of action and camerawork the distributors are
not used to seeing on these quickie, low-budget, straight-to-
video action movies, but that her name attached to the movie
would make it an easier sell for the distributor. We asked her
if she'd consider playing the leading female role of Domino.
She said that she had to go back to Mexico tomorrow for some
other business and that she would check her calendar. If she's
free, she'll come down next Monday for four and a half days.

We drove quietly back to Acuña to finish up the script and
any other business. I asked Carlos if he thought she'd do it. He
shrugged. I asked him if he thought we could sell the movie
without a name actor. He shrugged. I have a feeling we'll
never hear from her again. Maybe we should bite the bullet
and just load up the film with action and try to sell it for a
good price. I mean what would they rather have? A good ac-
tion-packed movie with no stars or a shitty movie with a famous soap opera star? I think I know the answer, but I'd
rather not think about that right now. I need to stay pumped
up for the work ahead.

Our music man, Juan Suarez, arrived. He had an hour and
a half for lunch. He sat down, and immediately I turned on
the video camera. I told him we were short on time and that
if he came up with a tune I liked, I wanted to be able to play it

back to him in case he forgets what it was he played. He started to play something that sounded really good and I said, "That's it! That's perfect! What is that?" He looked up at me, confused. "Nothing, I was just warming up."

I'm so desperate for music I'll take anything at this point. I told him that what he just played was perfect and we should develop that some more. I turned on my cassette tape recorder and told him to play it again, and see where it takes us. I recorded it on cassette as well as video so that Carlos can play back the video and learn the fingerings. We called the song "Mariachi Love Theme." That's original. I asked him if he could try and work out some words for it and come back in a few nights to record the song. He said he thought he could. We went on to another song. He strummed out an instrumental I think we can use somewhere. I taped that. In the last twenty minutes before his lunch break was over, he recorded a variation on an old traditional song for the bathtub scene. We rewrote the words to fit the script and I recorded this on Mariachi Audiotape #1. He left and we settled on getting together in a few days to record the first song with words. That way I'll have at least a couple of songs ready to use if we don't come up with anything better later on.

Carlos and I ate dinner and went to sleep at 9:00 P.M.

I finished writing scene 6 today.

Tuesday, July 30, 1991

Carlos left early this morning to get the blanks from a gun shop in Del Rio. He got back four hours late due to the gun shop's lazy owner who didn't open the store until noon. We tried out the blanks and they weren't good enough. They go bang and that's all. No smoke, no fire, nothing.

So far we've shot nothing. We still don't have a cash register for the hotel scene (the hotel doesn't have one, but the script does). No blanks, no guns, no Falomir (the special effects guy who's gonna rig the squibs, shoot the spark gun, and blow up the Chevy). We're trying to get the mayor's signature so we can borrow a couple of Uzis from the Police Department. We haven't found the police chief to sign the release permit for the weapons. Falomir did call and suggest some gun specialists to order movie blanks from. We ordered fifty full flash 9mm blanks.

I met the girls Reinol has a scene with tomorrow. They're perfect. They all look like Reinol. Things will slowly fall into place. I hope.

Carlos came in excited. He just ran into a girl that said she'd help us and that he thinks will be good for Domino. "You just ran into her on the street?" He explained that she works around the corner at a government office, and that he's known her for several years, but that he never thought she'd be right until he saw her just now. Her face is good, she's smart, she's a little older, about 28. I told him to bring her in.

Her name is Consuelo Gomez. Her hair was pulled back in a bun so I really couldn't tell what she looks like. I had her take her hair down. I grabbed the video camera and taped her as she talked to Carlos. I told them to just make up lies and tell them to each other. I told her to slowly dislike Carlos, getting angrier at everything he says. That was easy enough. She's alright. She'll be our backup girl if we can't find anyone else.

PRODUCTION

Wednesday, July 31, 1991

It was our first day of shooting. We met at Reinol "Azul" Martinez's house. He has a bedroom upstairs with a pool table, a refrigerator, and assorted junk that makes it the perfect location for Azul's hideout. There are several short scenes to be played in the hideout, so I decided to start the production by shooting these scenes first. They were fairly easy and a good way to get back into the groove of filming. Besides, Azul has only a few days to shoot all his scenes since he starts school in Saltillo next week.

We shot the scene where he wakes up and talks to Moco on the phone, all the scenes with him and the girls, and a few others where he scolds his henchmen. I shot the scenes silent, then had them repeat all their lines while I recorded the sound up-close with the camera off. Azul is amazing. He seems to be saying the lines the exact same way each time. That will help me when I sync the sound up to the picture in editing. I was rough and creaky and more than a little disoriented today. I'm glad we tackled the easy scenes as warm-up. Everyone's energy and enthusiasm helped us get everything we needed despite the scorching weather. Without air-conditioning and with all five actors, plus Carlos and me in the room, it turned into an oven. I couldn't imagine the heat wave we'd have in there with a big lighting setup. Instead, I used one practical in an overhead socket above the pool table and just let the sunlight come through the many windows all around the room. I used 320 ASA film. We had a gallon of really watered down Gatorade for everyone to drink.

I loaded the film there at Azul's house downstairs in a dark bathroom. Again, no air-conditioning. I was covered with sweat before we even filmed the day's first take. I've learned my lesson. From now on I'll load the film at Carlos's house so I can at least have air-conditioning and a fan. I'm sure it doesn't do the film any good to have sweat dripping all over it.

The cops were actually at the location before we were, ready to lend us the Uzis. We shot all the takes with the Uzis first so that the cops could go back to work. We also brought along Carlos's .38 special, Azul's friend's .38 automatic, and a few small .22s so that the weapon-filled guitar case would look well stocked.

We had only one problem at Azul's. Since it was so hot, he kept taking his leather vest off between shots. In one sequence he forgot to put it back on. I hope it's not too noticeable. Azul asked if we should reshoot the scene and he'd put the vest back on. I told him it wasn't worth wasting film on something like that and that if people noticed it, that means they're probably bored and we've lost the battle so we might as well keep going.

We changed locations and shot at the club Amadeus where Azul is served a drink by the assistant and accidentally picks up the wrong guitar case. At Amadeus, the assistant bartender was very nervous. We couldn't get him to calm down.

With my 250-watt bulbs I was getting more than an f2.8 light reading in the club scenes with my 320 ASA film stock. Not bad for a bunch of practical lights. We didn't have the cellular phone for the jail scene so we had to blow that off for today. All in all, things went fairly smooth. After we wrapped, Carlos and I got home to a huge banquet of a meal courtesy of his mom. (At Carlos's house, every meal his mom cooks seems like a banquet. She cooks as if ten people are at the table when it's only Carlos and myself.)

As we ate we figured out what scenes we'd shoot tomorrow, and after dinner Carlos got on the phone and started calling everyone and letting them know. We'll have to schedule everything on a day-by-day basis because everyone's schedule changes constantly.

Thursday, August 1, 1991

Carlos and I got up early and tried to track down a cellular phone. The one we were originally going to have fell through. I sent Carlos to Del Rio to cut his hair. I decided to save the long-hair look for the sequel. That'll make more sense, anyway. We're going to have to dye his hair, too. His natural hair color is too blond.

Carlos returned with short hair and a *Texas Times* article
about our movie. He's on the cover. They want to interview
me for next month's issue. Never. I'm more of a behind-the-
scenes man, I'll let Carlos do the interviews and be famous,
that's always been his dream, anyway. I just want to make
movies.

We went to see the blacksmith that is making us the pulley
for the bus scene. He gave us the pulley and some cable to try
it out with. The pulley looks sturdy enough. Only twelve bucks,
handmade.

We've tracked down a cellular phone and are still trying to
contact Lina Santos. She hasn't told us if her schedule will
allow her to come shoot our movie.

The local newscasters came over for a meeting. These guys
are the two main newscasters in town and are usually very
critical of just about everything that goes on in the town. We
figured that since we'll be running in the streets, firing blanks,
and causing a ruckus for the next two weeks it would be best
to have these guys on our side. So we cast them in the movie
as the Hotel Clerk and the First Bartender.

We've shot 1¼ rolls, or thirteen minutes. That's about 130
bucks of film already and we still have to develop it and transfer it to video. I told Carlos how much film we've used and he
got nervous. I told him that it was not a lot considering how
many scenes we've shot. I'm being extremely conservative. We
have to order the film a few rolls at a time from Kodak. Usually you would order all your film at once and get a discount,
but since we're not sure that this camera is going to hold up
or that anything we're doing is going to work, we decided to
bite the bullet and pay full price a little at a time and see how
it goes. If the camera breaks and we have to shut down for a
while or forever at least we won't have spent too much on
film.

We tried out the 9mm full flash movie blanks and they
looked good.

We set-dressed the upstairs for Domino's bedroom and tub
scenes. As I was moving furniture around, placing the tub on
a carpet and trying to fix up the bed using materials at hand,
I stopped and looked around and thought, "What the hell am

I doing? I'm no decorator. Why am I set dressing? This looks like shit." I guess that's what happens when you try to wear too many hats. You find that most of them don't fit.

Friday, August 2, 1991

Well, we got up early. All for nothing. The sky is black. Nothing will match. We went ahead and shot Carlos entering town, getting his shoes shined, etc. At midday we shot Carlos and Azul entering and leaving the Corona Club. We went to Del Rio for dinner, and rented *Escape From New York*, the movie that got us into filmmaking. When Carlos and I met in high school we talked about making movies like *Escape From New York*. Now we're making this movie and the gun Carlos ended up with is the same kind they used in *Escape*—a Mac-10.

Saturday, August 3, 1991

We tried to film at the jail (we got the cellular phone) but the place was packed!! Of course it was, they do their best business on the weekends. We'll have to come back on a Tuesday or Wednesday. Azul was all ready to go. At least now he knows his lines for the scene. We went back to the house and shot the scene where Carlos first walks into Domino's apartment. Since Azul was with us, he was able to help out by pulling me in a wheelchair for the long dolly shot into the bedroom. We borrowed the wheelchair from the hospital next door. Carlos's father was a surgeon at that hospital, so they lend us the chair whenever we need it and no patients are using it.

We packed up and went out to the eighteen-mile mark to shoot the scene where the Mariachi is trying to hitch a ride into town. Azul had found a turtle on the highway a few days before so we brought it along to try and include it in some shots. He turned out to be a great actor. I told Carlos that for fun we could have the turtle going to town at the same time as the Mariachi and that at the end of the movie when the Mariachi is leaving town, the turtle can be leaving too. We tried a rehearsal. Carlos got on his mark and put the turtle on the ground. The turtle wouldn't walk down the highway. Since it is a desert turtle, it tried to get away from us as fast as it could by making a break for the edge of the road. So I told Carlos to put him at the other end of the highway, and then to run back a few yards to his mark, start walking, and time it so that he and the turtle cross at the same time and to simply step over the turtle when they meet. Carlos put the turtle down and ran to his mark. I started the camera and Carlos started walking. When he got near it, the turtle ducked into his shell. After Carlos stepped over it, the turtle came out of its shell and kept walking. It looked great. I told Carlos I was going to splurge on this shot and shoot two takes. One take in a wide shot so we could see the turtle walking the entire width of the street, and then a second shot in close-up so we can see the turtle duck into his shell a little better. The turtle did the same thing each time and we got the sequence in two shots, one take of each composition. We'll need the turtle for the last scene so we have threatened Carlos's ranch hand, Roberto, with the loss of his job if anything happens to the turtle. So Roberto is feeding the turtle regularly.

As we were driving back to town we saw a coconut stand selling cold coconut milk right out of the shell. They chop a hole in the coconut using a machete then stick a straw into it for drinking. I thought it would make for a nice piece of business to have the thirsty Mariachi buy some coconut milk to quench his thirst as he enters the town. We shot the sequence quickly as the sun dropped.

For the shot of the ice bursting into the lens, I layed the camera down on the table with the wide angle lens on it and had the coconut man chop the ice really hard so that shards of ice would fly all around the camera. Some pieces hit or brushed right by the lens. I guess if this was my camera I wouldn't try and get shots like these for fear of messing it up. But it's not my camera.

We moved a little too quickly. As we were driving home, I realized we never showed the Mariachi paying for the coconut. Carlos asked if we should go back and shoot it really quickly. I told him not to bother. We can fix it in the narration by saying that the coconuts are free. A gift from the city to all entering strangers or something stupid like that.

Sunday, August 4, 1991

Still no word from Lina so I guess Consuelo will play Domino. I'm also trying to contact Peter. Carlos secured a crane from the local electricians for tomorrow afternoon. We picked up the little boy that had been hanging around the set during Azul's scenes (he had been looking through the camera lens and drinking our Gatorade). I thought he'd be perfect for the part of the little boy in the dream sequences. We got permission from his parents and shot all his scenes at once. He was loose and funny, imitating Carlos and cupping his hand to his eye as if filming his own movie. He thinks he's an actor now. He even gave me his long movie name: Oscar Manuel Fabila Menchaca. We shot all of his scenes in slow-motion to kind of build suspense . . . and extend the screen time.

As we were driving to one of the locations, we passed a really cool place. It was a buildingless door. It looked as if the whole building had been knocked down but the metal door and its door frame remained in perfect working condition. Carlos said he had seen it a while back and wanted to show it to me. I told him we can't pass up the chance of using freaky locations free of charge like this. We got out and I chose to use it for yet another shot of the dream sequence. When in doubt, have dream sequences! I got my Nikon out and shot some quick production stills of the door with the kid standing in front holding the basketball. That'll look good on the back of the video box. Make it look almost like an art film. I can't wait to go back to school and when people ask what I did this summer I can say, "I made an Artsy Foreign Action Film."

For the dream scene I had the kid bounce the basketball that I think later will turn into a human head. We have this foam rubber human head and we might as well use it somewhere. I can't think of any other place to put it so we might as well put it in the dream sequence. When in doubt . . .

Monday, August 5, 1991

Early morning. We got Jaime de Hoyos, who plays Moco's main henchman Bigotón (Mustache), and a few other guys to film the scene where they chase Carlos around the Hotel Coahuila. Most of what we shot was their running around, I saved Carlos's shots for a day when we can't get anyone to shoot for whatever reason. The cops stopped traffic and helped us fire off the Uzis. A huge crowd was gathered in the street and sidewalks. To get the close-ups of the fire belching out of the barrels I had to get close to the guns. I ended up with hot wax from the blanks riddling my body. Fun times. We also drove to a corner street to shoot the scene where Carlos runs up and over the truck as two bad guys shoot each other. It went great. I wasn't sure how all this was going to look. It works on paper but shooting it is a whole different deal. One problem we have with these guns we borrowed is that they are real guns. With movie guns, they put a smaller barrel inside the gun so that the shells can eject. Blanks have less force so if you put them in a regular gun they will jam, because there wasn't enough force to eject the shell. So here we have these cool machine guns but they only shoot one bullet per take. So I'm going to have to do an amazing editing job to make it appear that they have even semiautomatic weapons. I'll show one blank, cut away to the guy getting shot, cut back to another single blank going off and then put a sound effect over the whole section as if the gun was firing continuously.

We wrapped at noon because it was so hot and the sun was so high. We'll shoot the rest tomorrow morning when it's cooler. Carlos and I ate at the house along with Jamie De Hoyos. Since Carlos ran all over his truck the least we could do was share our banquet with him. We are trying to shoot our scenes quickly like we did today so that the actors will be more willing to show up for other scenes. For one thing, we don't want them to feel taken advantage of and if we finish with them early we won't have to feed them. After we ate, Carlos and I went out to shoot some of his other solo scenes.

We got home and Juan Suarez came over to record the love song with the words he wrote. It's called, "Ganas de Vivir."

Tuesday, August 6, 1991

Got up at 7:00 A.M. to go to the jail. Today is jail day. We filmed Moco's men entering the jail, slow-motion. While we were filming, one of the real prisoners was being loud so the guards took him outside so he wouldn't bother us. He escaped. They caught him an hour or so later and slapped him around. I wish I could have taped that.

We went to the ranch and filmed Azul and Domino's death scene. Afterwards, we shot Azul's scene in Amadeus where he enters and Domino serves him the beer in the bottle. Domino had to leave for the day so we shot the scene without her. I'll shoot her part of it later. Azul did a great job once again. He listens to what I tell him and can imitate even the slightest facial gesture. Too bad he dies. I wonder if we'll have anyone left for the sequel.

Carlos did a test ride down the cable set up in the backyard, then we went to Del Rio for pizza. In Del Rio we rented *Perro Rabioso 2*, which is the latest bigger budget straight-to-video Mexican action movie. Our main competition. It was awful, which really got us charged up.

Wednesday, August 7, 1991

We're up early. At the jail we shot Azul's lines in the cell. One of the cells was occupied by a drunk cop. He didn't move all day. He slept on the concrete floor face down. All the other prisoners were shoved into one cell so we could use the others. Later, I needed the shot of Azul's men pointing the guns between the bars of the cell. I didn't want to take the time to relocate the sleeping prisoners so we got permission to go ahead with the shot. As we did, one prisoner woke up, saw the guns pointed into the cell and started screaming. He'd been asleep the whole time and didn't know what was going on. The cops laughed. Great fun. We wrapped and left.

An article about us came out in the local paper. Front page! Pictures of dead bodies from the truck scene graced the article.

Carlos and I went to the outskirts of town to shoot some more walking shots. They were huge buzzards flying around him but every time I started to film they'd disappear. We went to Del Rio to mail our film off.

Today we shot Hotel Clerk (one of the newscasters) at the Hotel Coahuila. I shot as fast as I could to get all his lines in because he had to leave by noon. After Hotel Clerk left, I changed rolls to outdoor film and we shot the part where Azul is surrounded by the bad guys as they search his guitar case. It went well. Afterwards, we all went to La Posta to celebrate. It was Jaime, Azul, Alejandro, Carlos, and myself. The food is great here.

Peter came down from Austin. We cruised to the Corona Club and it was packed. We scouted for girls to play Peter's manicurist. Peter loves it here. "All this from being at the research hospital," he tells me. "Who would have thought . . ."

Saturday, August 10, 1991

We packed up the truck with food and drinks and headed out thirty minutes to Moco's ranch. We shot all of Peter's scenes for this location: the opening scene, the pool scene, the hair and nails scene. Peter looks great. This morning we had gone shopping for a white shirt and found an oversized guayabera. It looks funny on him.

Peter took one look at all his lines and freaked out. He can't speak a word of Spanish. I have to teach him the lines phonetically. I try and cut some of his lines down, but he still stumbles over the pronunciation, and has no idea what he's saying. I break up the lines into sections and tell him I'll film him saying half the line, then I'll cut away to the girl or his glass of booze or the phone or something so he doesn't have to say it all on camera, and then he can just read the script for the sound.

We end up putting sunglasses on him so that Carlos can stand right out of frame and hold the script up for Peter to read. If you look close you'll notice Peter is always looking down at something through his shades.

In the scene in the pool he had cheat notes cupped in his hand. He feels like shit for having to do it this way, but I tell him it's no big deal. All of five people will probably ever see this movie. The main thing is to look pissed off.

We were dead tired by the time we got home that evening but we went out anyway. We hit the Corona Club and Amadeus until 3:00 A.M. I was prepared for this since Peter is here for a short while and needs to be entertained. When he's gone I'll go back to my regular routine of staying home and relaxing after a long day's shoot.

Sunday, August 11, 1991

Today we went to the other ranch that's closer to Carlos's house for the ending scene of Peter with his men around him. I experimented with one of Peter's lines by shooting it in slo-mo. I had him spit as he said his line. We rigged him for squibs. He was ready to die. We told him it may hurt a bit. He was ready. He thought he was, anyway. *Boom!* The look on his face as his shirt explodes is priceless. We didn't want to put any more on him so we blew up a ground squib in front of him on the camera stand. The blood flew up in front of the camera lens. We cleaned up and went home. Peter napped while we set up for his last scene where he's talking to Domino on the phone as he plays some strange card game. It looked good. We went to Crosby's for a drink then we took him to the bus stop. He didn't want to leave.

Monday, August 12, 1991

No film!!! We've been buying film a few rolls at a time, so we could abort the project with a minimal loss in case our camera broke down. But our new shipment isn't here yet. I called Kodak and they said we should get it today so we were waiting in Del Rio. I was at Carlos's Del Rio house while he drove around town looking for the UPS truck. He found one but the driver didn't want to look for our package. He said that there were several trucks and he probably wasn't carrying it. Carlos was pissed. So we waited around and watched TV. Finally a UPS truck shows up. Same driver, same truck. He thought we were gonna beat him up. The whole day wasted. I'll never use UPS again, they've proven to be consistently awful. From now on it's FedEx. We checked out the Corona Club and plan to shoot there tomorrow. There were four bartenders hanging around. They have to be here early tomorrow to clean so we recruited them to be the bad guys in that scene.

Tuesday, August 13, 1991

We got up early for the Corona Club scene. The other newscaster showed up on time for his scene as the bartender. He's good. We went over his lines briefly then he practiced as I set up. Afterwards, I acted out the scene for him as I had it in mind when I wrote it, he did it, and we shot all his scenes. Next, we shot the scenes with the four bad guys. They're perfect.

When we were making the squibs, we had sent Roberto out to buy us some condoms. He came back with a few yellow ones. We filled them with fake blood. The blood dripped out of the tip of one of them. Carlos saw this and freaked out because these were his brand of condoms.

The squibs looked weak until I finally thought to put the explosive inside the blood pack instead of behind it. Blood sprayed everywhere. We shot everything except Carlos's lines. We filmed from 8:00 A.M. to 8:00 P.M. It's been our longest straight shoot yet. But considering all the shots and setups and nonactors we had to work with, not to mention going back at the end of the day and replaying the scenes for complete sound recording, I'd say we did really well. My back is killing me, though. We went home. I ate and slept.

Thursday, August 15, 1991

We got up early and shot Domino's first two scenes (movie order) at club Amadeus. We returned to the house for her scene with the pit bull. Then, we packed up and shot a few shots with her at the graveyard for the dream sequences. After that, it was off to the ranch to shoot the scene where Carlos finds Domino's dead body. Then we shot the final scene of Carlos's shots. We rigged his fake hand with a ground squib. I had to operate the camera and detonate the charge. It's times like this that you need an assistant. It worked fine.

We shot the Dead End Scene where Carlos uses the guitar case full of weapons to kill the bad guys. Then I got the shot where Carlos is walking through the busy street with a guitar case in one hand and the Mac-10 in the other. This is a Friday and all the tourists were driving by wondering what the hell was going on. Since I was without a crew down the block on full zoom, all they saw was Carlos. A day in the life in Mexico, they must have figured.

We returned to the Corona Club to shoot Carlos's lines and to record the audio for the Bartender, something we forgot to do yesterday and didn't think of until he had already left. I hope it matches up. All went well.

We went to the graveyard and shot a few things for the dream sequences so we could finish off the roll. I got a nice jump out of Carlos. We drove to Del Rio to drop off two more rolls of film. Carlos called for the crane again. We've been trying to get it all this time. It turns out that the people at the electric company were feeling kind of down. One of their electricians got fried yesterday . . . on the crane. We decided we don't want to use that crane anymore. Bad luck.

Friday, August 16, 1991

We did a pickup on the scene where the three bad guys get shot at near the black truck site. We rigged the squibs and shot them one by one. The funny thing was that each guy didn't tell the next guy how painful it was. So by the end, the last guy was kicking the others for not telling him it hurt.

We woke up right as Domino arrived for her scene. I set up quickly and we shot a few scenes before lunch time. After lunch, we shot the tub scene. I'm planning on getting wild sound of *everything* because last night I saw an awful movie on Cinemax that had been completely dubbed and the foley work was awful. It really scared me. It was unwatchable. I hope ours sounds decent or I'll die.

We shot all morning at Amadeus. First we shot the scene where Jaime walks in and asks Domino for the phone. Then I shot Domino's lines. Both did very well considering they hadn't been shown their lines until it was time to shoot. The assistant bartender showed up and we shot all his parts for cutaways. As we were filming Domino's scenes in the apartment, I got a call from Elizabeth. It seems Ben Davis called. They're going to need the camera back Tuesday. The guy that lent it to them needs it back. Some sort of emergency. Carlos looks panicked. I don't know if we can finish in time. We may have to cut scenes. And we have to shoot really fast now.

Saturday, August 17, 1991

At 7:30 A.M. we rigged the cable between a telephone pole and the hotel balcony. Actually, the man who built us the pulley rigged it up. He was there to supervise the stunt. Carlos swung across a few times for practice. Nope. Too low. I had them raise the wire. Carlos is supposed to glide above the bus. Then we'll cut to a shot of him landing on top. But it didn't look like we could get him high enough for that so I have to make it look like he lands on the hood. I got a shot from inside the bus of him landing on the hood. I like that better. Carlos was ready so we brought out the bus. The street was filled with onlookers. Carlos was sliding a little slow, so I sped up the camera to about 21fps. I was at the other end of the block on full zoom. Carlos only had to pass in front of the bus and the zoom compresses the action, making him look closer to it than he actually was. Easy. Carlos slid from the hotel balcony to the top of his truck on the other side of the street, where Fernando was ready to catch him. The bus started and Carlos waited. I told Carlos to go but he was still waiting. He finally went. I could tell that he was not gonna make it. I saw the bus slam into him, I was following all this on full zoom on a cheap stand so I tried to absorb the shakes, but I heard women screaming. I looked up and stopped the camera. I saw Carlos twisting around on the cable and Fernando caught him. Carlos looked at me for my verdict and I looked at him for his. He stuck his thumb out. I mimicked and yelled "Great! Next shot!" Carlos nodded in agreement. Our production assistant Roberto Martinez reassured the people around him that Carlos was supposed to do that.

After a few different angles of Carlos sliding on the wire and riding the bus like a surf board, we went in front of Carlos's house to shoot the scene where Carlos blows away a character named Taco from atop my car. I told Carlos that we should rig Taco so that he'd have one squib in front and one in back.

We'd detonate them at the same time. That way we can place him in front of his own car and blood will spray forward and onto his Bronco to look like the bullets made a clean exit. Well, we rigged him up and we were all set to go, when a car drove up. It was Taco's mom, wife, and little three-year-old daughter, arriving to watch the show from Carlos's porch. We blew Taco away. He slammed into the Bronco and was frozen, a look of complete pain on his face. He wouldn't move. I yelled cut. He still wouldn't move. Carlos ran over to him and asked how he was. He popped up and said, "Great. Didn't hurt a bit." His family was applauding. He was giving a real performance. Taco hopped in his Bronco with his kid as the wife drove the blood-covered vehicle away.

I finished off the indoor hotel scenes. I also shot some solo indoor stuff of Carlos. We changed rolls and shot the scenes where Carlos is getting chased through the hotel, jumping to the balcony, etc. Our multisquib panel was a dud, so we found someone to double for Carlos as he climbs over the balcony, so that Carlos would be free to detonate the ground squibs since I was busy running camera two stories below. I love this location. The staircases are narrow and very steep. The color is a weird aqua. I want to shoot here again. The ground squibs showed a little too much flame for ricochets. I wanted it to look like pieces of concrete are flying everywhere. So we rigged condoms full of dirt and put the squib inside. It looks good, the pieces of rubber that explode everywhere are dirty so they look like chunks of rock.

Later that night we shot all of Carlos's loft lines. (We already finished all of Domino's lines up here the other day.) Then at 11:00 P.M., we packed up and went to the club Amadeus's one-year anniversary party. The joint was packed and we announced that we were going to shoot a crowd scene. Everyone was excited. We got the shot of Carlos walking through the crowd with his guitar.

Monday, August 19, 1991

This morning we shot a scene with Azul's henchmen, a few motorcycle shots, running scenes of Carlos, and the rest of his dream sequences. We packed up to shoot the end scene with Carlos and the pit bull, but the motorcycle died. Bummer. And it started to rain! It never rains around here. I have to get the camera back tomorrow and this scene has to be shot at sunset. Carlos rushed to a garage to charge the battery, hoping it was just that. The rain finally stopped and the motorcycle started. The sun was going down and the location was eighteen miles away. We drove as fast as we could and I watched helplessly as the sun dropped. We got to the location, rigged Carlos's hand and strapped the dog on the motorcycle. I tried and got everything I wanted, even the turtle. We filmed them driving off but the dog kept trying to jump off. We strapped him on tighter. We got the shot. The sun was gone but I forgot the shot of his mechanical hand. I had to undercrank the camera and shoot at 8fps instead of 24fps so that more light would hit the film. Even at 8fps I barely got a 1.9 f-stop. We got the shot and we were gone. We ate and it was off for the final Amadeus scenes: Carlos singing "Ganas de Vivir," his first two scenes in the club, and a few other short scenes. We also shot three scenes with Domino. We finished it all, plus sound recording, by 3:30 A.M. A miracle.

Tuesday, August 20, 1991

I slept as long as I could: 9:00 A.M. We had to get a few last shots of the motorcycle, plus sound. We shot a few dream shots at my other favorite location: the buildingless door. I packed up and got ready to leave but Carlos couldn't remember what he had done with the permit for crossing the camera back to the US. He finally found it, and by 3:00 P.M. I was heading back to Austin.

I counted all the rolls of film we sent off. It added up to twenty-five rolls of film. Each roll is ten minutes long, so we did all right. We shot a little more than I wanted to, but with all the shots I got, I think there will be plenty to work with. If something, anything didn't come out, there is nothing we can do about it. If it all comes out, all I have to worry about is climbing into the editing bay and starting the real work—turning all these snippets of pictures into a movie.

POSTPRODUCTION

I sent all twenty-five rolls of 400-foot film to the lab for developing. At thirteen cents a foot, it came out to about $1,300. I then had them transfer the negative to ¾″ video with an "overall color correction." That means that the lab takes your negative and turns it into a positive image on video. This is a tremendous savings; since you don't have to make a positive work print first, you can go straight to making the positive on video. The "overall color correction" is correcting the first scene on the roll and then running the rest of the roll at that setting, making sure faces don't go green or what have you. Basically, it's a one-light print but with a little correction. That's all I needed. Since this was going to the Spanish home video market to compete against movies made with a lot less tender loving care, I knew my movie would still look pretty good, and be more than competitive even without the fancier, more expensive transfer and color correction.

The lab sent me back my ¾″ viedotapes which became my master tapes. From these I could go to any bottom-of-the-line ¾″ system and make straight cuts. I figured that if I was real careful, and planned as much as I could, I could make only one cut of the movie, and have that cut ¾″ videotape be the master tape that I could sell to the Spanish video distributors in Los Angeles. From that, they could make their VHS copies. I was hoping they'd accept ¾″ tape as the master tape since I couldn't afford to use digital tape or beta cam.

When I got my ¾″ tapes, I took them immediately to the local cable station and made some VHS copies so I could study the footage at home and make rough cuts using my old JVC VHS tape recorder and my RCA Pro-Edit video camera. While transferring from ¾″ to VHS, I got to watch my raw footage for the first time, which is a scary experience to say the least, now that it's too late to go back and reshoot anything if it didn't come out. But I was genuinely pleased to see all my shots exposed and somewhat in focus. Good enough, anyway.

I had prepared myself for a good amount of the material to be worthless, so I was pleased to see that there were no scratches or unusable shots. (I have a very lenient idea of what "usable shots" means.)

After transferring I took my tapes home and sat through all four hours of footage again. I think I have plenty to work with, even though I shot a lot of things in one take. It goes to show that if you plan carefully and have luck on your side, you can make a movie for less than $10,000. Even an action film. To think that four hours of film footage costs only . . . let's see with the twenty-five rolls of film I bought at full price coming out to be less than $2,400, developing at $1,300, then the transfer to video being about $2,800 . . . I've got this movie in the can with my master tapes and everything for about $6,500. We ended up spending a lot less than I thought we would.

Now I have to edit. No problem. There's a lot of places I can go to edit and it won't cost me a thing. As long as I pay for my videotapes, I've got a friend who has an old Sony 440 editing system I can use. I know there's some old equipment at school I can borrow, not to mention that the local public access station has the old Sony systems that they're getting ready to replace with better equipment, so nobody will be using the old stuff.

The first thing I do when I get my film back from the lab is *study* the footage completely and thoroughly. For an action film, four hours is not a lot of footage. There are a lot of things I would probably want to reshoot, but by studying the footage, you find that everything you really need is right there. It may need some rethinking and a lot of work, but it's all there.

Second, I begin editing immediately. But not the movie. Before even starting the movie, I need to get excited about the long journey ahead, so I cut a trailer. Like the kind you see in the movies before the main feature. The Coming Attractions. The process of cutting a trailer allows me to see what images from my film are the strongest, it gives me an idea of what the A material is, and how to exploit it. I want this movie to be fast paced so I'll make a fast-paced trailer. The trailer also gives me something to show people for the next few months when they ask me what I'm working on. Instead of showing them some lame, half-finished scene from my unfinished movie, I find that to sit them down and blast them out of their seats with a great trailer does wonders for your confidence and can give you the necessary creative juice to actually finish the movie and get through the laborious editing process.

The trailer will also come in handy when it comes time for me to sell the movie to the distributors, in that rather than having to get the buyers to block out enough time to sit and watch the movie, I can show them my two-minute trailer there at our initial meeting to get their interest.

Friday, September 5, 1991

Some old high school friends of mine called to see if I wanted to get together for a party they're throwing just across the street. I haven't seen them all in a while, but I told them no. I'm busy editing. It's funny how once you're locked into a project nothing else seems that important. You forget everything else your life is about and you hopefully pour it all into your movie. My wife is excited because she sees how focused I am. After all the work and money I've already put into this, I can't afford to be anything but focused. Even though this is a throwaway movie, I want to give it everything I've got because I know that I will learn so much more about filmmaking by making the experience as challenging as possible. If I'm going to do it, I really do have to go all the way or I'm wasting my time.

I'm editing a rough trailer for my movie here at home between my two VCRs. It's coming out really good. I'm cutting the trailer to Orff's "Carmina Burana" using my video camera to lay picture over the prelaid music track. I laid the music down first over black picture using the Audio Dub feature on my RCA Pro Edit camera. Then I play the parts of the movie I want to cut in over the music on my JVC, and lay the images over the music using the Video Dub feature on my Pro Edit camera. The Video Dub feature allows you to change picture on your tape without erasing the sound. These are just consumer products but you can really do a lot with them if you don't mind spending a lot of time. I've had a lot of practice so

I'm finished with this two-minute trailer in just a little over six hours.

Sunday, September 7, 1991

I've cut three different trailers. One is to Carmina Burana, another to some trailer music I swiped from another movie, and the last one, which is my favorite, is one that I took from *Drugstore Cowboy*. I rented the movie *Johnny Handsome* and at the start was a trailer for *Drugstore Cowboy*. The trailer had no dialogue from the movie, only cool music, some sound effects, and an announcer's voice reading off blurbs from the critics. His voice was booming stuff like, "Now, the most controversial film of the year. . . ." Then it shows clips of *Drugstore Cowboy* set to the music, punctuated with the critics' blurbs along with the names of the critics like Siskel and Ebert, saying that it was "a great movie" and so on. So what I did was record the trailer onto my RCA camera and I replaced only the images of their movie with images from *my* movie using the Video Dub feature. So it makes my movie look like a real movie and the trailer look like a real trailer, complete with stunning reviews. I've shown it to several people and it really gets them pumped up. Now I have to start editing the real movie. Damn. That's the hard part. With editing trailers you get that instant gratification you can't get with editing an entire movie until you've finished the whole thing. That takes forever.

Monday, September 8, 1991

I've decided to save myself a lot of time by doing a very rough edit of the movie here at home first, before going out and cutting on ¾" tape. By editing here at home I can block out the movie and know ahead of time how long the movie is, where the shots go, what works and what doesn't. Then I can take my camera into the ¾" editing rooms and use my rough cut as a guide in making my final cut. That way I'll just be working at cutting the movie smoothly on ¾" but do all the real work of blocking out the film here at home, where I can work whenever I want. I won't cut in any sound here at home, but that's all right. The picture is mostly visual. I'll have a good idea of how the movie plays.

Saturday, September 13, 1991

The movie is coming along. I've found a lot of mistakes but, fortunately, by really working with it I've found that just about anything can be fixed. The movie so far is shaping up to run pretty close to ninety minutes. I can't believe it. I must have formatted my script wrong. The script was only about thirty-five to forty pages. I thought for sure I was going to come up short.

Saturday, September 21, 1991

I went to the local public access station to edit a good version of my trailer on ¾″ for Keith Kritselis because he wants to air it on his public access show. So I cut the trailer to Orff's "Carmina Burana" again. I've gotten so used to the VHS version that this ¾″ version looks incredible. The cuts are a lot smoother, too. It took me ten hours.

Monday, September 23, 1991

Keith aired the Mariachi trailer on public access as part of his show. There was a lot of response from people who wanted to know how it was done. Keith had me get on the air and tell the audience what I was up to. I described the film, what I wanted to do with it, and so on. There was a lot of talk about low-budget movies, and how to make a good demo reel by shooting on film but transferring to video and editing on video for a much cleaner, more expensive-looking demo.

Wednesday, September 25, 1991

I started making backup copies of my master tapes there at the cable station. I'll need some backups in case the machines eat my master tapes. It's not unusual around here for that to happen, since the equipment is so old. The station is getting new equipment, but everyone's going to be using the new stuff, so I'll have to settle for the old. Fine by me, it beats renting an editing facility.

About all the edit time I can get away with around here is six to eight hours a day. I wish I had this stuff at home, I could edit around the clock and be done a lot sooner.

Thursday, September 26, 1991

I'm finishing the copies today. I can only get in here at certain hours but late at night there's no one around, so while I finish my copies in one room I edited a bit of my behind-the-scenes of *Like Water for Chocolate* in another room.

Friday, September 27, 1991

Now I have to think this out. I have all my sound on audiocassette tapes. I have my raw footage on ¾" videotape. Before I can edit the movie I have to transfer all the dialogue onto my raw footage. So what I'll do is take each cassette and lay the best audio takes onto the soundtracks of my copy ¾" videotapes, my backup tapes. That way I can play the copy tape on one machine and line up the dialogue lines to my master ¾" videotape, because I need the master tape to have the sound *in sync*, since that's what I will cut from. Cool. That should work. It'll take *a long time* but it should work. My guess is that it will take me about three days to line up all the dialogue. I don't have that much dialogue so it should go fast.

I start transferring the cassettes to my copy backup tapes. I'm halfway through my cassettes and it's taken six hours. Oh, well. Maybe I'll need more than three days to sync.

Saturday, September 28, 1991

I've finished transferring the dialogue from my audiocassette tapes to the copy videotapes. Chalk up six more hours.

Sunday, September 29, 1991

Tonight I begin to sync the dialogue to the master tapes. The lines don't sync up completely. They all start out OK but by the time we get to the end of the line, it's out of sync. That's all right, because whenever a line falls out of sync, I know that's where I will cut away to something else. A reaction, the dog, something. Then I'll cut back when the line is back in sync. That'll work. I hate rubbery lips. I'd rather cut away. I'm laying down the dialogue for Azul's opening jail scene. Line by line. It came out really good; I'm happy. But it took six hours. Uh-oh. Carlos and I wanted to sell this thing well before December so we could begin the next movie in January. At this rate we'll barely get this one to Los Angeles by Christmas.

Liz was sick and tried to go to work anyway. I told her to stay home, and that nobody wants her to go to work and get them sick. She stayed home reluctantly. Workaholic. She said she was in the mood for ice cream. I told her she shouldn't eat ice cream if she's sick. She ate a Häagen-Dazs Ice Cream bar anyway. She threw up. Goofy.

Tuesday, October 1, 1991

I synced Carlos and Azul in the Corona Club. I also did Moco's jail lines. Example: Azul has five lines in the Corona Club. It took me two hours to sync them. My back is starting to hurt again. Already? I've got a long way to go still.

Wednesday, October 2, 1991

I synced in the dialogue to Carlos, Bigotón, and Hotel Clerk in the Hotel Scene. Clerk's and Bigotón's lines match beautifully. Carlos's lines are awful, they don't sync up at all. I'll have to cut around it because I don't want to rerecord anything.

Liz is still sick. She's got some weird bug. One of her eyes is bigger than the other. It's protruding, and there's a blue ring around her iris, as if the pressure is pushing the eye out. We made eyeball jokes.

Thursday, October 3, 1991

Synced Domino's lines in scenes 6 and 11 and where she wakes Carlos up to give him money for a guitar.

Just when I was feeling a little worn out, I ran into a guy I met at school way back. I showed him the trailer and he was blown away. That got me charged up and I was able to finish the scenes I wanted in seven hours. Thank God I have these trailers to remind me of what the movie can be if I ever finish it. If it weren't for the trailers I'd probably just give up.

I took Liz to the doctor. She has pink eye. I have to be careful that I don't catch it from her. I can't afford to be sick right now. My back pain is enough to deal with right now.

Friday, October 4, 1991

I went to the campus and showed an old teacher of mine my trailer. He freaked. I ran into another professor, Charles Ramirez-Berg. I told him what I did and he wants to see the movie when I'm done. Today we went to San Antonio to visit the family.

Sunday, October 6, 1991

My back went out. No editing tonight.

Monday, October 7, 1991

I had to take more back medication today. I found out that the public access station closes in mid-November for renovations. I have to push myself harder if I'm gonna be done by then. We need to get to Los Angeles before Christmas. I refuse to be broke another Christmas.

I synced Carlos's scenes 6, 11, and 22.

Wednesday, October 9, 1991

I didn't get any sleep all day, one of those freak-out days. I didn't edit, either. I called Carlos. I need to come down and get some extra sound effects and ambient sounds. His lines from the bar scenes sound terrible. I need to get them again. I know why they sound terrible, too. We always do the sound *after* we finish shooting a scene. That night when we did all the bar stuff, it was 3:00 A.M. the last night of shooting after a long hard week. By the time we recorded the sound his speech was slow and slurred.

Friday, October 11, 1991

Liz and I drove to Mexico. Carlos and I recorded the sound we needed, including ambient sound from all the major locations.

Tuesday, October 15, 1991

Since I have been working nights, I have to sleep during the day. By the time I wake up, Liz is already asleep for the night. It's freezing outside and I'm dragging all these tapes around, my cassettes, all this junk, working my butt off. This movie better pay off. All we wanted to do was make back our investment and maybe a little more, but now after all this work I've decided that it better make us a good amount of money, or I probably won't make Part II. I told Carlos and he's feeling the pressure. He wants to make another one, but he knows that if this one doesn't at least double our investment, he can forget about Part II. This one is killing me. My back hurts, my eyes hurt, my head hurts, my wallet is empty. I keep trying to remind myself that I'm single-handedly replacing a crew of about 100 people, trying to feel good about that, but it's not working. The movie is starting to feel like work now. It was never that before. I've got to pull it together.

Friday, October 18, 1991

Synced the Loft Scene with Domino and Carlos. Domino is acting circles around everybody. I'm most surprised by her performance considering she was the least enthusiastic about making the movie. She also had the least amount of rehearsal time. Her lines are easy to sync because she's very consistent.

Azul's lines *always* match. He's like a robot. He says the line the same way each time, so I have no problem syncing him up. I remember that we'd shoot his line, then when it came time to record the sound, we'd ask him to do us an extra audio take slower because we thought he was talking too fast for the audio takes in comparison to the filmed take. But it turns out *we* were wrong. Reinol's fast line readings always match up.

Saturday, October 19, 1991

I'm finally finished with the syncing. I thought it would take three days. It's taken two weeks. The worst part is that this is the kind of work no one notices. When you have a bigger budget, you can afford to use the right equipment so when you get your film back your sound is already synced up. You don't have to do it this way. But I just spent two weeks doing something that, although necessary, no one would ever notice. I can just see myself showing this movie to people and saying, "See how great the sync is? Isn't that great! Watch their lips. It matches perfectly and it was never supposed to match 'cause we recorded the sound cold, ten minutes later! I worked really hard on that." And they'll say, "What sync? What? What are you talking about? Big deal!"

I've been listening to Peter Gabriel's *Passion*. I'll use that as my temporary score and it'll help to compose some music with my different music composers.

Friday, October 25, 1991

I went to see Eric Guthrie, a university student who dabbles in music. He has a great keyboard setup that I used on the short film "Pretty Good Man." I usually hate keyboard music, but he's got a sampler. I've stressed that I don't want the dreaded low-budget synthesizer sound and that, whenever possible, we have to use natural sounds and sampled instruments that sound realistic. I spent a good amount of time just listening to all the instruments he could call up on the key-board. Some of the stuff is pure cheese. The vast majority are unusable the way they are, so we tried to combine instruments to hide their fakey sound quality.

I played some music from *Passion* and from *The Mission* as a guide to the kind of music we can produce with his equip-ment. All I need from him are a couple of the action scene songs that are percussion heavy. The different drum sounds you can get from the keyboard are really good, so I'll leave that to the keyboard.

I think I'm going to leave the acoustic guitar music up to my cousin Alvaro and my brother Cecil. I already have a few songs that I got from Juan Suarez in Mexico. If I can find one more person to do some Sergio Leone–style music for the nightmare scenes, I'll be set. Those are the scenes where I really need some different sound and moody tunes.

Wednesday, October 30, 1991

I finished my at-home rough cut.

Now I'm going to use the ¾″ recorders at the local cable access station and edit my ¾″ master tape using my rough cut as a guide. I take my video camera into the editing room with me and I check my original choice of shots with the camera before laying down my edits on the ¾″ version. That way I don't have to rethink how I'm going to cut the movie. Instead I can concentrate on making each cut as smooth as I can, paying closer attention to pace and rhythm. The reason being that with non–time code video editing like this, once I make several cuts *I can't go back and change anything* without risk-ing messing up the rest of the film. If twenty minutes into the movie I want to shorten a shot earlier on, it's too late. The only way to do it would be to make a copy of the movie and shorten that shot. But then I'm dealing with a loss in picture quality since this would add a generation. Editing in this manner is extremely cost-effective, sure, but it requires a lot of work and complete attention to every detail. I've only got one shot at getting it right. This is a great experience. A lot of times on the set I had only one take. Now I've got a similar situation in the editing. So if the movie doesn't come out that good, at least I have every excuse in the world why it didn't work.

Thursday, October 31, 1991

It's Halloween. I've edited most of the jail scene. That's not too bad. This is going a lot faster than I thought it would. I owe it to my rough cut.

Saturday, November 2, 1991

I finished editing up through where Azul shoots everyone in the bar.

Keith Kritselis came in to check up on me. I showed him some of the bar shoot-out and he is completely amazed I was able to get those results with his busted up 16mm camera and two aluminum reflector lamps. He's ready to go shoot his own movie now. I told him it wasn't difficult as we'd been led to believe. He's convinced.

Monday, November 4, 1991

Today, something straight out of the movies happened to me. I was editing at the public access station when a guy named Dominic Kancilla saw me editing through the little window in the door. He burst through the door and said, "Man, look at that shot!" It was a shot of the Mariachi popping up into an extreme close-up, aiming a machine gun at the bad guys. I stopped the machine and told Dominic that if he liked that then he should check out the trailer. So I popped in my trailer tape, the one cut to "Carmina Burana," and he freaked out. I showed him my short film, "Bedhead," and he said that he works for the Texas Film Commission and wants to show my demo tape at the Producer's Conference they're throwing. Some bigwigs from Hollywood are flying down for the 20th anniversary of the Texas Film Commission. The Governor is trying to woo Hollywood into making more films in Texas, so the bash will be big. He told me that he's going to be on the plane that'll be carrying a lot of these bigwigs, so he'll have a captive audience and would like to show my trailer and "Bedhead" to them to show them the kind of work local Texas filmmakers do. I told him, "Sure." He gave me a list of people that are expected to speak. It's a big list.

Tonight I had bagged four minutes of the jail scene when my deck jammed. So I went home early. I've finished twenty-eight minutes so far.

Wednesday, November 6, 1991

I edited up to the scene where Domino puts the knife to Carlos's throat. This scene is going to have as many cuts as the previous chase scene.

I called Marc Trujillo about doing the nightmare music for the movie. I had heard some music on Keith's public access show that sounded really cool and he gave me Marc Trujillo's name.

Friday, November 8, 1991

Today is Elizabeth's birthday. We went out and had a great time.

The big Hollywood bash the Texas Film Commission was throwing fell through. Postponed indefinitely. I thought things were going just a little too easy. I still have the list of names though. Dominic told me I should still call some of these people when I'm in LA and show them my demo tape because he thinks they will respond to it. He said that it's solid work. He said to at least call the agent at ICM, Robert Newman.

Saturday, November 9, 1991

I met with Marc Trujillo; he was a fellow cartoonist at *The Daily Texan*. I went to his house today and was very impressed when I saw the equipment he had, or rather the lack of equipment he had. I heard some of his music on Keith's soundtrack and it sounded very full. But the equipment he had was bare minimum: an electric bass, an acoustic guitar, a Roland drum machine, and a high-speed four-track tape recorder. I told him he was perfect for this movie because the way he milks his equipment to make music is exactly how we milked the limited equipment and resources to make *Mariachi*. He's anxious to give it a try.

I charted the kind of song construction I need. Basically, I need the piece of music he writes to start quietly, build to a huge crescendo, and then drop back to its quiet, modest beginning notes and then start building again. That way I can edit it and place it anywhere in the movie and it will work, without his ever having to see the film. It will work because that is how I cut my scenes. They begin slowly, quietly, build with the edits getting faster and faster and then dropping back down to a slow rhythm.

He told me that he prefers not to see the film, rather to simply use his imagination and create music that can stand on its own, as well as work with the picture. He went at it. I showed him the trailer so he has some sense of what we're after and then I told him that he had one week.

Sunday, November 10, 1991

My brother Cecil called to say he came up with a song on the guitar that I might be able to use in my movie. I drove over to his apartment with my Marantz tape recorder and Radio Shack mike. He played the song to me. I recorded a temporary version onto my tape recorder with the mike positioned about an inch and a half away from the guitar. I told him I liked it and that it had potential. He said he would work on it some more and develop it further. I told him to keep working on more ideas because the movie is gonna be about ninety minutes, so I'll need a lot of music.

(Note: I never did rerecord that song. That rough, one-take version that I recorded in his apartment made it into the movie as is, and can be heard four times in the final mix of the film: the scene where Mariachi gets slapped by Domino, where he's talking to Domino in the tub after he sings, where he's in the bedroom with Domino as the dog sleeps, and then during Domino's confession to him.)

Wednesday, November 13, 1991

Carlos drove up to Austin and we wrote and recorded the final narration. We needed a studio to record it in so it would sound different from the other dialogue recordings I did, so we recorded it in my car. My Datsun. It gave Carlos's voice a nice metallic echo. That night we went to the public access station and typed up the ending credits on the character generator. We decided to call it A Los Hooligans Production. Since my daily comic strip that I had for three years was called that and it had gotten a good following, I figured if someone did see my movies, they would know it was the same Robert Rodriguez who did the comics. We got out of there at nine in the morning.

Tuesday, November 19, 1991

I went to Marc Trujillo's house to record the music he made. It sounds great. I used his four-track to mix different versions of the songs. I don't know where I'll use them yet, but I'm sure they'll work great.

(Note: I ended up using Marc's music in all the nightmare sequences, when Mariachi enters the hotel, and in several of the action scenes.)

Thursday, November 21, 1991

I finished editing all remaining visuals at a local editing facility that let me use their machines off-hours. I edited for twelve hours. From 8:00 P.M. to 8:00 A.M. They forgot I was in there so they turned on the motion control alarm system. I had to stay in my editing cubicle for ten hours without being able to go to the bathroom until the next morning when the janitor came in. I was in pain.

Friday, November 22, 1991

I recorded two acoustic guitar instrumentals my cousin Alvaro wrote. I taped them right there in my room with the same sound equipment I've been using all along. After two songs, he apologized and said he wasn't inspired. He left, promising to return in a few days.

I don't have a few days, so I'll just use the two songs I got. They sound fine to me, anyway.

(Note: Those two songs also made it into the final sound mix. The first can be heard over the end credits, and the second song plays five times. It's the guitar piece you hear the first time we meet the Mariachi, his theme song, and is used about every other time you see Mariachi walking around.)

Sunday, November 24, 1991

I'm finishing the sound effects track on my VHS camera here at home. I've been doing the sound this way: I already synced all the dialogue onto the ¾″ master, and when I edited the dialogue it ended up on the first of two audio tracks on my ¾″ master tape. I can't edit the sound effects on the ¾″ decks, because the ¾″ VCRs have terrible sound editing. Whenever you make a cut, there is a small audible pop before and after each sound cut. Therefore I am doing all my sound effects at home on my RCA Video Camera. Since my camera has a flying erase head I can edit each sound effect onto a bed of ambient sound, and the results are seamless audio cuts, including sound effects and ambiance, all on one track. The reason I can make it seamless without a change in ambient tone whenever I add a sound effect is that on location I made sure to record all my sound at the same level. I set my tape recorder to 7, and if a sound was too loud, I simply moved the mike closer, again, so that the ambient level wouldn't change. That way I have constant sound, they always have holes in the soundtracks. I'm putting a lot of work in so it will sound as real as I can get it. It's a lot of work but it sounds good, and the buyers will think the movie is more expensive than it really is. One thing about the other straight-to-video Spanish action movies I've seen is the sound is always awful. With a lot of work I can avoid that.

What I'll do next is transfer my sound effects track onto the second audio track of my ¾″ master tape. To add music, I'll have to sacrifice a generation and loss of quality by making a copy of my ¾″ that combines the sound effects track and the dialogue track onto track one of my new ¾″ master tape, leaving track two open for me to add the music.

As soon as I'm done with the film, I need a version to send to Carlos so he can show it to Lina Santos's mom. He told me that she is good friends with the head of Million Dollar Video company in Los Angeles. They distribute a lot of these straight-to-video movies. She can help us get an appointment with them. That will be good. I don't want to just drive up to Los Angeles cold like that, no contacts, no meetings set, just winging it. That'll never work. We need a game plan. Then again, we wanted to learn the business; no better way to learn the business than just plunging in.

I edited for fourteen hours tonight. I couldn't use the restroom all night again because of the motion control alarm system. I should just ask them for the code since they keep forgetting I'm in here. One more day, I think, and I'll be done.

Monday, November 25, 1991 and Tuesday, November 26, 1991

Another thirteen-hour bathroomless night of editing. I should have brought in a plastic jug or something. But at least I finally finished the movie! I sat back and watched the whole thing while I made a VHS master copy of it. I think I had tears in my eyes, or maybe it was just the pain of not going to the bathroom. It's such an incredibly great feeling to be able to sit back and watch your finished movie, and know that you've completely exhausted yourself in making it. Funny thing is, that after I sell it and I have some money in my hand I'll have forgotten how much work it was and be ready to make another one.

Physically, I don't feel very well today. My schedule the past two days has gone like this. Sunday I edited sound effects all day until 7:00 P.M. I then edited in the bathroomless editing cubicle until 8:30 the next morning. I slept three hours, then went to work at school for two hours. At 4:00 P.M. I edited some things at home preparing for my last night of editing. I then edited at the bathroomless cubicle from 7:00 P.M. to 8:30 this morning.

I got home at 9:00 A.M. I'm feeling sick, now. I think I got piss-poisoned from holding it in so long. Liz came home and made me go to sleep. Later on I dropped by Tommy Nix's house to tell him the good news. I showed him my videotape, telling him I'll give him a copy later, but that I'm finally done. He told me I look like shit run over. My eyes are glazed over, my skin is pasty white, and I look like a crusty corpse. "But I feel good!" I told him.

I celebrated with a big, fat, juicy steak at the Ruth Chris Steak House. I'm going to take it easy for Thanksgiving. I'll catch my friend Mike Cardenas's wedding on Saturday, then it's off to Los Angeles.

Liz wants to see the movie. She hasn't seen any of it and is anxious to see how it came out. I'm not that anxoius to show it to her. After all that work, I was starting to think that maybe the movie was coming out OK. But what if it blows? I'd hate to have her sit through the whole thing, not like it, and then have to tell me that she thought it was great. She's seen me practically kill myself making it. She propped herself up in the bed and I put on the tape. I layed silently beside her while she watched it. She laughed a few times but I thought she was bored. It was the most nerve-wracking experience. About seventy minutes into it she turned to me and said, "This is paced really well." I got excited. "Really? Because this is where it actually starts to pick up again," I told her.

After the movie I turned off the tape and asked her for her honest opinion. She told me that she gives it 3½ stars, for the movie itself, but then knowing all the insane work I put into it, and considering I did it without a crew and with crude equipment and very little money, she said she gives it 5 stars. I have mixed feelings about what she said. One, what she said was great and makes me feel good, but then again . . . she's my wife. So I don't know if she's just biased or if the movie *is* good. After working on something for so long you completely lose perspective. I just hope we can sell it.

HIGHWAY TO HELL

Sunday, December 1, 1991

Carlos arrived in San Antonio to pick me up. We packed blankets and other necessities and headed out. It's 8:00 P.M. and we're going to drive down Interstate 10 straight through to Los Angeles. We don't want to stop, so we'll take turns driving. In addition to looking for a distributor, I plan to take Dominic up on his advice and call Robert Newman at ICM. Maybe I can get him to watch my demo tape or maybe he can refer me to someone who will watch it. I'm bringing a ten-minute demo tape that has the "Carmina Burana" trailer from *Mariachi* to grab his attention, then it goes right into my short film "Bedhead." I'll add a cover letter that says the trailer is from a low-budget movie I made for $7,000 with no crew, and that the short film has won thirteen national and international film festival awards. I kept the tape short so he'd be more likely to watch it.

I'm also taking along my master ¾" tapes of *El Mariachi* in my briefcase. Ready to be sold, I hope. We've also got a list of Spanish distributors' phone numbers and addresses that we got off the backs of the Spanish action videotapes. There are several companies we are going to be visiting.

Monday, December 2, 1991

We arrived in LA at 5:21 P.M. We made it in twenty-one hours. Not bad. A blood-red sun was setting to the AC/DC tune "Highway to Hell" playing on the radio. I had to catch all this on video so I pulled out the RCA camera and taped it.

We waited outside of our friend Jorge Campo's apartment until he got home from work around 9:30 P.M. He's also from Acuña and is going to let us crash at his place while we're here in town.

Jorge let us in and told us to pick a spot to sleep in. He has extra blankets. He sells furniture door to door on a rent-to-buy program and his apartment is his office/warehouse. Full of furniture. We'll be out and about most of the days, so this will work out great. We're in Sherman Oaks, not too far from where we have to go for meetings.

Tuesday, December 3, 1991

Our first stop is a company called Film-Mex. We dropped in and found the owner himself, Mr. Frank Cinelli, stylishly decked out in his Members Only jacket and itchy pants, as he was leaving. We tried to talk to him but he evaded us. He said that he had to leave the office but to talk to his secretary. She had very little information to give us so we decided to come back later.

We decided to try Mex-American next. They at least have cool looking video cover designs. Hopefully, they're a classier joint. We went to their office on Wilshire and met with Anna Maria Sancho. I started off by showing her my trailer. Then I lied. I took out my master ¾" videotape of the entire movie and said, "You know how trailers are, they show the best parts and the rest of the movie is slow. Not this movie. The whole thing is that fast! I have the tape here for you to watch with us later." (All the action is in the first thirty minutes, so if she asks to see it, I can stop the tape after a half hour and say, "The rest is just as fast paced" or something like that.)

I told her that I was a Latino filmmaker from San Antonio, and that the only way Latinos can get into Hollywood is by making our own movies so we can show them that we have talent. I told her that the video market they have can be a great training ground for Latino filmmakers and that they should encourage quality instead of the junk they crank out for quick profits. I told her my plan, that I was training myself to compete with Hollywood movies by making several Spanish video action movies first, in order to teach myself feature filmmaking. *El Mariachi* is the first one. If she bought my movie to release it in Spanish video stores, I would make them at least two more sequels, each one getting better and better in quality since with the profits from the first one I'd be able to put more money into each film. I didn't tell her how we made the movie or how much we spent. If she knew it cost less than $10,000, she'd want to buy it for $5,000. Or less. So I said, "I need at least $*100,000* to keep the quality up for the rest of the series, so I can at least turn a profit. (I kept the figure high knowing that they'd lower it as much as they could. We're hoping they'll lower it to $50,000. But probably $30,000 to 40,000 is the ballpark because we didn't get a soap star to help sell it.)

She said that she had to talk with her boss, Javier. She said she would like to buy it but that she can't clear anything unless it's through him. Anna Maria set up an appointment for us to see Javier on Friday. She asked if we could leave the tape. "No. It's our only copy and we take it with us wherever we go. If someone wants to watch it, they watch it with us," I said.

She liked us so I think this place is for real. Thank God. We still have at least three other Spanish video distributors here in the LA area to go to.

Next we drove down the street to Million Dollar Video, also on Wilshire. We tried to meet with Miguel Kahn, who is a friend of Lina Santos's mother who is a friend of Carlos's family. So in a way Miguel Kahn, the #1 guy here at the company, is a friend of a friend of a friend. I hope.

We went into the big building and found out that it looks like they're doing a lot of business. There were a ton of secretaries and everyone was hanging around. We asked to see Miguel Kahn and they gave us the runaround. We told them we had a tape to sell and they set up an appointment with Miguel Kahn on Thursday. OK. Thursday.

There was a Christmas tree up in the lobby. We just hope we go home for Christmas with some dough in our pockets.

Our last appointment for the day is with Tel-Star. We got to their office and found out that it's completely low rent. Their posters and cover art are terrible and no one in charge was anywhere to be found. We figured we would have a better shot at getting the price we want at someplace that could afford it. So we left.

The sun was going down. We did pretty well our first day, we've seen just about all the big companies. Tomorrow we have to drive to San Diego. There is another big company called Cine-Mex with their offices down there. They put out a lot of tapes, so we don't mind making the trip. Should take about three hours to get there.

On our way back to the apartment we stopped by the Hollywood Book Store and I bought the script to *Road Warrior* so I can have something to read, and so I can finally see how to format a script. My script for *El Mariachi* was completely mis-formatted, which is why my thirty-five-page script ended up being a ninety-minute movie.

Later that night we watched *El Mariachi* with our first recruited audience: Jorge. He was excited to see it since we shot it in his hometown. In a way his opinion will be biased since he grew up with everyone in the movie. We told him to be honest and to pretend he just rented this from the Spanish video store. After the movie he told us he liked it. I asked if he thought it was too slow, because I thought it was too slow. No, he thought it was just right. The action? The action was good, he said. It lacked maybe one explosion, if it could have only had just one explosion, that's all that seemed like it was missing he told us.

Carlos and I cursed because we knew how close we came to having an explosion. The special effects guy, Falomir, was going to blow up that junk car Chevy for us. Too bad. I knew that an explosion would add tremendous production value so we could really make the distributors think we spent a lot of money on the movie and get a better price.

At least we'll know what to do for the sequel. We asked Jorge if he would tell his friends to see the movie, and he said he would. That made us feel better, but then again, Jorge's our friend, so what else would he tell us?

Wednesday, December 4, 1991

Carlos and I headed for San Diego at 4:00 A.M. to make our 9:00 A.M. appointment at Cine-Mex. We needed to eat breakfast, so we grabbed a couple of burgers and shakes at Fat Burgers since it was the closest thing that's open twenty-four hours. Tasted pretty good. Settled like a brick, though.

We made it to San Diego and met with Omar, the president of the company. We sat down with him and told him that we have a great movie that we'd made, action packed, very different from what he's used to selling, high quality, etc. I told him that I wanted to show him the trailer. He said no. He told me he doesn't need to see the trailer. He'll know if it's good by watching the first twenty-five minutes. Perfect.

He took us out of his office to his video showroom and played our video through all the suspended TV sets around the room. There were about fifteen to twenty people in the store shopping for bad movies, but after a few minutes they all turned around and started watching our movie. It was great. Here the president of the company wanted to see the first twenty-five minutes to get a sense of the movie, and everyone in the store stopped what they were doing to check it out. They realized that this was different from the Spanish videos they usually rent. It's a good thing I packed all the action into the first thirty minutes. After the bus chase, he turned off the tape and went back into his office.

He asked who the cast was. We told him. He had never heard of any of them. I told him they are "new stars."

He told me about how bad business has been. He told me that he liked our movie, that we'll go far, and that we should consider going to a bigger foreign distributor like Miramax.

I tried to tell him that he *needed* to put out a movie like this. The movies they are making are getting worse and worse, and that if he puts out ours, we'll make him several more before leaving the Spanish video business and heading for Hollywood.

He knows his business is sliding down the tubes. The best he could do was make us an offer where we wouldn't get any advance money, and if the movie did well and sold a lot of videos then we might make something down the line. The way he made it sound, by the time they release it and collect their moneys it would be July before we'd see anything.

No thanks.

Before we left I asked Omar if he liked any of his movies. He just smiled and quickly said, "No."

Carlos and I packed up and left. We talked about it and put our bets down for Anna Maria over at Mex-American. She seemed to be the early contender for the contract.

Thursday, December 5, 1991

We went back to Million Dollar Video to meet with Miguel Kahn. After sitting in the waiting room for what seemed like an hour and a half, the receptionist said that Miguel Kahn was busy. I asked if there was anyone else we could talk to who had some responsibility in the company.

A few minutes later, one of Miguel's underlings talked to us. Someone named Benjamin. Benjamin sat us down in his big office and asked what we wanted. I threw him my big enthusiastic sales pitch telling him that I want to make quality movies for his video company so that he'll have good product and I'll have a good filmmaking training ground. He acted really stuck-up with us so I popped in the trailer and watched his reaction. He knew that I was watching him and he was clearly impressed, but he did a bad job of hiding it. He tried to discourage us by saying we should have cast a soap star in it to help sell it. I argued that we wanted to make a *good* movie. All the shitty movies have the soap stars in them. I told him that everyone knows that if you rent a movie with a soap star the movie's gonna blow. We wanted to make a *good* action film that actually had *action* in it and not cast a soap star so people would know they weren't renting the same old thing. We didn't want to be connected with those terrible movies, I told him. I asked Benjamin directly if he felt any of the movies they make are any good. Does he take any of them home at night and watch them for entertainment. He shook his head no. He knows they suck. I told him the reason they suck is because they're made by a bunch of businessmen trying to make a quick buck and it's killing their industry. The video market is oversaturated with bad movies. Their sales have dropped drastically since the video boom in the mid-eighties and it doesn't take a genius to figure out that business won't last unless the product improves. If their company puts out a few decent movies, everyone else will have to raise their standards in order to compete. Benjamin got lofty again and acted like he was doing us a huge favor (as if he had anything else going on around here). He asked us to leave him a tape so he could show it to Miguel Kahn. We told him we couldn't do that. We would have to watch it together. So we left.

Carlos thinks we should have hung out longer. I told him to
forget it. I think we have a better shot over at Mex-American.
At least they don't pretend to be busy over there.

Friday, December 6, 1991

We went back to Mex-American for our meeting with Javier,
but Anna Maria told us he was still out of town. We had to
move the meeting to Monday. Great.

Saturday, December 7, 1991

Carlos and I are on a one-meal-a-day diet, since we could
conceivably be here until Christmas. We don't have enough
money to eat like we do in Texas. Everything is expensive here.
Even the food in the grocery stores is expensive. It's cheaper
to live off bad hamburgers.

The weekend sucks. I wanted to settle a contract and go
home. During the weekend everything is closed. We have to
sit around and do nothing but wait.

Everything is so expensive here that I decided to pass the
time this weekend constructively. I went to Michael's Art Supply and bought a few boards and some acrylic paints. I might
as well teach myself how to paint. I've always wanted to learn
but could never find the time. I've got plenty of time now. Who
knows how long we'll end up being here.

Monday, December 9, 1991

Finally. We got to the Mex-American office and met with the
co-president, Javier. The other co-president is in Spain producing a movie. Fortunately, Javier has enough say to buy our
movie if he wants to.

He wanted to see the trailer. It was obvious Anna Maria had
told him all about it because he seemed very interested in
seeing it.

We showed it to him. He asked us how much we made the
movie for. What do you think? I asked him. He said it looked
like at least $70,000 to $80,000.

I said, "Yeah, well . . . it cost something like that. That's why we need to make back enough to go make some more. We need to pull this whole industry out of the rut and the only way is by making higher quality movies."

He agreed. *So he offered us twenty-five thousand dollars for the movie!* (I looked at Carlos. It's a good thing we didn't tell him how much it cost or he would have offered us five bucks.)

I told Javier that we couldn't possibly go that low or we'd lose everything and we couldn't make another one. He told us that he couldn't go any higher, and that if we wanted to try another company, to go to Miramax or MexCinema. He said that there was a man he knew at MexCinema, an older gentleman named Señor Blascoe. He could help us. If not, he said, his offer is $25,000 up front and we could come back if we didn't turn up a better offer.

We told him we'd go see MexCinema first to see if Señor Blascoe would give us a fair price. We left.

Carlos and I talked about it a bit and were happy that at least if all went wrong we could get at least twenty-five grand for it. Carlos isn't satisfied. We went into this hoping we'd get thirty-five or forty grand at least.

Oh, well. It looks like we'll have to crawl back to Million Dollar Video and at least get an offer. We can tell them we have a $30,000 offer over at Mex-American and try and get them to give us a few thousand more. We should also go back to the first place we went to, Film Mex and try and get an offer there too. It helps that we have an offer we can give the other companies to try and top.

Tuesday, December 10, 1991

We went to see Señor Blascoe. He runs the company with his son. They watched our trailer and liked what they saw. We told them about the offer we had already and they said that they would talk to their partners in Mexico and make an offer tomorrow.

I went home and painted some more. It's helping me think. The paintings are coming out OK, considering I don't know what I'm doing. I'm painting a *Mariachi* movie poster.

Wednesday, December 11, 1991

We talked to MexCinema and Señor Blascoe offered us a $10,000 advance and a share in the profits of the movie, meaning we won't see any additional money until June or July. No good. We declined. Damn.

I called Mex-American and told them to make up the contracts and to get a check ready for $25,000. That way they'll be ready, and we'll just hold on to them until we are sure no one will give us a better offer.

We dropped by Million Dollar and asked to talk to Benjamin again. We asked him to set us up with Miguel Kahn. We had an offer at Mex-American and we wanted to give Miguel a chance to counteroffer. He set up a meeting for next Wednesday. Great. Another week here.

I decided to occupy my time with other business. As long as I'm in town waiting I might as well try and see some of the people on this list I got from the Film Commission party.

I looked in the phone book for ICM (International Creative Management). It's one of the biggest talent agencies in the world. I call the number and ask for Robert Newman. They hooked me up with his office. That was easy. His assistant's name is Warren. Warren asked what I wanted. I told him I was going to attend the same seminar in Texas that Robert Newman was going to speak at a few weekends back. "Oh, yeah, I set that up for him! What happened to that anyway? Newman was all set to go and it was canceled at the last minute."

"Yeah," I told him, "it fell through. Anyway, I've got this demo tape I was going to show him in Texas, and it so happens that I'm in town selling a movie I made to some Spanish distributors. I was wondering if Robert Newman could watch my tape and let me know what he thinks." Warren asked me what it was.

I held my breath then I said it, "It's a demo tape guaranteed to knock out anyone who sees it. It has a two-minute trailer from my latest movie and my award-winning short film, "Bedhead," which has won 13 film festivals." Warren said to bring it by. I felt stupid making such a hard sell, but I was desperate.

Carlos and I quickly drove to the ICM Beverly Boulevard office and I saw Bette Midler hanging out in the lobby. I had the receptionist call up to Robert Newman's office and speak to Warren. She told me, "They want you to take it down the hall and give it to the mailroom." I gave it to the guys in the mailroom and left.

Carlos was waiting in the car outside. "Did you meet him?" he asked.

"Nope. But I saw Bette Midler."

On our way home we dropped by Wendy's for today's meal. They had 99 cent specials so I got a couple of junior bacon burgers, a frosty, fries, and a cup of water. We thought about maybe calling a studio like Paramount and seeing if they had a foreign video division we could maybe sell to. The idea seemed so far-fetched we didn't even call to find out. We'll stick with the Spanish videos first, see where that gets us.

Friday, December 13, 1991

Warren from Robert Newman's office called today! Wow, I thought. They watched my tape already? That was fast.

Warren said, "Uh, Robert Newman tried to watch your tape last night but his VCR ate it."

I said, "You're kidding me. I can make another one and bring it by."

Fortunately I had my video camera, so I hooked it up to Jorge's VCR and made another copy of my demo. At least Newman tried to see it that day. Maybe he'll watch it over the weekend. It's nice to see that some people move fast around here.

We drove to the ICM office again. This time, though, the receptionist told me to go up to Robert Newman's office. I took the elevator up to the seventh floor. I was looking for his office number but all of the doors were tall and gray with no room numbers! What the hell? It looked like some sci-fi setup. Numberless, closed-door offices. Kinda spooky.

I found Warren, who quickly, very quickly ushered me into Robert Newman's office. Warren said, "He has a meeting in three minutes so you've got some time." He talked so fast it took me a few seconds to register what he said.

Before I knew it I was sitting in Robert Newman's office while he finished a phone call. He talked faster than his assistant. He hung up the phone and said, "Well, you look like a director anyway. Nice ring."

He meant the ring on my right finger. A skull ring with a moving jaw bone. I told him it was a present from my mother. She brought it back from Mexico, thinking it was the kind of thing I'd be into. I told him that I wear it because it reminds me of my mom. I could tell he didn't believe me.

Warren burst into the room. "Meeting in two minutes."

"Right," Newman said.

Warren disappeared.

"So what's on the tape?" Newman asked.

I told him that it had my award-winning short film on it that had won thirteen festivals and then a two-minute trailer for a feature that I shot with no money and no crew.

He asked if I had been approached by any agents. I told him that I was from Texas and that I was only here to sell my movie and that he was the first agent I had met.

"Who are you selling it to?"

I told him that I made it for the straight-to-video Spanish home video market.

He asked if that was a big outlet.

I told him that I was trying to find out if it was. I told him my plan to make three of these and sell them to the video market to gain experience making films, to have extra work to put on my demo reel, and to make some extra money for a real movie later on after I had gotten some practice with the Spanish films.

"The movies are in Spanish?"

I told him they were. He seemed impressed.

"That's pretty cool. So you'll make like your Sergio Leone series before making an American feature," he said.

"Yeah, something like that," I replied.

"Cool plan. Does anyone know you're doing this?" he asked.

I told him no, that I was going to keep it quiet so I wouldn't get naysayed to death. Make three films, if they worked out, I'd just show up in town some day with a huge demo reel looking for work. I told him I wanted him to watch my demo tape and let me know if he thought that I was on the right track and maybe offer suggestions as to what to include on a demo reel.

He told me that he would and that I should continue with what I'm doing. Sell the first one, make two more, and then come back. "How much are you selling it for?"

"We have an offer for $25,000. We're trying to get more," I said.

"How much you make it for?" he asked surprised.

"$7,000."

"$7,000? Really? Not bad. Your first feature film and you're already more than tripling your money. You're considered a huge success in this town if you can do that. Do you like Sergio Leone's films?"

I told him I hadn't seen them in a long time.

He told me that I should rent them and check them out and that he'd watch my tape and get back to me. We shook hands and I left.

Warren shook my hand as he battled with the incoming phone calls. This place is a war zone.

I left somewhat shell-shocked. Carlos was waiting in the truck outside. He asked me how it went. I told him I'd kill to have gotten my video camera in there and tape the whole thing. From the numberless doors to the mile-a-minute talking agent. I told him it went well and that Newman liked our plan and said we were a huge success in this town because we have more than tripled our money on our first film. Carlos thought about that logic and we realized that we were doing pretty well.

Carlos and I stopped by the video store and rented *The Good, the Bad and the Ugly*. We went to Michael's Art Supply on Ventura Boulevard and I bought some more paints and boards. I feel like I'm on a roll even though I'm nearly broke. My *Mariachi* painting came out good. Carlos wants me to make another one for him, because he's convinced himself it will be worth millions someday. I told him he's putting too much pressure on me.

Sunday, December 15, 1991

Jorge asked us if we wanted to go downtown with him to pick up a few things. I didn't really want to go. I was in the middle of a painting. They convinced me to go. You know how you get a bad feeling about something just before you do it? I had one of those but went along anyway to see if anything would happen, or if I was just being stupid. That makes sense doesn't it?

We crammed into the cab of Jorge's little truck and I strapped myself in tightly. They laughed at me for grabbing the seat belt so fast as if I already thought we were gonna wreck. I said nothing.

Jorge took us downtown and gave us a tour. We were driving down Broadway and the street scene looked like something out of *Dawn of the Dead* and *Blade Runner* melted together. Trash was everywhere, it was overcast, newspapers were blowing around. It was really creepy-looking. It would make a great location for a futuristic movie. Then I noticed a landmark that I saw in *Blade Runner*. The Million Dollar Movie theater. It was showing Spanish films. That's why the name sounded familiar. I pointed it out to Carlos and he told me that Miguel Kahn owns that theater. He knew about it because one time Lina Santos had to go to a premiere for one of her movies there.

Jorge picked up a typewriter for his new secretary and we headed on back. He told us he was going to drive us towards the Galleria. Carlos was talking to him and there was a Porsche that stopped in front of us to turn left. Jorge didn't see it. I yelled, "Look out!" as *slam!* He rear-ended the Porsche. He actually turned a bit at the end there but still hit the thing. We turned a corner and stopped. Jorge said he probably would have kept going but he blew his tire out on the Porsche. He said he had a suspended license.

The Porsche guy pulled up behind us. The rear was smashed in enough to rub against his rear tire. He wasn't going anywhere. The driver was a kid who started yelling at Jorge for insurance. "Call the cops. I don't have insurance," Jorge said.

The cops came and told us that they would have to cart Jorge off to jail. Jorge told Carlos and me, "Oye, no me sacen, no me sacen. I'll spend the night in jail, and that's it. Don't waste your money trying to get me out." Carlos and I looked at each other—what money? Bailing him out was the last thing on our minds. He gave us sixty bucks to tow the truck back to the house. We went home.

Jorge called us later on, really happy. It turned out that he was taken to the Beverly Hills jail house. He said that it was full of male prostitutes having a good time singing and dancing. Nothing too bad. He said the food was great there, too. "Fucking Beverly Hills. For dinner they serve you a big hamburger, an orange, an apple, lemonade, and a nice big bed to sleep in." He sounded happy.

Monday, December 16, 1991

Robert Newman called! He told me that he watched my tape over the weekend and loved it! He's showing it to some colleagues at the agency right now. He said he wanted to work with me! I think for a minute about how weird this is. He said he liked the short film a lot, but that he loved the two-minute *Mariachi* trailer. He said he *really* loved the trailer. He said if nothing else, I could definitely have a career cutting trailers.

"How much did it cost again?" he asked.

"$7,000," I told him.

"Really? That's pretty good . . . most trailers usually cost between $20,000 and $30,000."

I paused for a moment, trying to make sense of what he had just said. Then I said, "No, the whole movie cost $7,000."

"Really? That's incredible, do you have it here? Can I see it?"

I told him that the copy I had was in Spanish but that as soon as I got back to Texas I could subtitle it using a character generator at the public access station, then send him a subtitled version.

He said to please keep in touch and to send a copy of *El Mariachi* as soon as I had a subtitled version.

"Ah," I think to myself, "there's the catch." I knew this was too easy. I made a great trailer. It's a lot better than the movie, probably. He'll watch the movie thinking the whole movie is as crazy and as fast-paced as the trailer. He'll see the movie and say, "Well kid, try again." But that's all right! That's what I was going to do anyway.

Carlos and I talked about it and we realized that this was the plan all along. Make three Mariachi movies and hope that the second or third would be good enough to get a movie deal with. So if we get an agent from the first one, that would be great. If not, we continue with Part II and really work hard on that one. The fact that we know that we can ship it to a big agency like ICM is definitely more incentive to work hard. Damn, if it was this easy to get their attention we should plan on really blowing it out on the next movie, and we'll do great. We're charged now. Even if we don't sell the first one for the price we want, we can make a second one, get an agent, and get started on a *real* first film that we can shoot in English and put in film festivals and all that. Great news today!

Tuesday, December 17, 1991

Jorge came home. He said that Beverly Hills was just for the first night. Monday morning they shipped him off to LA County jail. He wasn't happy anymore. But he said at least the wreck is cleared. He spent his two nights in jail so it's over with.

We meet with Million Dollar tomorrow. If they don't make a good offer, we'll take the $25,000 Mex-American offered and go home. I'm broke and I don't want to miss Christmas. I'm tired of LA, anyway.

We went to Mex-American to pick up the contracts. They showed me a check for $10,000 and a contract. I asked why the contract said only $10,000.

They told me that they were waiting for the Mexico contract to come in. They are paying $10,000 for the US distribution rights, and $15,000 for the Mexico distribution rights. The

$10,000 contract is for US only. They have a sister company in Mexico that has to send the $15,000 contract. I asked how long it would take because I didn't want to sell the US rights without selling the Mexico rights and getting the Mexico check at the same time. She said it should arrive any day now. Did they really expect me to sign a contract for US without Mexico? All they'd have to do is make copies and sell them in Mexico anyway. How could I stop them?

Wednesday, December 18, 1991

We met with Miguel Kahn finally at Million Dollar. We showed him the trailer. He said he'd try to help us. He would think about what he could do for us. He liked us and our trailer, he said. He didn't want us to get ripped off so he'd try to come up with a good offer.

I finished my first painting last night. I called Elizabeth and she told me that "Bedhead" won the Black Maria Film Festival. We're on a roll.

Thursday, December 19, 1991

I called my sister Patricia and wished her a happy birthday.

I asked Anna Maria at Mex-American if the Mexico contract was in yet. She said that she had asked them to send it overnight but that they are slow. She said that if I want to go home with money I should just come in and sign the US contract and take the $10,000 so that I'll have some money until the $15,000 comes in. That sounds too much like a trick. I told her no thanks. I'll wait.

Friday, December 20, 1991

No check still. I asked if they think it will be in on Monday. They said it should. If not, it will be in January, because next week is Christmas.

Monday, December 23, 1991

We called Javier at home. No check. We told him to let us know when the Mexico contract and $15,000 comes in and we'll sell him the movie.

Carlos and I packed up and drove home empty-handed. We're really broke now. We didn't get an answer from Million Dollar Video so we're just going to wait. We tried to convince ourselves that it would be safer and worth our while to wait for the extra $15,000. Seeing that US contract and check written out in my name for $10,000 was really tempting. But we worked too hard to make only $3,000 profit.

So we'll go home broke and just do everything by mail. When they get the contract they can mail it to us, we'll sign it, send it back with the tape, they'll send us our checks, etc.

Trying to put a positive spin on things, I told Carlos that at least one good thing came out of this trip. I got noticed by ICM. I'm surprised that all this is already happening with the first Mariachi. It is more than I expected.

Tuesday, December 24, 1991

I got back to San Antonio for Christmas. Elizabeth was waiting there for me. I'm empty-handed. Oh well. Merry Christmas.

THE CHASE

Monday, January 13, 1992

ICM called me today. They also called last Friday, to secure a subtitled copy of *El Mariachi*. Robert Newman himself called today to tell me they want to work with me. He had a list of questions. Q: How long did it take for you to shoot the movie? A: Two and a half weeks. Q: How much did it cost? A: Seven thousand. Q: Aw C'mon!!! A: It's true. I was the entire crew!

He asked if I had any other scripts or treatments. I said yes, two treatments. He asked what I was doing in film school. I told him I made "Bedhead" in film school. He asked what I was still doing in film school. "I promised my parents I'd get a degree," I told him. He's anxious for a copy; he said he had shown my reel to a few associates and they all want to see the new movie.

Thursday, January 23, 1992

I edited all the subtitles for the subtitled version of *El Mariachi*. Tonight I'll go back and add the music and I'll be done.

I got to work and checked my messages. ICM had called saying, "As always Robert, call us collect." I called Warren and he said, "Robert Newman, Dave Wirtschafter, and myself are excited as hell to see it!" I said, "Hope you enjoy the movie." He said they would send Federal Express to pick it up and that they would pay for it. I said, "Great, is there anything else I can do for you guys?" He snapped back, "No, no, no, the question is what can we do *for you!*" I laughed. This is too much.

I went at 1:00 A.M. to finish editing the sound onto the flick. I finished and made my master tape, plus a copy for ICM.

Friday, January 24, 1992

I'm still waiting for the contracts from Mex-American or an offer from Million Dollar Video. Nothing yet.

I slept until 12:20 P.M. when Warren of ICM called to ask about the movie. He said Federal Express should be here within two hours to pick up the tape. I hope they like it.

Monday, February 3, 1992

ICM called. Robert Newman said he saw the flick and so did an associate, David Wirtschafter. He said that they want to represent me and that he'll send a contract right over. "I look forward to working with you Robert, we're gonna make a lot of money together." Today's been a great day. The Year of the Monkey begins Wednesday. I'm getting a head start. I asked him what he thought about sending the movie to Miramax. He said that it was a tough sell because it was a low-budget movie, no stars, in Spanish, and that it was too small for them. I'd be better off selling it to the Spanish video market for $20,000. I asked if he'd mind if I sent it to them anyway on my own. He said to go ahead if I wanted, but not to get my hopes up.

Wednesday, February 5, 1992

Today begins the Year of the Monkey, my year according to the Chinese calendar since I was born in '68. Well, I'm off to a smashing start but I'm sick today. Maybe tomorrow everything will kick in.

I called Miramax and asked for Acquisitions. I talked to a guy named Patrick McDarrah. I told him I had made this film and I was recommended to send my movie to Miramax. I told him I could send him a videotape of it, that it was subtitled, and that there was a two-minute trailer at the head of the tape. All I want is for him to watch the trailer. If he likes what he sees, watch the rest of the movie. If he's not interested after seeing the trailer then he can send the tape back and I'll understand it's not for them. He said, "Sure, send it up!"

Thursday, February 6, 1992

I was home sick and Warren called. He confirmed my address and said that they are processing the contract. He said that at least six agents are excited about seeing the movie. ICM never picks anyone up just like that, since they're so big, they usually don't pick someone up until they've done really well. He said that I should be ecstatic.

Black Maria Film Festival called and they said that "Bedhead" is a smash! The director of the festival talked to me about it and said audiences were raving about it. He said that they go crazy when Becca summons the water hose. I told him how we shot it and he can't believe the primitive equipment we used. He said that it has a professional feel and style to it. He loves it. I have to send them more stills and a ¾" and ½" copy. He also wants to see the trailer for *El Mariachi*.

I called Charles Ramirez-Berg at school and he said he loved *El Mariachi*. He put it on late at night, he was tired but started it up anyway, saw the trailer and didn't turn off the tape until the movie was over. He thought it was great.

"Bedhead" tied for First Place at the Atlanta Film & Video Festival.

Friday, February 7, 1992

I received the contract from ICM by Federal Express. I took it to work and gave it to our office patent lawyer. She looked it over and evaluated it. She informed me that they were standard forms approved by the State of California, and that if I had a problem with any of it I'd have to go through California law with a California lawyer. She said she saw nothing unreasonable about it except for a small inconsistency I might want to mention. On Article 9 of Rider D (the Directors Guild minimum guarantees) it says ICM cannot cash my paychecks without a signed revocable instrument from me. But, on the provided instrument it states the agreement is irrevocable. So I called the contracts department and the lady said I was probably the only person to ever read Article 9, and said I could change it. So I signed the contracts and sent them Federal Express on Monday.

Tuesday, February 11, 1992

I called Miramax today to see if Patrick in Acquisitions had seen the flick. He said he had and that he thought it was great.

He passed it on up the totem pole to Mark Tusk and said that I can call back or they'll call me with a response. He told me he was expecting a great payoff at the end and got it! He loved the trailer. He said it was a good idea to include that at the start of the tape.

Friday, February 14, 1992

Scott Dinger, owner of the Dobie Theater in Austin, called to say he is taking copies of *El Mariachi* to the Berlin Film Festival to show prospective buyers. He wants to show it at his Dobie Theater very badly. I got the ICM contract back, my copy, fully executed and signed. Now what?

Tuesday, February 18, 1992

I called Anna Maria at Mex-American Video again. I told her I still haven't gotten the contracts and that I'm ready to sign the movie away. Send the contracts and we can get going. She says that she's still waiting on Mexico. ICM called. Robert Newman wants to send *El Mariachi* to Cannes.

Thursday, February 20, 1992

Louis Black wrote up a great little article about me in the *Austin Chronicle*. I called to thank Louis about the article and he remarked on how he and the late Warren Skaaren (screenwriter on *Batman, Beetlejuice*) had judged the local video contest two years ago when my short anthology "Austin Stories" was in competition. He said how they talked for a good while about how good it was before awarding it first place, and how Warren Skaaren wondered aloud how the filmmaking would be affected if I ever moved to Hollywood and started making bigger movies with bigger equipment. That was the last time Louis talked to Warren before he passed away.

Tuesday, February 25, 1992

I called Scott Dinger today to find out how the trip to the Berlin Film Festival went. He said the distributor of *The Van-*

ishing saw my movie but Scott had to leave for a screening and didn't get to talk to him about it. He said the problem comes in trying to market a foreign language picture by an American director. John Pierson, the producers' rep, also requested a copy of my movie.

I visited Kevin's new Funny Papers comic book store in Austin. He's throwing another autograph session this Friday and wants me to crank out some more copies of my comic strip compilation book *Bootleg Hooligans*. He said that all my others sold out.

I called Mex-American Video and Anna Maria said that the contracts for the rights to *El Mariachi* were in the mail. One for me one for Carlos.

Tuesday, March 3, 1992

Today is my little sister Becca's birthday. It's also the day that my agent at ICM called to alert me that I would be getting a call from Kevin Mischer, Vice-President of TriStar Pictures. He saw *Mariachi* and wants to talk to me. Stephanie Allain from Columbia Pictures saw *Mariachi* and will also be calling. She discovered John Singleton and wants to talk to me. This is getting weird.

I got home and found a message on my machine from Kevin Mischer saying he saw *Mariachi* and was "mesmerized." He also said he was showing it to some colleagues and in the next few days he'd like to fly me up to LA, have a sit down and see what we can "drum up."

Thursday, March 5, 1992

Stephanie Allain from Columbia called today and said she "loved" *Mariachi*. She's showing it to colleagues and they may want to fly me up for, if nothing else, a "get to know ya" kind of thing. She's going to start looking for a project for us to do, or if I have a script that I want to make, we can work out some kind of deal, she says. "I'd like to wait and see if I can find something for you to do before bringing you up, otherwise it's just more Hollywood bullshit." She sounds cool, laid back.

Last night ICM called and I told Warren what was going on. He said that every movie company has a copy now and they all love it: MGM, Universal, everyone! He also said that, "everyone at ICM" knows who I am now. I said, "what?" He said he was serious, and that if you were to walk into ICM and say "Robert Rodriguez" everyone would say *"El Mariachi."* I laughed out loud. He assured me he was not exaggerating. I find the idea kind of spooky, really.

Monday, March 9, 1992

This morning Chris Melendandri from Dawn Steel's company Steel Pictures called to say he *loved El Mariachi.* He said he wants to work with me seriously and couldn't believe the level of accomplishment I got with a 16mm camera, a shoestring budget, and no film crew.

TriStar Pictures called me back, Kevin Mischer said that they were flying me up at my leisure.

I called Miramax's Mark Tusk. He finally saw the movie but remarked that successful foreign action films are few and far between, except for the occasional *Nikita*, and *Nikita* this ain't. I thanked him and decided not to tell him how much I made it for, and how it was put together because in the end that shouldn't matter. I had a feeling that if people just saw it as a movie, without knowing the sacrifices that had to be made to get it done, that it would be a mediocre movie at best. Even I'm impressed that a lot of the things we attempted actually came out, but that's not what makes a movie great.

ICM told me that they would notify the other companies that I'm coming to town and that if they wanted to see me they'd have to put me up for a night. They also said I should come to the meetings prepared to discuss at least two specific projects I'd like to work on. Unfortunately, my wife is in school so I'll have to fly solo.

I plan on reading Stephen King's *The Langoliers* on the plane ride.

Tuesday, March 10, 1992

I got a call from Chris Lee at TriStar. He thought my movie looked like a John Woo film. He loved it and wants to show me Woo's *Hard Boiled* and *Bullet Through the Head*.

Wednesday, March 11, 1992

Mischer called me at work to tell me the details of the trip. A limo (?) picks me up from the airport and drives me to the Loews Santa Monica Beach Hotel. A rental car will be waiting at the hotel. The next day I go to the lot and meet with everyone at 2:30 P.M. Then the rest of the day is mine. I fly back to Austin the next morning. He tells me to relax and not to be nervous about Monday's meeting, I'm only meeting with the entire production company. (About ten people.)

Everyone at work was excited for me, if a little scared. I told them that it'll be fine, that this sort of thing probably happens to people every day. The studios have their feelers out, that's their job. They meet people like me daily, then probably forget about them. Everyone at one point or another gets a little attention, then it's all over before you know it and you're back to your regular life. At least now I know that getting their attention is easier than I thought. *Mariachi* is decent, but I know I can do much better simply knowing people will see it. I'll put more work and planning into the next movie, shoot carefully, work hard and then have something great to show as my demo reel. So if nothing comes from this trip, they'll at least know who I am and I can just keep making movies, keep practicing, and send in a better movie next time, along with a script for a bigger film. That's a good plan. I'm charged.

Friday, March 13, 1992

Robert Newman called and told me Elaine Colit at Disney saw *Mariachi* and was extremely excited. She's passing it around right now.

Dave Wirtschafter, my other agent (I've got two now at ICM) got on the phone too and they had me give my TriStar pitch so they could help me shape it, since I have no idea what I'm doing. They were extremely helpful. "As a rule, *no matter what you are pitching,*" he told me, "you should be as positive as possible about your ideas. You should tell TriStar that you have a few ideas that are not completely fleshed out, but that you would welcome a collaboration with TriStar in helping you develop them. That is the language you should use."

He then told me a bit about what they want to set up for me—I get my first lesson in Hollywood biz in this five-minute conversation: "If you have a script, it is more beneficial monetarily to say you want to do this story and have them say OK we'll give you X amount of dollars to write the screenplay. By doing that, you are in a good position to be writing for a company like TriStar, both externally and internally. Internally ICM can start spreading the news throughout the industry that you are writing for TriStar, and if you were also writing a separate script on spec, ICM could start letting people know this and create anticipation for whoever is looking to acquire your spec script.

"If TriStar likes an idea of yours they will make a development deal with you. Since you're a new writer they would pay you to work on this script with them and for them. You will be paid to write a treatment, then first draft, and then a second draft, known as the "three-step deal guarantee." If they were to put you up in this development deal you could expect to see a minimum of anywhere from $50,000 to $75,000 to write the screenplay, guaranteed. Your back-end to do this, which is the money you would make if the movie were made, would be in the range of $150,000 to $200,000. That's just for writing. As a director they would pay you scale which is $120,000." David mentioned that these are just conservative figures he is throwing at me. Conservative figures?

Now, spec work can be much more lucrative, they told me, and you can have much more control, but what he tells all his new people is that as they work on spec they should also work for hire, to get the experience, to get paid, to interact with the studio to see what they like about it and what they don't like about it. Even when you write on spec, when a studio options or buys your script then you are in partnership with that studio. So what I'm doing is good prep for that. David said that what will benefit me is that if I come up with a project in this arena that is as good as *Mariachi*, I can expect my position, monetarily, to change dramatically from this job to the next. On spec you are always judged by what you got paid for last.

In other words, let's say I make this movie for TriStar. I'll get paid $250,000. If this movie bombs and no one wants to see it (I did credible work but let's say because of the subject matter it just didn't happen), my writing fee up front will at least double. My directing fee would at least triple. Let's say I write a script and it doesn't get made, and I write it on spec. People pay in steps of work "to be done." Right now my step is zero. If I were to get even a minimal deal with TriStar on assignment I will be already $50,000 ahead of that by taking a studio job first.

I hung up the phone and couldn't help but feel more than a little strange. I make movies for fun, I have a fun time making them. It's my creative outlet. But if I work for these people I could make more money on one fun project than my parents make slaving at work for several years. It's crazy, completely crazy. All this time I thought I was going to have to go to UCLA or something to be a filmmaker and it turns out I've been one all this time. I can't help but wonder when all this is going to disappear. I can see it already. I go up to LA. I meet with TriStar. They are mildly impressed but a few days later someone more talented eclipses me and I'm forgotten. My agents decide they've got more important clients to deal with and cut me loose. I go back to making Mexican action movies for a tiny profit. Things could be worse. At least I'll be self-employed, making a little bit of money doing the things I love. That's all I ever wanted.

Robert Newman called back to say that although I am going to see TriStar, they went ahead and set an appointment for me to see Trilogy, who are the hottest writer/producer team in Hollywood right now. They wrote and produced *Backdraft* and *Robin Hood*. Robert showed my tape to Richard Lewis of that group and he loved it. They have an overall deal with Columbia. Since they are producers and not a studio, Dave and him decided to set up an appointment to see them since they're on the Columbia TriStar lot. So I'll meet with them at 4:00 P.M. then walk on over to the TriStar meeting.

Sunday, March 15, 1992

I left on a Delta flight from Austin to Dallas, then transferred and flew to LA. The limo chauffeur was there to greet me, holding a sign that said "Rodriguez, Loews Santa Monica." He asked if I saw Olivia Newton-John on the plane. I hadn't. The limo was huge, spacious. Television, phone, the works. We arrived at the Loews Santa Monica Beach Hotel at 9:00 P.M. I got to my room, 858, and spent a few minutes checking it out. Two televisions, one pops out of the bureau, and the other one in the bathroom. I can access my messages on channel 88 of the TV. There are luxurious bathrobes (I'm taking one) and, a minibar stocked with champagne, wine, beer, sodas, chocolate bars, chips, cookies, beef jerky, peanuts, liquor, Perrier, Loews Hotel sunglasses, and suntan lotion. I picked up my telephone, which has two lines, and a desk clerk immediately answered, "Yes Mr. Rodriguez." Just like in *Barton Fink!*

I have a rental car waiting in the valet-parked garage, a dark blue Honda Accord. If I want it I press Garage on my phone and valet parking brings it around the front for me.

All this for a short meeting tomorrow. They're trying to jazz me. It's working.

I showered, relaxed in my luxurious bathrobe (I'm taking one, I tell you), and watched TV. This is a great vacation. I can't help but think about the last time I was in Los Angeles. Sleeping on that furniture in Jorge's house. I had the same movie to my credits but I didn't have an agent back then. I can't believe they tried to tell us in film school that we should think about if we wanted to get an agent or not. What's there to think about? With an agent your interests are taken care of; without an agent you're sleeping on a nightstand in Jorge's house.

Monday, March 16, 1992

I woke up at 7:30 A.M. and couldn't go back to sleep. It was about sixty degrees and beautiful outside. I got up and hit the beach. It's too polluted to swim in so I just looked at it from afar.

I got dressed and cruised in my Honda Accord to ICM for my lunch date. The ride was about thirty-five minutes, nice and slow. I listened to cassette tapes I brought. At ICM I met the president of the company, Jim Wiatt. Steel Pictures, Disney, etc. were calling my agent lamenting that they would have flown me up first if they had known TriStar was jumping on it. So Disney wants to fly me up ASAP and they want exclusivity also.

Robert Newman and David Wirtschafter took me out to eat lunch at the Pane Caldo, where I guess Roger Moore, 007 eats lunch since he sat at the table next to us. Robert Newman was saying how people are already asking him, "So who's this Robert Rodriguez guy?" Word is getting out, he told me. I asked him and David if they as agents could just pick anyone off the streets and create a buzz like this around town, set them up in meetings, and cause all this commotion with just anybody, because it's sure starting to feel that way. They looked at each other and laughed. Dave said, "Yes. I guess we could do that." Robert laughed in agreement. David added, "But of course it's much easier if the client actually has some talent. It makes our job easier anyway, because if the client was just some no-talent then it wouldn't be long before people around town realize the client has no talent and they wouldn't hire him." We all thought about that a second or two. "Then again . . ."

Afterwards I drove to Trilogy Entertainment and met Richard B. Lewis and John Watson. They are two-thirds of the writer/producer team that made *Backdraft* and *Robin Hood*. Richard told me how impressed he was with *Mariachi*. He said that he sees demo reels all the time and they are nothing compared to *Mariachi*. I showed him "Bedhead" and pitched a feature length "Bedhead" idea to them and Richard said, "I love it. Let's do it." He also said he would be thinking of projects they may already have that I could do for them. Phillip Noyce called while I was talking to Richard, for a prep talk before meeting "Arnold" on making *Count of Monte Cristo*.

I went to my TriStar meeting and talked about *Mariachi* for a while. I pitched them a couple of ideas and we talked about future projects. I gave them a copy of my short film, "Bedhead," to watch, since it's a family comedy. I want them to see another side of my work.

That was it. A twenty-minute meeting, a few handshakes, and I was out the door. Back to the hotel and then I fly home tomorrow. All this for a twenty-minute meeting. I like these guys.

Tuesday, March 17, 1992

One of the maids gave me a free bathrobe. The limo took me to the airport and I flew home to Austin.

Kevin Mischer called me in Austin to tell me TriStar wants to make an action movie with me and that I should think of some action movie ideas and keep in touch with him. Something in the eight- to ten-million-dollar range! I wonder what happens if I bring it in under budget. Can I keep the rest?

Robert Newman called to say Disney is flying me up Monday and that Kevin Mischer wants me to write them an action movie. I said I'll get cracking. Steel Pictures asked him if TriStar and I discussed remaking *El Mariachi*. He answsered no, so that is a possible future project.

Wednesday, March 18, 1992

Stephanie Allain from Columbia called to say she was flying me up next Thursday. She is thinking of projects she may have that I can do, also.

I got a call from Robert Newman telling me Columbia wants to fly me up. He said to start thinking ten million dollars, *big canvas*. I said, "OK." He told me to get cracking! I said, "I am, I am."

Thursday, March 19, 1992

I'm thinking about the research hospital where I raised the money for *Mariachi*. TriStar liked the stories I told them about what I went through during my stay there. Possible script? Why not. Working title: *Needles*.

Monday, March 23, 1992

Columbia is not flying me out until next week and Disney is trying to schedule their people so I can meet everyone at once. Robert Newman asked if I wanted any scripts as airplane reading. Sure, makes sense. If they want me to write scripts I better start learning what they look like. I gave Warren my wish list of *Godfather, Jaws, Raiders of the Lost Ark, Darkman, Robocop, Sea of Love*. He said he'll FedEx them ASAP. They said I'm easy to please.

Tuesday, March 24, 1992

I spoke with Chris Meledandri from Steel Pictures. He told me they want me up there ASAP and as soon as people are scheduled he'll fly me up. I asked him about remaking *Mariachi* and he said that he personally wants to do that. He's got to figure out how to sell the marketing division on it. He said that he'll call me back tomorrow after he has collected his thoughts.

That would be cool. The movie's just going to rot on my bookshelf otherwise, so I might as well milk it for all it's worth.

Wednesday, March 25, 1992

I was doing some kind of filing work at the office when I got a call from Hollywood. My coworkers get excited whenever I get a call now, they think something big's going to happen. I assured them that this kind of thing happens to everyone who tries to get into Hollywood at one point or another and passes after a few days.

I answered the phone and it's Ann Templeton, she's with Dino DeLaurentiis Productions. She said, "I'm sorry I'm calling you at work . . . Hollywood calling, I'm so embarrassed,

I'm sorry, but I loved your movie." She said she was going to show it to Dino, who she's sure will love it.

Thursday, March 26, 1992

Robert Newman called to tell me that David Kirkpatrick ex-president of Paramount Pictures called to say he loved *El Mariachi* and is showing it to Paramount Chairman Brandon Tartikoff. Robert said, "See we're working for ya." I told him I know he is, and thanked him.

Monday, March 30, 1992

Adam Leipzig from Touchstone Pictures called me to say he wants me up that week and, to make things easier on me, he's going to allow me to see the other companies if I choose so as not to be flying me back and forth so much. I thanked him.

His secretary set up tickets for Thursday at 6:00 P.M. I'll be staying at the Sheraton Universal, a rental car will be waiting at the airport, and I'll get $200 spending money. These meetings are becoming profitable. Too bad I can't just do this full time. Who says there's no such thing as a free lunch? I've made it a habit to order a big fat juicy steak and two desserts whenever someone in Hollywood takes me out and pays. You never know when this will dry up.

I called Mex-American Video. They told me that the contracts were in the mail, but I never got them. They're all out of the office.

Tuesday, March 31, 1992

My flight to Dallas included a midflight scare. It was raining and a loud *bang* was heard outside the aircraft, followed by our right side jerking down followed by the left side doing the same, after which the craft was finally stabilized. The passengers screamed and gasped. It sounded and felt like our right wing was struck by a lightning bolt, sending us seesawing like that. Our kind pilot never bothered to tell us what it was that took place. It gave everyone something to talk about until we go to Dallas. Great, I've got to get on another plane for a three-hour flight. I don't like planes.

I arrived in LA at 9:30 P.M. I got my National rental car, a maroon Corsica, and drove out to my Sheraton Hotel across town. With my road map handy I got lost only twice, arriving at my hotel at 11:30 P.M. Fast food restaurants were already closed (?) so I settled for a $12 hamburger in my hotel room. There was a fax waiting for me at the front desk. I have a meeting with Chris Meledandri at 9:00 A.M. at Steel Pictures on the Disney lot.

Wednesday, April 1, 1992

I got lost trying to find the Disney studios. I was fifteen minutes late to my meeting. Disney Studios is a funny place. Little streets with names like Dopey Street and Mickey Avenue are filled with strange architecture and lots of trees. Happy workers shuffle around. Steel Pictures is in the Animation Building and I spent a few extra minutes walking the hallway, eyeing the original sketches and finished animation cels from all the Disney classics, right up to *Beauty and the Beast* and the yet-to-be-released *Aladdin*.

I met with Chris Meledandri and his crew, Jordi Ross from Spain and Mark something from Chicago. I talked to them about the *Mariachi* remake and they offered their take on it. Chris Meledandri wants to know if we can make him an electric guitar player and set it in Texas. He also told me his idea of having Mariachi end up on an Indian reservation and being nursed back to health and trained in fighting techniques by a mentor, so he will be prepared for the big battle. He asked about the culture and if they have an old ancient way of fighting, kind of like karate, something hand to hand, and if maybe the mentor could teach him these things. They started talking about the Hero Paradigm (I think I read that in Wehmeyer's class at UT–Austin) and how to mold Mariachi to fit it. Chris asked Mark to run through the beats of that paradigm. Mark went through the beats effortlessly as if this were required study before applying for a job at this studio. (I found out later that it is required reading around here.) They remarked on the

Mariachi's hand being shot and noted that in these movies the near fatal injury to the hero is usually placed earlier in the film ". . . so maybe if we moved that up a few beats . . ." they said.

I almost dove out the window. They all realized by my silence that I was not taking the disembowelment of my story too well. I too realized that although I came here ready to work on anything, desperate for work, that I knew it was not going to be as easy to sell out as I thought.

In all fairness, I understand they have to make movies that make money, and the way I envisioned *El Mariachi*, it was never supposed to make money. It was supposed to be an offbeat action comedy for a very small marketplace. The only way to make it commercial would be to rip it to shreds. Oh well, I'll have to follow my instincts now, and consider doing something else.

We went on to other business. I showed them "Bedhead." They flipped over it. I pulled out my comic book, *Bootleg Hooligan*, and it prompted the question, "Wait, you wrote *and* drew this?" I told them that the book represents three years of a daily comic strip that features only one of my ten siblings. Meaning I have tons of material for a family television series, or a half-hour weekly comedy or series of films. They loved the idea.

We went to lunch and I tried to order something hefty, since this is Disney's tab. I ended up with a little pile of pasta with strips of grilled chicken layed carefully and sparsely on top of it. It tasted like paper and didn't fill me up so I asked for more bread rolls.

I went back to Disney for my 2:30 P.M. appointment at the Team Disney Building. It's a stone building with the seven dwarves as pillars. I met Adam Leipzig and his associate Bridget Johnson. I told them about myself, about my family, about how my mom used to take us all to the revival theater where she'd sneak the food in under the diapers. And to make it worth our time and money, we'd see the movie at least twice. Old Hitchcock, MGM musicals, Marx Brothers, etc. I explained how daddy was Mr. Gadget and bought the first VCR in town. I showed them "Bedhead" and they enjoyed it thoroughly. I showed them my comic book. They told me they'd love to work with me.

I went back to ICM to check in and find that Robert and Dave, my tag team agents, are having way too much fun stirring the pot. Dave told me Adam Leipzig called to say they thought I was a genius and that they loved me and want to work with me. Dave dropped the ax. He advised them that Columbia, Paramount, and TriStar are ready to make serious deals with me. Adam freaked out over this. Dave reminded him that it was his idea to allow me to meet with other companies on their dime. Adam lamented, "Why did we do that, oh no!" Dave advised them to figure out what they want and offer a deal, because he can bet the others are already doing that. Adam went away freaked out.

Robert and Dave took me to meet Mark Wyman, an attorney at Sinclair and Tennenbaum; they represent Ridley Scott and Peter Weir among others. They tell me later that Mark's extremely tough on the deal. I'm going to need an attorney very soon, so they suggested him.

Robert took me to eat at the Daily Grill. Spike Lee walked in wearing a jacket with a huge *X* on the back in the colors of the flag. I remember reading his books on filmmaking. He said that he wanted to demythologize the filmmaking process. I'm slowly learning what he was talking about. This business is really strange.

I drove to my hotel, watched TV, and relaxed. A fax told me I meet with Disney again tomorrow.

Thursday, April 2, 1992

At 11:00 A.M. I went to meet Dawn Steel. She sat next to me and said, "Well, what a good-looking guy!" I like her already. I showed her "Bedhead" and my comic book and told her about my ideas in shooting Texas movies. She said that I should do something that I know as a first film, which is something about my family or a remake of *El Mariachi*.

Chris Meledandri and I went to eat at the Animation Building. I choked down a Toad Burger with chips and fries. I listened to his "Why it's good to work for Disney" pitch. I told him that I knew that when he spoke of the Mariachi with an electric guitar on an Indian reservation idea he was just brainstorming, throwing ideas out, trying to figure out how to take a movie that wasn't extremely commercial and make it more commercial. I told him that we'll see what happens. I'd love to set up my ideas at different places and I am still considering the *Mariachi* remake with Touchstone, if we could come to a good compromise conceptually. I thanked him and left.

I drove down to Paramount Pictures to see David Kirkpatrick. I talked to him about the making of *Mariachi,* and we watched "Bedhead." He loved it and we talked some more. I told him about my research hospital experiments and about the script it inspired, he laughed and said, "You're an original." He seemed impressed. I left feeling happy and confident; maybe they'll offer something good.

Later, Agent Dave told me Kirkpatrick wants to do whatever it takes to get me at Paramount. So let's see, if everything came together, conceivably I could develop the script for "Bedhead" with Kirkpatrick, work out some kind of *Mariachi* remake with Chris Meledandri at Disney, and maybe develop one of my action movies with Trilogy for Columbia or TriStar. Get to work with everyone at once to see who's got the best setup and who's best to work with.

Stephanie Allain from Columbia took me to see *Basic Instinct* and we almost got in a car wreck on our way to eat dinner at Musso and Franks. I ordered filet mignon and a baked potato. Two desserts. Stephanie talked to me about the other studios. I love hearing each studio tell me how the other studios are no good.

Friday, April 3, 1992

I met with Disney President David Hoberman and Executive Vice-President Donald De Line at Touchstone, along with Adam Leipzig again and Bridget Johnson. I went through my little presentation with them and found myself speaking to Donald De Line the most since he seemed most into what I had to say. After our little thirty-minute meeting I shook everyone's hand and left. Hoberman seemed bored with me the whole time. Too bored.

I went to Columbia and sat in a meeting with Stephanie, Yalda Tehranian, Wendy Wasserman, Christine something, Amy Greene, and some guy. They seemed to really like my stories, my comic strip, my ideas, and they are all young, fresh minds. We had a great time talking. I told them how I had also financed my short film "Bedhead" with the money I earned at the medical research hospital by testing a speed healing drug. They wanted to see my scars and I covered my arms and said, "You get me a deal, and then I'll show you my arms."

I think there's a point in Hollywood when you realize you've become a whore. This was the point for me. I want to work so badly and I think Columbia seems open to most of my ideas, to the point that I could earn great pay while at the same time having fun making a few crazy movies. Things are looking great. I told them I liked Trilogy and Stephanie said, "We have a contract with them. Let's do something with Trilogy!"

I dropped by TriStar and talked to Mischer. He wants to hook me up with a producer. He told me he has sent the movie to Demme, Donner, DeVito, Levinson, and the producer of *Robocop*.

I went to ICM and Mark Platt called. He's the President of TriStar and he just saw "Bedhead" and is ready to make a deal based solely on that. He told my agent Dave to call him back, and not to forget! Agent Dave said that this means serious business and that things are heating up. He added that Disney is taking matters to the Katzenberg level and that alone will heat things up considerably and send waves through the community.

Agent Robert asked if I wanted to go to an advance screening of *The Player*. Sure, I guess. "Is that the movie about making movies?" I asked him. I'd read about it somewhere. It was set to open in a few weeks.

It turned out that Robert wasn't taking me to a screening, but to the premiere of *The Player*. We walked into the Directors Guild theater and flashbulbs were popping all over the place. Not at us, of course, but at the people standing all around us. There was Nick Nolte, Brion James, Mimi Rogers,

Jeff Goldblum, Peter Strauss, Brian De Palma, Sydney Pollack, Michael Bolton, Kathy Ireland, Teri Garr, Elisabeth Shue, Jack Lemmon, Fred Ward, Powers Booth, Graham Greene, Virginia Madsen, Christine Lahti, Faye Dunaway, Sally Kellerman . . . I felt a little stupid trying to introduce myself to Nick Nolte, Powers Booth, Jeff Fahey, and Fred Ward, they probably shake a hundred hands a day, but they were all nice and they even asked who I was. I told them and they seemed interested.

Watching the film was probably the most surreal experience I'd ever had. I just spent the past couple of weeks meeting studios, pitching story ideas, just like in the movie *The Player* . . . except that while I'm watching this movie, I'm surrounded by people who are in the movie. It was too weird. I think I'm going to tell my agents that I'll make a deal with anybody that lets me stay in Texas. That will be the new requirement. Not the money, not the most lucrative deal, but who will work with me and let me reside in Texas. What good is money and a hefty deal if you're cursed to live in Hollywood? In small doses like this it's interesting and pretty funny, but any more than that and I'd flip out.

Saturday, April 4, 1992

I woke up to a call from Adam Leipzig who wanted to apologize for Hoberman's seeming disinterested at our meeting Friday. He said that he just wasn't feeling well and that he liked me and is taking my films to Katzenberg. I almost told Adam that I saw Hoberman at the premiere for *The Player* and almost didn't recognize him because he was smiling so big and having such a great time. Quick recovery. I didn't mention it, though, and simply thanked Adam for a pleasant stay and visit, and bid him farewell.

I called Kirkpatrick and he told me how much he wants to work with me and that he is showing the films to Brandon Tartikoff. Although he doesn't need Brandon's approval, he likes to show him what's going on anyway. Kirkpatrick used to run the studio before becoming a producer on the lot. He's ready to make a blind deal, figuring out the project later. I thanked him.

My agents suggested I go home and think about what has happened, get out of the house, take a road trip or something and stay away from the phone.

I flew home to Austin, puzzled but elated.

Monday, April 6, 1992

I woke up late, around 1:00 P.M. and checked messages. I got a lot of calls including some from Stephanie Allain, Kevin Mischer, and ICM.

Agent Robert and Agent Dave called to tell me that TriStar offered me an overall deal. "What does that mean? Is that good?" They tell me it means they're offering me a home. A casa. Which means they'll pay me to develop "Bedhead," *Mariachi*, *Needles*, whatever, and that they have a first look at anything I write, but if they don't want to make it I can take the project somewhere else. I called TriStar and Kevin Mischer told me that Jonathan Demme is looking at the tape right now. He said that he knows I'm looking at other companies and that if I don't join with them, he'll understand and knows we'll probably work together in the future.

Michael Nathanson, President of Columbia called and told me he saw *Mariachi* and "Bedhead" over the weekend and is dying to work with me. He mentioned that I really should work at Columbia because he is also offering me a home there and that they are a young, vital company and that Stephanie Allain has a network of great talent like John Singleton and myself and that she is able to provide us with a working environment that is free from studio interference. He explained that Mark Canton, the chairman is watching my tape as we speak and that he is only forty-one. He said he's sending Stephanie Allain down to visit me in Austin.

One of the persons who was in the first Columbia meeting, Yalda, called to tell me that she loved "Bedhead" and that I must have this innate talent to have performed so well with so little money. I confided in telling her that it's really not that big a deal. I really owe it all to video, that's where I got to make movies for very little money by trial and error, and that after several years and many many terrible efforts, the movies actually began to improve. "Bedhead" and *Mariachi* are the latest in a long line of home movies. She said that she could never do that, she doesn't have that kind of time to spend. I guess that's the main part of it. Very few people have a lot of time to dedicate to one hobby. I was fortunate to have started so young, because when you're young you have nothing but time. Hours and hours to burn up on something as silly as a movie. I told her I felt bad that I was always screwing around with the video camera or with drawing instead of studying, but now I realize I was preparing for my future career. She said it meant a lot that Michael Nathanson called me himself because he never does that.

Stephanie Allain called to say she *and* Richard Lewis from Trilogy Entertainment want to come down Wednesday to see me here in Austin. She says Columbia wants to give me a home. She said, "How about remaking *El Mariachi* with Antonio Banderas?" Could we really get him to be in it? I guess we could if he was interested. This is spooky. *Mariachi* was a practice film. To take that and remake it into a film with Antonio Banderas would be freaky. In a good way, though. It's just such a mind trip right now. Too much information, options, and questions all at once. Even my instincts are confused.

She said she'd get back to me on the Wednesday trip, and that they're very busy and that's why they want to come down, because they want me to know they are serious. They told Agent Dave about the offer and he, cool as ice, told them that *everyone* is offering the same thing, so stand in line. He's a tough one. She wanted to remind me that unlike Disney or the other guys, they have already made my kind of movies without interference.

I talked to David Wirtschafter and he said that he told Kevin Mischer at TriStar that Columbia is flying people down here to see me. He asked David what he can do and David told them to get on the ball. Kirkpatrick is also getting to Tartikoff and asking for things, and Dave tells me that Disney is also foaming at the mouth. He told me that Columbia wants to offer a two-picture guarantee to write and direct, and that pay would be scale plus 10%. David told them that with that kind of money they're not even in the ballpark. So Columbia is going back to rethink the numbers.

David told Columbia to figure out what a hit filmmaker at the Sundance Film Festival would have gotten for this sort of deal since my movie has generated much more interest than even that.

David also told me not to make a decision until Stephanie Allain is good and gone. Oh, and Steven Spielberg is getting my tapes. Have fun, he told me. This is getting interesting and it will only get more interesting.

Tuesday, April 7, 1992

Columbia has made the first offer. They were all asked not to talk numbers yet, but they called up with this latest offer anyway. If I go with Columbia I will be *guaranteed* at least a quarter of a million dollars. They will pay me $100,000 for a two-step arrangement for *El Mariachi:* a first draft and one rewrite. My back-end will be $250,000 (if it gets made). To direct I'd get about $200,000. For the second script, probably "Bedhead," I am once again guaranteed $125,000 for the first draft and a rewrite with a back-end of at least $350,000 (if it gets made).

I gasped. David said that TriStar will be making an offer very soon. So will Disney. He told me that he had originally kept the numbers conservative so he would look good when the real figures came in. Once again, I'm impressed. What's an agent for again? Oh yeah. To protect your interests.

Agent Robert brought up something interesting. He said he might be able to sell my original *Mariachi* tape after all. If Columbia really wants to remake *El Mariachi*, he'll sell them distribution rights to the original tape. Since this is a studio, and studios like to control everything, it would be in their best interest to buy my original $7,000 tape. Since they'll spend several million dollars to remake it, they're not going to want the original to get bought and released on video at the same time their remake is in theaters. So he said he'd ask for a good sum of money, so hold off selling the rights to the Spanish video market. Wow. Good thing they never got the contract together.

Mark Wyman, the attorney I met from Sinclair and Tennenbaum called to ask if I would consider making him my attorney. I told him I completely trust David and Robert and that they told me that if I wanted a good honest person who is ferocious on the deal, that he was the guy. He says sometimes when dealing with these people you have to be an asshole. Cool. So he's on my team.

Wednesday, April 8, 1992

Stephanie Allain and Richard B. Lewis arrived in Austin. Liz and I picked them up and we went to our favorite Mexican restaurant, Tio Tito's. They devoured their fajita plates. I called Dad to bring the kids up. We headed back to the apartment and they asked how long it will take me to write the script and said that contractually I'd have three months. I told them I think I can do it quickly and that I'm used to working fast. Mom and Dad, Lizzy, Dave, Bec-Bec, and Tina arrived and Richard and Stephanie tried to sell Mom and Dad on the idea of me working for them. They admitted that this was a new experience for them and that they had never flown down to do this for anyone before. They felt like they were recruiting for a football team or something.

For dinner, we all went to eat at County Line and ordered big rib plates with milk shakes for dessert. Richard took me aside and advised me that I should not sign an exclusive with anyone. I should try and work for both TriStar and Columbia. Get a first look deal with Columbia and then get my movie made with someone else if need be. He told me he knows the offer already, $100,000 for *Mariachi*. $25,000 to start and onward. I said it sounds like a hell of a lot of money to me, and he said that it was a lot. He didn't start getting money like that until his fifth script. He also said that with the economic slump Hollywood is in right now this is unheard of, and that it won't last long because everyone is tightening their belts, so to get in while the getting's good.

My agents called to tell me that they've made a counteroffer to Columbia and that if Columbia doesn't respond by late Friday, then school's out and I fly back up to meet with everyone again including Warner Brothers and Fox.

Friday, April 10, 1992

I got a call this morning from Donald De Line, Executive Vice-President at Disney. He remarked at how sorry he feels for me right now, having all these Hollywood nutsos hounding me. I told them it was difficult to choose because I had planned on working with everybody in some way. But now that everyone's offering an exclusive deal, I'll have to pick only one, yet I don't want to offend the ones I don't choose. He told me he was upset that I didn't choose Disney and that they were all hurt that Columbia jumped the gun and made an offer before it was time to make offers. They felt that if they hadn't played by the rules, things would have turned out differently. I told him the decision wasn't an easy one and that there are no clear-cut winners in this. I felt that *Mariachi* would get the proper treatment at Columbia, yet a family film liked "Bedhead" would obviously benefit from the Disney banner. He told me he hopes I have a long career ahead of me and that I can work with them in the future. I told him that if Columbia doesn't respond to the counteroffer we have made, then the game will reopen and I will be able to fly back up and discuss in further detail just what it is we can do. He wished me luck.

David Wirtschafter and Robert Newman called to tell me that they are making enemies because of me. Supposedly everyone is calling them up and chewing them out for letting Columbia pull a fast one. They told me that even Jeffrey Katzenberg himself was calling the President of ICM, Jim Wiatt, to try and muscle me over to Disney. Things have gotten out of hand.

Kevin Mischer called to tell me Jonathan Demme saw my movie and loved it. I can't believe it. Kevin told me that I am doing myself a great disservice by moving to Columbia before I get to have a sit-down with Jonathan Demme. I told him I feel bad about that since I am a big fan of Demme's. He told me Mark Platt, President of TriStar, is flying to New York Monday to talk to Demme. A sit-down could happen as early as next week. I told Kevin that if Columbia refuses our counteroffer, then I will be flying out to see everyone again and that maybe that meeting can take place at that time.

Jordi Ross called very depressed and asked what he can do to get me to reconsider Disney. I explained that Columbia was allowing me to keep the *Mariachi* story in Mexico and the main character Latino. I also mentioned that the moment I saw Stephanie Allain she asked me, "What do you think about Antonio Banderas as *El Mariachi?*" Jordi said that he can be my champion and tell Diney that that's what I want. He also said that he knows Almodóvar and can get me a meeting with Antonio Banderas if I want. He said that Disney can get me Antonio Banderas. I told him that if Columbia doesn't accept my outlandish counterproposal, then he can talk to Disney so that when I go back up to meet them, we can discuss those possibilities.

Ed Saxon called me. He's one of the producers from *Silence of the Lambs*. He told me that he and Demme saw "Bedhead" together this morning and thought it was great. They also saw thirty minutes of *El Mariachi* and thought it was great. Demme demanded a copy of it ASAP. He told me the benefits of working under guys like Demme and himself and talked about the New York advantage in filmmaking. I told him I was confused. He gave me his home number in case I want to talk about what's going on.

Robert, Dave, and Mark called to finalize the proposal. They filled in the new points and the additions. They asked if I agree. If I say yes, we close. They are excited because even Jim Wiatt thought this deal was incredible. For someone who has never written for Hollywood, much less directed for Hollywood, the freedom and compensation I'm being granted is unprecedented. Or in David's words, this is a "coup." Robert said that the trades are calling him to find out what the hell is going on. They told me there would no doubt be a story about all this in the *Hollywood Reporter* and *Variety* next week. David told me I owe them a big dinner. They asked me if I want the

Columbia deal. All I have to do is say "yes." This deal makes us all look good, me, Columbia, and the agency.

I said "yes." They told me to go and celebrate.

Stephanie and Richard called screaming with delight. They will call me Monday so we can get started.

I called home and told Daddy, and I called my sister, Angela, in New York. Carlos is here when it all goes down and I have the pleasure of telling him that the original *Mariachi* will get sold after all—to Columbia's distribution. They want to control those rights. So, Carlos will get paid back and so will I. It all worked out after all.

COLUMBIA PICTURES

Tuesday, April 14, 1992

I went to school and caught up with the Dean of Students. He was someone I had to beg only two semesters ago not to kick me out of school due to poor grades so I could take a film course and make "Bedhead." Back then I had shown him my comic strips and my short video movies in order to convince him I'd make a good student despite the bad grades, so he endorsed my staying enrolled. Today I met with him to tell him the good news concerning *Mariachi* and thanked him for letting me stay in school, illustrating how much power he wields by possibly making or breaking a kid's future. He was speechless.

Thursday, April 16, 1992

I got a call from Mark Wyman, my attorney. He said that the contract negotiations are in Stage Three, and that I should have a contract to sign and some money by early next week. He explained a few clauses he managed to get for me, such as reversion rights for three projects, *Mariachi*, "Bedhead," and the Hospital Project (meaning something to the effect that they could develop the material but I would get it back after a certain amount of time if it wasn't getting made). He also explained a bit of the three-month extension specifications; such as that during the time after the two-year deal, if Columbia extends my contract for the optional three months, I have to give them at least three ideas of something I want to produce at that time.

Friday, April 17, 1992

I got a message from Jordan Cronenweth, director of photography on many films, including *Blade Runner*. His neighbor goes to school with my wife, Elizabeth. Before I knew what was happening Jordan got a copy of *Mariachi* and "Bed-head." I called him back and spoke to his wife Shane for a while. She told me how much she loved the films and that Jordan had seen *Mariachi* several times. I was flattered beyond expression since I've seen Jordan's films many times as well. I told her about the Columbia deal and she was ecstatic. Jordan joined her on the line and said that he wanted to be my cinematographer and I told him that I could never afford him. He said I was right, because he would bring about twenty electricians with him. They invited me to Santa Fe to meet with them sometime. I thanked them.

Robert Newman told me that the word was out on the streets about the deal and that people had been asking him, "Who's this Robert Rodriguez guy?"

Tuesday, April 21, 1992

I got a call from Mark Gill, head of the publicity department at Columbia. He read me the announcement they are sending out to the trades this week. It sounds good. Stephanie Allain called to tell me that they are flying me up Wednesday and I'll be back in Texas on Saturday.

Wednesday, April 22, 1992

A huge white limo picked me up at my apartment complex today. Some of the neighbors wondered why this kid in overalls was getting into the big white limo. The driver apologized for the big car, he was supposed to be in a town car, but didn't have time to switch vehicles. I told him it was all right. The people at my apartment complex probably think I'm a drug dealer now.

This is my first plane ride first class. It's great. Since I'm 6'2" I can finally stretch my legs out all the way in my chair. They served red and white wine and champagne. I got a tossed salad with sourdough roll and fresh shrimp. Then a big plate of baked potato and filet mignon, finished up with a hot fudge sundae. I got to LA and called Newman from the car phone. I was driven to the Westwood Marquis. They wanted a $400 deposit for incidentals. I gave them $60; that's all I had. I went to my suite. Two big TVs, stocked fridge, stocked pantry, robe (more souvenirs). The works.

I went to the agency and Robert gave me a copy of the press release that hits the stands tomorrow. David, Robert, and I went to some fancy restaurant. The food was awful, but I did see James Coburn there, so maybe I ordered wrong. Whenever I tell my agents I'd like us to go to a normal restaurant that serves good inexpensive food they just laugh.

Thursday, April 23, 1992

I woke up to a ringing phone at 8:30 A.M. Robert Newman asked, "Have you seen the trades? Go get it then call me back." What's wrong? I asked. "Just get it and call me." Click! I thought the worst. I showered and found a newsstand. Good news! I made the front page in *Daily Variety*! I called Robert back and he said, "Congratulations! I think it's a good day for you to come by the agency."

I sat in Robert's office as other agents poured in with their congratulations. I thanked them and after each one left I asked who they were. I met Lou Pitt (Arnold's agent), Joe Funicello (Jodie's agent who said, "Front page! When Jodie got her deal all I could get was third page!"), Jack Gilardi (Van Damme's agent), CEO and President Jeff Berg (Cameron's agent).

Stephanie took me to South Central LA to John Singleton's set of *Poetic Justice*. Singleton came over and congratulated me. I met Steve Nicolaides and Stephanie's husband Mitch Marcus. Steve and I talked about making movies. He's really cool and laid back.

After that, Stephanie and I ate at an Italian restaurant where I saw Chris Lee from TriStar. He said, "John Woo is in town, want to meet him?" I said yes, definitely. But Chris Lee left before I could find out where I could meet him.

Back at the lot, Steph's assistant Chris Thompson gave me a tour of the lot. I saw the high-definition room, where an artist rendered a frame of *A Few Good Men* with a pixel pen, turning an actor into the Joker with a few pen strokes.

I met Michael Nathanson and then Mark Canton, who told me that he saw *Mariachi* finally, and can happily say he is in agreement with everyone else that was raving about it. He mentioned that this doesn't always happen. He likes stuff they don't, and vice versa. He told me that he hadn't been this excited about new talent since he saw Tim Burton's first film *Frankenweenie* and gave him *Pee Wee's Big Adventure* to do. He made a few suggestions about the *Mariachi* remake and told me he thinks that the remake should definitely be my first film project there at Columbia because it's such "a great fucking story." The guitar player, the guns in the case . . . all that, he told me.

He asked Stephanie if I had received the Columbia leather jacket yet, and she said no. He told her to send me one quick! He also told Nathanson to get right on securing the rights for the original *Mariachi*. Since we're remaking it, they want to control the rights on the original. He asked me if I sold the distribution rights to the Spanish video market. I told him I hadn't. I had come close to selling it, but that I still controlled all the rights. He said the last thing they want is to spend five or six million remaking *El Mariachi* and then have the original pop up on videotape somewhere.

He also said that he's getting a copy to Peter Guber to watch this weekend. Steph said that Canton called her on the car phone to tell her he was really psyched.

Friday, April 24, 1992

Richard Lewis and I talked about the story, about crew choices, about the logistics, etc. He told me that he's going to make sure Columbia sends me a PowerBook so I can get started on the writing.

At Columbia I met with Sid Ganis. He is head of marketing and told me the thing he loved the most was the editing in *Mariachi*. "Who did the editing, was it you?" I nodded, and told him that if he looks at the credits real close, he'd notice that my name creeps up quite a bit. I stuffed the credits with a bunch of made-up names in an effort to disguise the fact that we didn't have a crew. We were afraid that if the Spanish video market didn't see a lot of credits they would pay us less for the movie. I wanted the movie to look complicated and expensive so we could justify asking for a higher selling price. He laughed.

Mark Canton exited the building with Peter Guber and Mark said, "There he is!" Guber shook my hand and welcomed me aboard and said that he was looking forward to seeing my film.

Robert Newman took me to eat at the Ivy where I sat next to Roger Moore again! (He's shadowing me.) I ordered a mesquite steak and potato, and two desserts. Later, I flew back to Austin.

Sunday, April 26, 1992

I woke up at 9:30 A.M. with Elizabeth who is now finished with school. This is the first time we both get to sleep in late together in a long time. This is nice. She's been commuting to Houston for three days of classes then coming back to Austin for three days of work in order to finish her degree.

We laid in bed until 11:00 A.M. I finally said, "Well, I better get to work. Pass me the movie listings." She hit me. I really like my new job. Really really.

Monday, April 27, 1992

At school I saw Nick Cominos who elbowed his way out of the elevator to congratulate me. I told him I made the film he told me I couldn't. He said, "I know, I know." He tried to give me some horseshit about how I should never have told them I made it for less than $10,000. I told him that he knew that's what the budget would be. He was even willing to put some money into it. He said that now they'll take advantage of me, knowing I can make good movies cheap. He said that it would have been more beneficial to have said it cost $70,000. I told him that made no sense. I didn't need $70,000 to make that movie. I want them to know that I can put a film together regardless of budget because I preplan and think things through. Everyone who's seen it has told me they've liked something different: camera, the directing, the editing, etc.

He said they say that because no one sees the whole picture. He'd rather them say it's a great story, and that's all, because that says more about the movie. I told him that they did say that, and in fact, they like the story so much they want to re-make it! "Oh!" he said. Some people can be so negative.

Tuesday, April 28, 1992

Stephanie Allain called with good news: Peter Guber *loved El Mariachi*, she said. He loved it so much that *he actually thinks it's great as is!*

She also said that tomorrow I can look forward to some gifts! "What?" I asked. "A surprise!" she said.

Thursday, April 30, 1992

Robert Newman called twice today. He said Harvey Weinstein, President of Miramax, called him to tell him not to sell *Mariachi* (the original) because he'll kill for it. He wants to release it theatrically as is. He told Robert that "This guy is Jim Cameron, this guy is Luc Besson!" So Robert is excited because he can sell the movie now for big bucks, more than we ever imagined. He also said that Arnold Kopelson, who produced *Platoon* among other things is extremely interested in the rights to the original *Mariachi* as well.

The original one? What for? Who wants to see that? There are no actors in it, it's in a foreign language. I told Robert to tell Miramax that I sent them the movie a long time ago and they passed. They passed before they knew about how it was made, sure, but they passed on its merits as a picture that can or cannot stand on its own. I told Robert I'd rather remake it and do a good version than show the original around. That's my practice film. It would be like publishing my trunk novel.

Richard Linklater, a fellow Austin resident and director of *Slacker* and the upcoming *Dazed and Confused*, called. I'd never met him and he basically called to find out who I was and what I was doing. He heard about *Mariachi* and that it was a cross between Peckinpah and Almodóvar. We had a good time talking about making films and all that. He wants to see the tape, so I'll be dropping it by his office where I can check out his office setup, his script-writing programs, etc.

Stephanie Allain called to tell me I should be getting my surprise in the morning via Federal Express. She said she's glad I'm not living in Los Angeles. The rioting over the Rodney King verdict Wednesday afternoon has caused a huge uproar. She's glad? I'm glad I'm not living in Los Angeles!

Friday, May 1, 1992

We drove to Houston for Liz's graduation ceremony from Rice University.

Monday, May 4, 1992

Robert Newman and David Wirtschafter called today to tell me their plans on letting Columbia in on the bidding for the original *Mariachi*. They want to propose a price of $250,000 for the rights to *Mariachi*. I told them that a few months ago, before I signed with the agency I couldn't give it away for $20,000. They also say that I owe them a big dinner.

Joe Rosenberg, who handles Luc Besson, is supposedly going to call this morning to tell me how much he liked *El Mariachi*.

Tuesday, May 5, 1992

I got a gift from the studio today! A PowerBook.

At home Robert Newman called to give me an update. He said he told Darrell Walker to tell the big boys that we want $250,000 for *El Mariachi* and 15% of the gross profits that the film makes. Robert says Arnold gets that. Darrell said that he's going to talk to the boys and see what we can do because they want it badly also. I'm still waiting for my advance money.

Thursday, May 7, 1992

I went to campus and visited Charles Ramirez-Berg and he told me that his class screenings of "Bedhead" and the *Maria-*

chi trailer were a huge success. He said the class went nuts over it and that we should have questions/answers over it sometime.

Agent David called and said that the contract is almost finished and that we are still discussing the fate of the original *Mariachi*. I told him I needed money. He called back telling me he was faxing me a paper to sign and fax back to him and I'd get $25,000 *advance* on my advance tomorrow. I was excited for all of two minutes, because then Mark Wyman called back saying he's not sending the paper because that would make negotiations harder for us since then Columbia could say, "Well, we already gave him money, and blah blah." So it's a good thing I've got Mark Wyman on my side, looking out for my best interests. Even though I'm broke.

Stephanie called to say they are flying me up May 18 for a meeting with Canton about possibly changing the ending of *Mariachi* and the fate of the original, whether or not they'll release it on video, shelve it and remake it, or what.

Richard Lewis called to say hello and tell me what he thought was going on. He got the impression that Columbia wanted to release *Mariachi* the original and not do the remake. I told him I didn't get that impression, but if that's the case, then I'm with him in getting this film remade and the *Mariachi* original shelved or maybe sold to another company like Miramax. So we'll see what happens in the neverending *Mariachi* soap opera.

Friday, May 8, 1992

Robert Newman called from Cannes. He said Columbia called back with their counteroffer of $100,000 against 50% net theatrical and 25% video. He said he was surprised by the offer, because he had figured they would either tell him to kiss off on his original asking price of 250 grand or just pay it. I told him they were flying me up the day he gets back anyway, so we can wait until then to hear what they want to do with it before we decide to take it or haggle.

I got a little worried. I mean the money sounds great, but are they paying that much because they think I have a film print, or do they know that the movie only exists on videotape? If I tell them that I never cut the negative and don't even have a work print, they might not pay the money. I asked Robert. He said if they want a film print they can make it themselves.

Well, it's not that easy, I mean it would have to be reedited or conformed at least and I don't have any kind of timecode or, ah . . . not my problem.

Wednesday, May 13, 1992

David Wirtschafter called and said that Mark Wyman is very close to finishing the deal and it should be done today. Also, that Columbia has now upped their offer to $150,000 for the rights to *El Mariachi* the original (25% royalties). Since the price to get this up to speed is so low, he thinks I'll make a good amount of money on this deal. He and Mark suggested that we take that offer. He also mentioned that he will send the original forms to Columbia and they'll send me my $25,000. He also reminded me that they owe me $75,000 for the signing, and another $37,500 as a first writing step on the *El Mariachi* sequel. And if they green-light *El Mariachi*, they'll owe me acquisition rights fee for the movie, which is another $150,000, my pay-or-play fee as a director of $200,000 (whether the movie gets made or not), and then a back-end writing fee of $250,000. So he tells me that conceptually this could happen next week, which means 150G plus 125G plus 250G plus 200G which is as he said, "a lot of money."

I realize that even if things go badly at Columbia, I'd be set up to go somewhere else and still find decent work. So, I think I'll do alright. I came from nothing and I can always go back. But I should keep stocking up on souvenirs, just in case.

Friday, May 15, 1992

Mark Wyman called to update me on the status of the negotiations. He also mentioned that the paperwork I signed will need to be resigned. He said that the version I got hadn't gone through him and needs revisions. So dinero is at a stall again.

I hocked my video camera for some extra dough. We're

down to the wire. I know I've hit rock bottom when I'm hocking my most valued possession for food money.

Sunday, May 17, 1992

A car picked me up and dropped me off at the airport, where I am writing this. I will be staying at the Westwood Marquis again and eating good food. It's a strange split; here in Texas my wife and I can barely buy lettuce but as soon as I get to LA I'm eating like a king 'cause it's all free. I would get a loan to keep us afloat until the money comes in, but I'm so afraid they'll change their minds and the money might never come in. (I grew up in a family where loans were always considered bad news.) I guess that's one of the main reasons I wanted Carlos and me to put our own money into *Mariachi*. That way we'd be a lot more careful spending it, and then at the end we could sell the movie and not have to pay back any lenders.

Tuesday, May 19, 1992

I got up early to fix up the *Mariachi* treatment.

I went to Columbia and Mark Canton, Stephanie Allain, and Michael Nathanson were there for a discussion on mainly how to end the movie a little more *upbeat?* Is that the word? They're afraid that if they release the original on video, it doesn't set up for a sequel very well in that the Mariachi loses use of his hand completely and will never play guitar again. They think that's too depressing.

So the compromise we came up with was that the action would remain the same, but that I would change the last few lines of voice over narration. So the girl still dies, the Mariachi still loses his hand, *but it won't be a permanent injury.* In the original version he says at the end that "with this injury, I will never play the guitar again." They want me to change it to "I *don't know* if I'll ever play the guitar again." Then he still rides off with the guns and the dog. I can live with that. Too bad I don't have to reshoot the ending. If they were to send me back down to Mexico with a 16mm camera and a $2,000 budget to reshoot the ending, I'd end up reshooting half the movie to try and make it better. If I had known people might see this movie I'd have worked harder on it.

Now we have to wait until Thursday to decide if we should just go ahead and release the original on video and not remake it, but instead continue on with a sequel. Or should we just shelve the original and remake it? I'd rather shelve it, but we'll know by Thursday.

Stephanie said that I should have my money before I leave and that I have an interview with the *LA Times* about the ICM/Columbia deal. So I'll be here until Friday at least.

I went to Trilogy. Their office was lined with posters from *Robin Hood* and *Backdraft*. They told me that they were afraid Columbia would want to just release my original *Mariachi* and not remake it, but rather do some kind of sequel. This takes us from what is essentially a go picture into a whole development deal where we have to sit down and actually write a sequel. It could take forever is what they're saying. We want to avoid that, they said, because the main reason I came to Columbia was that I thought I'd have a go picture and be behind the camera again as soon as possible. So, we'll see.

Robert Newman and I went to the *Alien 3* premiere. David Goldberg appeared and Robert Newman introduced us. He said he saw *Mariachi* last night and flipped out over it. He said he really enjoyed it and wanted to introduce me to someone. He moved aside and I saw a shock of white hair. Billy Idol. "Hi, nice to meet you," he said. David told him about the movie and that he wanted to show it to Billy. Billy said, "Oh, yeah, I'd like to see it." We arrived at the main floor, and there was the red carpet thing and the journalists behind the ropes. I started walking down the rug. Then before I knew it the guy in front of me stops to face the photographers. Jean-Claude Van Damme. He was standing there for the cameras so I walked behind him real slow so I could get on TV. I also saw Apollo Creed, Bill Paxton, Lance Henriksen, Kathryn Bigelow, Walter Hill, Al Bundy and I got to meet Ted Tally. (*Silence of the Lambs* writer.) Robert Newman ragged on the movie all the way home. He said, "There's no guns? An Aliens movie with no guns? It's not gonna make dick at the box office!''

Wednesday, May 20, 1992

I came up with a way to get them to shelve my original *Mariachi*. I told them that if they were going to release my original that I would want to fix it a bit, do some additional shooting. I told Steph how originally there was supposed to be a huge action scene in the third act that we never got to shoot because we had to give our camera back. If people are going to see the movie, I'd like to at least have the opportunity to go shoot what was always supposed to be there. Maybe beef up some of the action. I told her it wouldn't cost anything, a couple of thousand dollars. They spend that kind of money on my hotel. Why not put it on the screen? I'm cheap.

Stephanie told me to send her a wish list of all the things I would want to shoot or reshoot. So I wrote up a huge list of stuff, anything I could think of, and faxed it over for Mark Canton's review. I figured that if the list was big enough, they'd say, aw forget it. Might as well remake the whole film (boy, was I wrong).

Stephanie Allain called to talk about what I'm thinking. I told her what I wanted to do. I wanted to remake *Mariachi* and not release the original, because the original is not a good sign of the kind of movie I can make. It's too rough, I mean I had no money. It's a home movie! Why show my home movies to the world? I'd rather do something that knocks them out. They'll take one look at *Mariachi* and shrug and say so what? That's not the impression I wanted my first film to make. My first real film, that is. I don't consider this my first real film; this was practice. I mean, I'm glad you all like it but to me it's practice.

Stephanie said I should express my ideas in these meetings without reservations. Mark Canton and Michael Nathanson won't get offended, they've heard it all. She asked if I liked the Trilogy guys. I told her that I did. She suggested I meet other producers, like Steve Nicolaides, etc. because what I would

really need would be a line producer, a nuts and bolts producer. I told her I was game to that.

David Wirtschafter called and told me that I should decide
what I want to do. If I want to meet other producers, I'll have
to sever the relationship with Trilogy altogether. I told David
all I want is as little interference in the initial writing process
as possible, whoever is involved in the producing end. David
called back later to say he spoke to Pen Densham and Pen
understood.

Thursday, May 21, 1992

I went to ICM for the interview. This was an interview that
the agency sets up to kind of announce the new kid in town. I
was ushered into a room with Robert Newman and the writer
for the *LA Times*, Andy Marx. Grandson to the great Groucho
Marx. You figure that after a while you'll start running into
offspring and relatives of famous people.

I gave Andy the full story, or at least as much of it as I could
in one interview. We talked a lot and had a great time. Both
Mike, the ICM publicist, and Robert agreed that the interview
went great. Mike said I was honest and interesting and mentioned everything. Cool. They told me to get used to it because
I'll be doing a lot of interviews.

I got to our meeting with Canton and they watched the end
of *Mariachi* to see if the ending would still be too downbeat,
even with the change in the narration. As they watched it, they
said that they were still amazed at the work. They asked again
how I managed to shoot all this material for such a low budget. I simply told them that when you're making a low-budget
movie like this you have to have all your shots lined up, really
see how it's going to be edited in your head beforehand, so
you only shoot the stuff you know you're going to use. Plus it
helps to not have a crew. Because even if you have a crew that
works for free, you still have to feed them and that adds up. I
told them I basically shot it like you would a documentary,
with no crew, but with a lot of preplanning.

Mark told me that they've decided they want to make a film
print, and screen it for an audience. Then once we get audi-

ence reactions, we'll decide if we want to distribute only in Mexico and South America and remake it for American audiences in English, or also release it in limited art houses in the US and then make a sequel.

I figured it was time to put my foot down. I told them that quite honestly I couldn't imagine anyone ever paying $7 to see a $7,000 movie. It's just a home movie, and I wouldn't feel comfortable seeing it blown up and screened to audiences in real theaters. Mark Canton waved my thoughts away with his hand and said, "You don't know what you're saying. You haven't even had the benefit of seeing this in front of an audience to see how it plays. Am I right?"

I nodded.

He said, "That's right! So what we're going to do is, at least, let you see it in front of an audience before you throw it away and do it all over again. You might have something great here. Give yourself the benefit of seeing it in front of an audience before deciding, and afterwards if we decide to shelve it we can shelve it and move on." He's walking us out the door.

I think I have him now. I go for it. "But we can't screen it in a theater because I don't have a film print. I never made a film print, I only edited on video."

Mark stopped walking. He thought for all of two seconds. Then he waved his hand in the air again and said, "Don't worry, we'll make you a print." Stephanie smiled.

Hmmm. Even I can't refuse that. If they want to spend the dough in making me a 16mm or maybe even a 35mm film print just to screen it to an audience, I might as well shut up and stick around. I'd love to see how my home movie looks projected onto a big screen.

Robert Newman and I talked about what would happen if *El Mariachi* was released and then didn't perform well. Columbia might then blow off making a sequel altogether, which means that I will not be behind the camera again anytime soon, which was the whole reason I made the deal with Columbia to begin with. We'll discuss it more tomorrow. He said, "We have to get you behind the camera as soon as possible on a real movie so that you can show people what you can do with a real camera and a real budget." I agree with that completely.

Friday, May 22, 1992

Robert Newman and I both talked to Steph to clear things up. She said they weren't expecting *Mariachi* to perform at all. No matter what, they'll still want to do something with the character. It's just that they don't want to shelve the film unnecessarily, for it could be something good, and until they test it there will be no way of knowing. So Robert was more at ease. He later mentioned to me that the *Mariachi* deal was actually really sweet. Not only will I get $150,000 up front for distribution rights to the film, but they will also pay 25% on video sales. This means that if we sell 10,000 videotapes, I'll make another $125,000.

I had lunch with Steph and got ready to leave on my four o'clock flight. The car never showed up and I didn't have money for a cab, so I missed my flight. I did get my paycheck though, $13,000 after taxes and commissions were taken out. As soon as I got the check, Mark Wyman called and said not to cash it. He said that since I'm incorporating, cashing this check with taxes withheld would only complicate matters. Damn! So now I've finally got a check in my hand but I'm still broke cause I can't cash it! I can't win!!!!

I guess these guys don't know what it feels like to be completely broke, and to be holding a $13,000 check in your hand that you can't cash. I'm sure they're thinking, "Can't he just wait a bit longer? What's he gonna do, run out and spend it?" They don't realize you *can't* wait for something like this! Your mind starts believing the money will never come. You start thinking that maybe Columbia will change their mind and not write out the real check when I'm so close to getting paid. I'm freaking out.

So I waited over at Steph's house until the midnight flight. I watched TV. It was Johnny Carson's last night on the "Tonight Show." The car showed up and took me to the airport. I didn't arrive in Austin until 9:00 A.M. An old classmate from film school was on the same plane flying to Austin for graduation.

He saw me in the first class section and asked what was going on, because he'd read the article in the Austin paper and it seemed like all hell was breaking loose. I told him about the Columbia deal and all the crazy stuff that was going on. We left the plane talking.

Usually the driver is supposed to be waiting outside the gate, but he wasn't there. I figured something had gone wrong again so I continued walking, figuring I'd catch a cab.

As I talked and walked, my driver appeared. It was the same guy who had dropped me off. He waved knowingly, took my bags from me and walked away. I acted as if this were all normal behavior. My classmate asked who that was and why he took my bags without saying anything, and I explained that Columbia was paying for the flight and the driver. We walked outside and he spotted the driver putting my bags into a huge black limousine. We both laughed. I told him it's supposed to be a regular town car, but sometimes they don't have time to switch vehicles. "Whatever," he tells me laughing.

Wyman called this morning and told me to go ahead and cash the check. He said that we'll just go ahead and incorporate and apply only the new checks to the corporation. We got to the bank and deposited the money. Thank God!

Sunday, May 24, 1992

Liz and I slept until past noon. We went to Sam's Discount Warehouse and bought a ton of food, some new underwear, socks, shoes, a file cabinet, a high-powered fan, a wide slice toaster, and a garment bag. Hallelujah.

POSTPRODUCTION, TAKE 2

Monday, May 25, 1992

Jimmy Honore, the Senior Vice-President of Postproduction at Sony Pictures, flew in to Austin late this morning. He was here to see what kind of shape my original materials for *Mariachi* are in. Since he's in charge of making the 35mm film print, he needed to see where I have my sound, what format it's on, what condition my original footage is in, etc. A car brought him to the house and I showed him my setup with all my sound on ten cassette tapes, the Radio Shack microphone, and the Marantz tape recorder I used to record the sound. He couldn't believe it. He offered some suggestions on how to make the print.

I asked if he thought we'd have to replace any of the sound because I kind of liked the sounds I got from location and it was a hell of a lot of work syncing everything up.

He said that I shouldn't have to redo anything because "you want it to sound fucking natural! You clean it up too much and it won't sound fucking natural!!" Jimmy's hilarious. We dropped him off at the airport and then the car drove me back home.

Tuesday, May 26, 1992

I got calls from Jimmy Honore requesting original footage from the movie so he could make a 35mm blowup test along with a sample of my original sound. I called my lab and had them clip a piece of film at the end of roll 23. I also made a sample audiotape for Jimmy Honore, and FedExed it.

Thursday, May 28, 1992

The Music Department at Columbia called to discuss my musical needs on the movie. I told them that I didn't need any extra music because the agreement was to put *Mariachi* together on 35mm with the same sound and picture as the original. That was the deal. Since they wouldn't let me reshoot anything, they can't change my music either. If they want to spruce it up they'll have to let me reshoot first. I can't let them fix up one part and not fix up another and then say it's the $7,000 movie.

Friday, May 29, 1992

Jimmy Honore called. They made the test and it looked great. They want all the film stock sent on over. He also wants all my original sound. So they're flying me up next Tuesday or Wednesday for three to four weeks of supervision while they conform a work print to my videotape. Since there are no slates or any identification on any of the film, they'll need my help finding the right shots.

Stephanie faxed me the *LA Times* article due out Sunday. It looked pretty good. The story sounds really weird, though. He wanted to make a film so badly he sold his body to science to pay for it, wrote the script in the science lab, and met his main bad guy there, too. When I read it out altogether like that I come off sounding like a freak. Am I a freak?

Robert Newman thought the timing was perfect. He said that things will only get better.

Monday, June 1, 1992

I picked up two copies of the *LA Times* Sunday edition at a local bookstore. I want to send copies to Mom and Dad.

Robert Newman said that he's been getting lots of great calls from people who have seen the article.

Wednesday, June 3, 1992

I convinced Elizabeth to sleep in with me this morning. I had the driver drop her off at work on the way to the airport.

I was at the elevator at the LA hotel when a bellhop asked if I was Robert Rodriguez. He had seen the *LA Times* article.

Mark Wyman and Robert Newman called to talk about the whole per diem thing. Chris from Steph's office also called about that. They are all going to find out what happens if I don't spend all $2,000 per week (doesn't include rental car or airfare). Do I keep it? Or what if I go over? Do I pay? I can't really go over, seeing as how I'd have to spend $285 dollars per day. (The hotel suite at the Marquis is $185). I told them that I loved the Westwood Marquis and that if I had to spend money I would stay there, but if I could keep whatever was leftover, then I'd rather stay at the Howard Johnson and keep the rest. I have nine brothers and sisters, ya know. They tell me no one has ever asked this before. Most people just spend it all and live it up.

Steph said I'll start editing tomorrow.

Thursday, June 4, 1992

I called an electronics store out of the back of a video magazine this morning and ordered the Canon L-1 Hi-8 video camera. I need to start recording all of the crazy stuff that is going on and I need something higher quality than VHS or regular 8mm.

I went to Columbia at 10:30 A.M. Jimmy Honore introduced me to an editor, George Hively, and we checked out the editing room where we will be doing the cutting. George usually cuts TV versions of movies for television or airlines.

I met with Barry Josephson. He said he wants me to tell him sometime about how I made *Mariachi* for so cheap.

George Hively and I watched *Mariachi* and noted the repeated shots. I told him I repeated a lot of shots since that's so easy to do on video, not thinking I'd ever make a film print. I told him that the reason was to stretch it out to ninety minutes to sell it to the Spanish video market. Now it doesn't have to be ninety minutes, so if I eliminate the extra shots and repeated action, it would be easier to conform and it would be a lot tighter, which is what I would prefer anyway. If it was up to me, I'd rather the film be seventy-five minutes and fly like a bullet. Tomorrow we'll watch the blowup test.

A lady came by to take me to my new office over in the Lean

Building. I checked it out. It's cool. I was about to sit at the desk and the lady said, "No, that's where your assistant sits. Your office is in here. She opened the other door to a bigger office, much nicer. They're supplying me with a fax, phone, VCR, monitors, etc. This is so strange. What am I going to do with an office? I'll just be editing all day over in the editing room. What am I going to do with an assistant?

I went to ICM to talk with my agents, Agent David and Agent Robert. They told me that everything is cool with Trilogy.

Friday, June 5, 1992

I went to work at 10:00 A.M. I got to the editing room, which is around the corner from the Cary Grant Theater.

The funny thing about this editing room and about George my coeditor, is that this place is where they cut the TV and airline versions of the movies. So on the desk is a listing of all the parts that need to be cut out of *Thunderheart*. I heard George running down the list over the phone to someone to double-check it. It's fun hearing ol' George, a guy probably in his early 60s, rapid fire through cuss words like "fuckin' badger, sum-na-bitch, fuckin' question, fuckin' cop, fuckin' hubcap, militant bullshit, you asshole, etc."

We listened to the 35mm magnetic sound print, which they had taken from my ¾" edit master. It sounded OK. So if we cut the film print to match my videotape, then just slap the soundtracks on from the video master, hopefully that will be good enough to screen the film with. It would be a nightmare having to recut all that sound from my original audiocassettes. It would take forever.

After lunch, our 35mm blowup came in. This is my 16mm film blown up to 35mm so we can cut it. We took it to the Thalberg screening room. The movie looked so different on the big screen. The color was richer, the image was huge. I couldn't believe it. I've gotten so used to seeing it on video.

I met with producer Arnold Kopelson (*Platoon*). We sat and talked about how I made *Mariachi*, how much it cost, my other ideas. Arnold told me how disappointed he was in not getting rights to *Mariachi*. He asked when my one year exclusive was up and promised he'd start calling me to take me away from Columbia. He loved my stories about making the movie in Mexico and said that Carlos was wonderful, and that the girl was fantastic.

Monday, June 8, 1992

I got to my office and figured out the phone system. I called Denise Grant. She said the corporation is set up. I owe them $695 for the Texas fee, preparation fee, first year's agent fee, and minutes book. So I guess I'm Los Hooligans Productions, Inc. My comic strip name has served me well. So I should keep using it.

Tuesday, June 9, 1992

I called Robert Newman and asked what it is I'm actually selling to Columbia, so Layne Lauritzen, my accountant, and I can figure out exactly who they should pay the check to, me or the corporation. He said I'm selling them the world distribution rights for perpetuity, not the underlying rights, such as the soundtrack, sequels, characters, etc. Maybe merchandising, I'd have to clear that up with Wyman.

I went to a computer store and bought a scriptwriting program called Final Draft.

Thursday, June 11, 1992

Well, I've been here a week and we've edited one minute of screen time. I told George that we'll never finish using this method so I suggested a new plan of attack. Instead of trying to conform the film to the old soundtrack, we should just cut it straight, using the videotape as a guide. Then we can get soundtracks of each element, the dialogue stem, the sound effects stem and the music stem from my tapes in Texas, and cut that if necessary to match wherever it goes out of sync.

I told him it's not doing me any good to sit here and watch him cut and that I need to have my own kem so I can cut too.

I know the film better than anyone and it will save a lot of time. He said that this was a union lot and I shouldn't be cutting on it and if we did that we'd have to keep the door closed so no one can complain. Fine. I really don't care about the unions as much as I care about me having to stick around here for three months cutting something that should take three weeks.

I went to see Jimmy Honore while George was on his post-lunch bank trip. I told Jimmy that he has me cutting this movie with union editors that are used to spending a year cutting a TV version of a film, and that I don't intend to hang around that long so we need a better method of editing this picture. I told him that we had only edited one minute in two days. He agreed we had to do something and he called George in. We decided to go with my plan on recutting the film so they brought me in my own editing bench, a Kem Jr.

Friday, June 12, 1992

Chris called me with the news about the mysterious per diem. I basically get $2,000 a week. Whatever I save, I keep. So what I can do is pay for my hotel out of my own pocket and they can just write me a check for $2,000 every week. Great! So this is what I'm gonna do. The corporate apartments are a lot cheaper than any hotel; in fact I'll save almost $4,000 in one month's time, since I'm making $2,000 a week in per diem and I can keep the rest. Cool. I can put my brother David through school with that money. Incredible.

Tuesday, June 16, 1992

I got a visit from Raul Perez from the Music Division this morning to discuss movie music rights. They told me my musicians would have to sign new contracts that are about ten pages long. After the cue sheets are drawn, they can get a copy and immediately join BMI or ASCAP. They were saying things like, "What about resale rights? No it's nonunion . . . negative pickup. No problem. Take care of it all in one form." Supposedly the performers and composers will earn royalties every time the movie shows somewhere if they join the ASCAP or BMI. That's cool. They'll like that.

Wednesday, June 17, 1992

Single White Female came in for the TV version, and Barbet
Schroeder came in to use part of our editing room to look at
the last reel, and a problem they were having with the music.
I wanted to meet him since I was a big fan of *Barfly*, and I
wanted to tell him how it was one of our favorite movies when
we were locked in the research hospital, but I left him alone.
I'm still a nobody.

Elizabeth arrived to visit me for my birthday. We went to
eat dinner at the Ivy with Stephanie Allain and Mitch. Before
we left, they gave me my birthday present from Mark Canton,
Michael Nathanson, and Stephanie. It was a Sony Laserdisc
player!

After the dinner, Liz and I went to Tower Records and I
bought the *Aliens* deluxe laserdisc box set.

Saturday, June 20, 1992

It's my birthday! I'm twenty-four years old. Liz and I had
free tickets waiting for us at Universal Studios. It's weird, last
year I had no money and couldn't buy a thing. Now I've finally
got some money but now everything's free.

Sunday, June 21, 1992

Liz had to fly back to Austin so I drowned my lonely sorrows
in a *Close Encounters* Criterion Edition and *Taxi Driver* Criterion Edition laserdisc rentals.

On the *Taxi Driver* disc Scorcese said something funny; he
said that shooting a movie is a horrible experience. All day
long people ask you questions questions questions, all day
long, what do you want to eat? what color should this hat be?
etc. That's why shooting *Mariachi* was so much fun! I never
had anyone ask me questions because I had no crew. No wonder. Everyone that sees it thinks it was an incredible amount
of work and that it must have taken months to shoot all by
myself. You'd think that it would be more work and money
without a crew, but I tell them it was the complete opposite.

Tuesday, June 23, 1992

George Huang brought me the bootleg tape of John Woo's new movie, *Hard Boiled*. As I edited I got a call from Carlos. He drove into town to check out the editing. He came onto the studio lot and soaked in all the sights. He drove here in nineteen hours straight. He broke our last record. He went to sleep.

Later, Carlos and I watched *Hard Boiled*. It was exhilarating. It made us want to go out and make another *Mariachi*.

Sunday, June 28, 1992

I woke up at 5:00 A.M. because the room was rocking back and forth. I got up, and realized it was an earthquake. I stumbled to the living room and saw the lamp swinging from side to side. Carlos was half-asleep and staring out the window saying "Robert, I'm scared!" He thought the building was going to cave in on us. I was standing under the doorway laughing. It was great fun until I started feeling motion sickness from the rocking. It stopped and I went back to sleep with a slight headache. Another quake hit at 8:00 A.M. I laughed then, too. It didn't last as long, but it was kind of fun anyway. I told him it wasn't that bad, or we'd have really felt it. I was wrong. We watched TV and it turned out to measure 7.5 on the Richter scale. The reason we didn't feel it as much was because it went off in the desert.

Wednesday, July 1, 1992

George and I went to see Jimmy Honore today, we talked about bringing in another cutter, kem, and video playback. We need this film cut ASAP.

I told him that I was cutting as fast as I could, but what everyone underestimated when they took on this project was that yeah, sure, it's the little $7,000 movie and it should be easy to conform, but this little ninety-minute movie has got over 2,000 cuts in it! That takes time to conform.

I went on up to Steph's and we talked about the editing delays, and she said that from now on if I feel something isn't working to tell her so she can straighten it out. She's my contact. I edited until 8:30 P.M.

The new editor assistant came over and met us. His name is Chris, he's from Texas, in fact he graduated from UT in '83. He's an editor's assistant.

I tried to get into the *Dracula* test screening next door but it was for nonindustry people only.

Thursday, July 2, 1992

I was talking about how much easier computer editing would be. Chris was telling me that most people still edit on film and that a lot of TV shows are edited on film. What? I told him I thought film was the slowest thing in the world. I hate film editing. I told him that as soon as they get these computers editing in twenty-four-frames-per-second mode, no one in his right mind should edit on film.

Friday, July 3, 1992

Today everyone was off for the Fourth of July weekend. I went in to edit at 10:00 A.M. and left at 8:30 P.M. I ate when I got home and went to sleep. Too tired to write or draw, much less work out.

Sunday, July 5, 1992

I've edited all weekend. My back hurts. I just want to get the hell out of this town and go back to Texas. I'm editing as fast as I can now.

Wednesday, July 8, 1992

We finished cutting the picture, finally, and we should be done syncing dialogue tomorrow. The sound effects and music should take another day and a half and then we can screen it.

Today I received the contract for my overall deal. *Finally!*

Saturday, July 11, 1992

I'm editing from 11:00 A.M. to 11:00 P.M. cutting sound effects into the picture. All I've eaten so far today is the candy Elizabeth sent in a care package.

Saturday, August 3, 1991. On my "crane" for the shot of Mariachi walking to town. Azul (Reinol Martinez) and Mission Impossible (Roberto Martinez) look on.

Saturday, August 3, 1991.
El Mariachi himself,
Carlos Gallardo. We're so
proud of our camera,
we'll take any opportunity
to get a photo with it.

Tuesday, August 6, 1991.
Mariachi shows Domino
(Consuelo Gomez) the
lines for her death scene
for the first time.

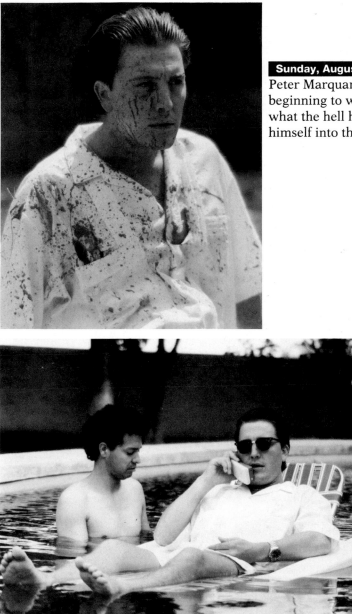

Sunday, August 11, 1991. Peter Marquardt is beginning to wonder just what the hell he's gotten himself into this time.

Saturday, August 10, 1991. Mariachi was in charge of pushing Peter into the frame. Notice Peter's left hand is cupped to conceal his "cheat sheet." He wears dark glasses to hide the fact that he's looking down to read his lines.

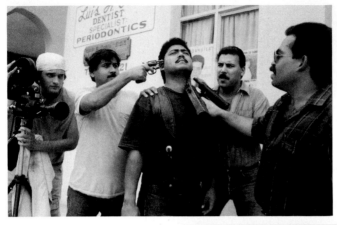

My crappy camera stand and all-purpose blood-soaked towel.

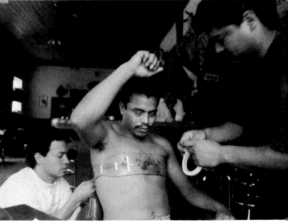

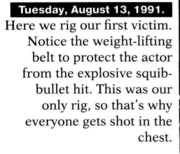

Tuesday, August 13, 1991.
Here we rig our first victim. Notice the weight-lifting belt to protect the actor from the explosive squib-bullet hit. This was our only rig, so that's why everyone gets shot in the chest.

The first wave of bad guys wore suits. The second wave wore T-shirts and jeans. Now, all the bad guys left in town are these fifteen-year-olds. We killed off all the big guys in town too quickly. . . .

Wednesday, July 31, 1991. Azul wanted to have a scene where he'd be in bed with three women. I told him, "You find 'em, you've got 'em." He found 'em.

Saturday, August 3, 1991. I'm riding on my "dolly cart," the wheelchair borrowed from the hospital next door. Azul, who films a scene next, is available to push me back for our long dolly take.

Monday, September 7, 1992. I'm with Harvey Keitel at the Telluride Film Festival.

Sunday, September 13, 1992. At a seminar/panel discussion at the Toronto Film Festival with co-panelist and writer/director Quentin Tarantino.

Tuesday, September 15, 1992. On another panel in Toronto, this time sitting next to Baz Luhrmann, director of *Strictly Ballroom*.

Sunday, March 16, 1991. With Laura Esquivel, novelist and screenwriter of *Like Water for Chocolate.*

Thursday, December 12, 1991. Standing in front of the "cash machine," the old ICM building.

Wednesday, August 7, 1991. The demanding director. Notice how full my pockets are. A one-man crew needs deep pockets for lenses, motors, compressed air, etc.

Sunday, July 12, 1992

I edited for fourteen hours and finished the sound effects track. I celebrated with a double king burger from Fat Burger on my way home for the night. Eating that at 2:00 A.M. made me sick.

Wednesday, July 15, 1992

Stephanie Allain called with good news this morning. She read me a fax that said *Mariachi* has been invited to the Telluride Film Festival.

We got our quote back from the people who are going to be doing our subtitles. They want to charge us $3,000 to spot the movie! Meaning to figure out where the subtitles go on and off and they need *three weeks* to do it. I told them never mind, that I'll do it myself in three days for free this weekend. No wonder movies cost so much in this town. Three weeks. What a joke.

I worked cutting the music tracks until 3:30 A.M. I hadn't eaten since yesterday so I went to Fat Burger and wolfed down a double cheese king burger. I felt sick again. I'd stop doing that, but everything is closed at that time of night and Fat Burger is the only thing still open. I thought this was the city that never sleeps. Or is that New York?

Friday, July 17, 1992

Harold Becker *(Sea of Love)* arrived to cut screen tests for his new movie with Nicole Kidman and Alec Baldwin. He was in my cutting room working on the other kem.

I really liked *Sea of Love* so I was hoping he'd catch a glimpse of what I was editing. I pretended I was studying the chase scene in my mind.

Sure enough, it got his attention. He asked what I was doing and I told him all about *Mariachi*. As his assistant editor cut, he would come over and watch some of *Mariachi*. He told his assistant, "This is more interesting over here." I told him how I shot it and he was impressed. I told him how the actors learned one line at a time and then forgot about them and that by not having a crew I was able to get all my setups in fourteen days for $7,000.

He said, "That's great, but don't ever do that again." I told him a few more tricks I used and he finally said, "Maybe we're working too hard."

Monday, July 20, 1995

I spotted all the subtitles this past weekend and today I sent off the list along with all the translations, etc.

Thursday, July 23, 1992

I edited the last of the sound effects in for this dub. The new dubbing station they have here on the Sony lot is incredible. It's completely computerized. I guess they don't care how much this is costing them since it's all internal anyway. They can use it as a write off. I'm glad I don't have net points on this movie because they can justify costs of who knows what just for using the studio lot when I conformed and mixed sound. What a scam.

We dubbed until 8:00 P.M., finishing through roll 6. It sounded awful. The dialogue track we used from the videotape was full of hiss. You can't tell from the kem but on a good speaker system it sounds like shit. To get it ready for the festival, it'll take me another three weeks to fix. I guess I'm not going home anytime soon.

Friday, July 24, 1992

We finished dubbing at 10:30 A.M. It sounded good except for the dialogue, of course.

Tenny, my dialogue mixer, told me to bring in a sample of my original dialogue straight off of my original cassette tapes and we played it through the mixing room speakers. It sounded great. Damn. Tenny told me that it'll be a lot of work for me to first find all the original lines and then resync them by hand, but that it will be worth it, it will sound a lot better.

This is gonna be rough. All this for a few festival screenings? Is it worth it? I told him I'd think about it.

We screened the subtitled print for ourselves. I can't believe the subtitle people misspelled so many words when I gave them the list spelled correctly as a guide. I can't imagine how bad it would have been if I had paid them the $3,000 to translate it and spot it as well. Incredible.

Monday, July 27, 1992

The screening was this morning and everyone was there: Mark Canton, Michael Nathanson, Doug Taylor, Amy Pascal, Stephanie Allain, Kevin Jones, International Films guys, the music guy, Jimmy Honore, etc. Before the screening, Jimmy said that the film was a rough work print, all chopped up, no color correcting, final mixing, etc. I added, "And if you have any comments, criticisms, or if you just don't like something, please keep it to yourself . . ." The screening went well, scattered laughs here and there, applause at the end.

Doug Taylor, the publicity guy, called and said he hated me. He hated me for going out and doing what he's always wanted to do: make a movie. He said he couldn't believe I made it. He was amazed, congratulatory, and all that.

Tuesday, July 28, 1992

I talked to Telluride about the festival; Bill Pence is sending me a packet on Telluride to get me psyched. He also mentioned that I'm scheduled for opening night!

The studio wants me to fix the sound. Transferring off the ¾" just won't cut it in a theater. So I have to bite the bullet and transfer all my raw dialogue takes from my original cassette tapes to 35mm magnetic stock, then resync everything to the film print. I have to listen to each audio take and find the right ones all over again. Not only do I have to resync all the dialogue, but many times I used different parts of different line readings to make up one sentence. To have to go back and match that by ear is going to be suicide. Plus I never marked any of the takes, so I have to make a sound log at night so I can identify them during the day while transferring. Plus, I'll have to retransfer all my sound effects and ambience and cut that back in sync as well, then I have to find all my music cues, transfer those and recut those back in as well. The worst part is that even if they wanted to hire someone to help me, they couldn't, because no one else would be able to make heads or tails of the material. I'm the only one even remotely familiar with any of this sound since I cut it the first time; so it's a one-man job again. If they did hire someone it would cost them a mint to do all that this is going to take.

I'm here in the transfer room and they have all the DAT machines and 35mm mag stock recorders and patch cables sticking out everywhere and here I have my little Marantz tape recorder patched into the 35mm mag recorder making my transfers. The guys working here ask me, "What are you doing? Is that sound for a temporary soundtrack?"

"No," I told them. "This is for my final soundtrack. This Marantz is what I recorded my dialogue, sound effects, and music with." They all laugh at me.

Thursday, July 30, 1992

Robert Newman called to tell me Toronto Film Festival called and they were going ballistic about *Mariachi*, they loved it and want it in the festival.

It's going to cost $1.30 per title for the subtitles and $70 per reel. So the whole process will be less than $1,000. I did the most expensive part myself, I saved Columbia over $3,000 on the subtitles alone. Not that they'll care, these studios are used to spending money like there's no tomorrow. It's so funny that when you make your own movie and edit on tape, all it takes to make subtitles is a shitty character generator you can get for free at any local cable access station.

Thursday, August 13, 1992

I stayed until 1:30 A.M. fixing subtitles, cutting in sound effects. I wonder to myself who usually takes care of this sort of thing on real movies. Do they just hire a bunch of people and then bring it to the director for approval? They must have to redo a ton of stuff. No wonder movies cost so much and take so long. If you want to do it right you've got to do it yourself.

Monday, August 17, 1992

I'm feeling sick. Got a cold or something. I transferred the rest of the sound effects, and I cut them in all night while the boys did backgrounds and cue sheets.

Thursday, August 20, 1992

I went to the Vincente Minnelli dub room at noon, and Danny DeVito came out to use the phone. He was working on *Hoffa*. I found the room I was supposed to be in, next door, the newly refurbished Room 6. This room is great. It has a pool table, a big buffet spread out on a table, a refrigerator, extremely comfortable leather sofas. This is a workplace?

The mixing went quickly. Since I don't have many tracks we got through half of reel 3. The music mixer asked why all my music was on one track. I told him it was mono. He said, "No, why is it all on one track? Usually you spread out each song from the others on separate tracks. But yours are all together, yet they fade in and out on their own." I realized I was doing it the cheap way. Instead of putting each song on a different track, I simply butted each song up against the next, making my own fades by scraping the magnetic stripe with a razor blade into an arrow so that the sound would get louder or softer.

Friday, August 21, 1992

Today we didn't finish roll 6, so we'll have to come back tomorrow for an all-day run. Yeah.

Saturday, August 22, 1992

We're finishing roll 6 and moving on. We have to print master today also. I haven't felt this tired in a long time. I can't remember the last time I felt this tired.

Wednesday, August 26, 1992

We watched roll 1 at Technicolor. The work print and the corrected dupe ran side by side for an astonishing and gut-wrenching comparison. The original work print straight from my negative looked beautiful in comparison to the "corrected" one-light dupe we just got. That one was muddy, flat, and dark. It actually looked like someone wiped their ass with it. The boys at Technicolor said they could make it look better, but it would still be flat. We're letting them correct half the roll from the internegative, and half from the interpositive, to see how much they can fix from the negative, or to see if maybe the interpositive is OK, and only the negative is screwy. We'll see.

Thursday, August 27, 1992

I saw the print at Technicolor. It's a vast improvement from yesterday, but again, I didn't have anything else on the screen to compare it with. The problem is definitely in the interpositive. So to fix the movie they're going to have to treat this as an original negative. It'll take them time to do this.

Friday, August 28, 1992

I met with Jerry Greenberg today, a really nice guy who's edited movies for Coppola, De Palma, etc. and who's now an executive here at Columbia. He talked about the editing, etc. and he's going to try and help me on this movie by viewing the film on Monday with me. If it's not up to par he'll help me fix it.

Wednesday, September 2, 1992

I watched what I could of the movie, and then had to fly home to Austin to pack up my things. I'm leaving for the Telluride Film Festival tomorrow morning.

TELLURIDE AND TORONTO

Thursday, September 3, 1992

We flew into Telluride on one of those little puddle jumpers and a volunteer picked us up at the airport and took us to our hotel, the Ice House. We ate at Florandora and took a nap. The air is thin up here, but it's definitely a cool town. Part of our Featival package awaiting us in the hotel was an invitation to a dinner party.

At the party I met Ken Burns, The Quay Brothers, Kathryn Bigelow, while Peter, Paul, and Mary played some tunes. I also hooked up with the guest festival director for this year, Guillermo Cabrera Infante, the great Cuban writer. He's the one who chose my movie for opening night. He's featuring other Latin films this year during the festival.

When I told people that it was my first visit here, they all told me that I will never forget this first visit to the Telluride Film Festival.

Friday, September 4, 1992

Liz and I met Roger Ebert at the opening night party out in the middle of the town. Ebert snapped some pictures of Liz and me. He had already heard all about the movie and was anxious to see it. (Oh great, now I really wish I had gotten a chance to reshoot some of this movie. If he hates it he'll write a review that will go out next week dogging it.)

I was nervous already. Fortunately, there was another film premiering at the same time, so all the pressure wasn't on me to deliver the film that would set the tone for the weekend. As we walked to the theater where *Mariachi* was to be shown we saw that a lot of the people from the opening night party were heading off in the same direction. We got to the theater and I had to videotape the huge serpentine line of more than 600 people standing waiting for a seat. Holy shit! I was really freaked out. They're gonna lynch me, I kept thinking. What happens when they get in there after hearing that this is the opening night movie, expecting something great, and then all they see is my blow-off Spanish home video mexploitation flick? I see a lot of older people here too. Real festival lovers, people that have been patrons here for ten, fifteen years. What are they going to think of this ultraviolent shoot-'em-up? I'm screwed. On top of this I had to do what I fear most. Speak. They wanted me to talk to the audience for about five minutes. All 600 seats were full. I had a spotlight in my face and a microphone in my sweaty hand. I started by saying that they were never supposed to see this movie. Then I sort of ran through the rough outline of why this movie came about and how it got here. From the medical experiments to the hustling and agenting. Some of which got big laughs. I told them I wanted Columbia to give me $2,000 so I could reshoot half the movie but they wouldn't let me. As I spoke there was enough laughter that made me realize that to a crowd this size, my life story sounded like a comedy routine. They laughed at all my misfortunes and applauded the victories. I finished my "speech" and sat back in my seat, nerves shot. The movie began. I wanted to bury myself.

So began the first public screening of *El Mariachi*. The audience included Kathryn Bigelow, and the producers of the documentary *Visions of Light*. Someone from Peter, Paul, and Mary was there too, I think it was Paul (he told me later that he loved the movie).

The screening was a success. People were polite, they laughed at all the right places, which I found really surprising, since there were a lot of jokes that I thought were only funny to me and a handful of people in Acuña. There was applause at the end and a lot of people stuck around to congratulate and generally speak positively about the film.

Outside of the theater, after the crowd had moved on to whatever movie was next in the festival, Mark Gill, from Columbia publicity, was standing outside the theater with a big smile on his face. He told me the last time he saw a response like this was at the Cannes Film Festival with *Boyz 'n the*

Hood. He sure looked happy. Sid Ganis came out of the theater and walked right up to Mark Gill, took him by the arm and said smiling, "We have to seriously talk about giving this movie a theatrical release." Mark smiled and said, "I agree." Uh-oh.

There was a second screening that night about thirty minutes later at a smaller venue, seating about 300 people. I was just as nervous this time around, probably more so because I noticed that Roger Ebert was watching it this time. Now I know I'm screwed! If he doesn't like it, I'm doomed. One review and it'll be dead. My career will be over. I remember that joke trailer I made last September with the *Drugstore Cowboy* blurbs with Roger Ebert's review saying "A Great Movie." Now one year later here's my chance to earn the real thing and I'll probably drop the ball.

Fortunately the screening went extremely well, the audience had a good time, and laughed at all the right places. They even laughed during a few extra scenes that shouldn't get laughs. But hey! That's all right, I'll take what I can get!

Mark Gill told me not to go ask Roger Ebert how he liked the movie afterwards. He said "Ebert never talks to the filmmaker after he sees his movie, so stay away."

Saturday, September 5, 1992

Today is the last screening. It's at the Nugget theater at 9:00 A.M. I didn't expect many people to show, this isn't exactly a nine-in-the-morning kind of movie. But, amazingly, I had a full house. People have been saying that this is the low-budget "freak show" movie of the festival that can't be missed. Although I hear there's a *really* strange flick premiering here this weekend called *The Crying Game* that supposedly has strange plot twists.

My morning screening went great. The audience was a lot younger and afterwards I had a lot of eager young people tell me how inspiring it was to see someone just go out and make their own film their own way against all odds and end up here. That made me feel good. Even if people don't like the movie, if it's inspiring to them then at least it's worth something. I told them that I would have loved to have heard a story like this a few years ago when I was depressed and couldn't get into film school because of my grades. If I had known you could go out and make your own movie by yourself for comparatively very little money I would have done something like this a lot sooner.

One of the Festival people came up before the screening and announced that due to popular demand *two* more screenings of *El Mariachi* had been added for the weekend. So I guess I'm not done, yet.

I had an interview with *Premiere* magazine. At least it's getting easier doing interviews. I even had a good time giving my speech before the third screening audience.

I ran into the director of the Miami Film Festival, Nat Chediak, who wants *Mariachi* to show at his festival in February and actually asked me to bring H. B., the pit bull in *Mariachi*, to the festival for a personal appearance. I think he's serious.

Sunday, September 6, 1992

We ate breakfast with Robert and Dave, then went to the Brothers Quay show for a collection of their short films. As I was walking down the aisle to find a seat, a photographer appeared at the other end of the aisle with a zoom lens and snapped a rapid succession of flash pictures. I found a seat and sat down as he ran up and shot a few more pictures. This is getting weird.

After a nap I went to the fourth showing of *Mariachi*. Vic Argo, an actor I've seen in a lot of Scorcese movies and in *Bad Lieutenant* told me how much he liked *Mariachi* and wants to introduce me to Harvey Keitel tomorrow after the Harvey Keitel Tribute.

We went to the screening of *Reservoir Dogs* at 11:30 P.M. I'd been waiting to see this since I heard about it from my agent, Robert, who saw it in Cannes. I'm also interested to see it because when we go to the Toronto Film Festival I'm supposed to be on a discussion panel with the writer/director of *Reservoir Dogs*, Quentin Tarantino.

The movie was really cool and everyone was into it. The

place was packed with 600 people. Harvey Keitel and Tim Roth were there to present the film. As the movie ended and the credits rolled, people were filing out. As I sat watching the credits someone exiting through the aisle flashed a couple of pictures of me. Liz asked if someone was taking pictures of me. I told her I wasn't sure. "I think so." This is very strange.

I finally talked to Roger Ebert who said that the article and review for my movie should come out Sunday. All he would say was that it was favorable and that I should enjoy it.

Anyway, he said he knew what my shooting ratio was and that I really knew where to put the camera. He mentioned John Ford and I told him about what George Hively at Columbia said when he saw my raw footage: I'd made a John Ford movie, where at the end of the editing I would carry all my trims home in a shoe box. I also told Ebert about how I'd been making videos since I was twelve years old, and that my editing between two VCRs is what taught me previsualization of an edit. He said this is what Coppola predicted years ago, when he said soon a kid would be carrying around a whole studio on his shoulder.

Tuesday, September 8, 1992

I had two last interviews and then packed up to leave. I really liked it here. I wish it could continue. At least I shot lots of videotape of the place, the screenings, etc.

At 4:30 P.M. we got back onto the puddle jumper and flew to Denver.

Mark Canton called to congratulate me. I told him he was right, people *did* like the movie and I was glad he made the film print for me or the movie would be sitting on a shelf at home with all my other home movies.

Thursday, September 10, 1992

Dave Wirtschafter called to tell me about the *Mariachi* review in *Daily Variety*, page 2. It was great. Azul is going to love it, it says all kinds of cool things about him and his performance.

Saturday, September 12, 1992

Back in Austin, El Mariachi himself, Mr. Carlos Gallardo arrived for his trip to Toronto with us. The car picked us up and took us to the plane, where we got to fly first class to Toronto. In Toronto, Doug Taylor was there with a luxury limo to greet us. We rode to the hotel with the roof open.

Carlos's eyes were bugging out of his head with excitement and I got it all on videotape. We got to the Sutton Hotel where they goofed with our room assignment so they put us in a deluxe suite for the night. In fact, Tim Robbins had just checked out of this room. It's huge. A hot tub in the bathroom, a full-sized kitchen, a living room, two TVs, and a stereo with a connecting speaker near the hot tub. The tile in the bathroom floor is heated so that you don't wake up to cold floors. They'll probably move us in the morning.

Sunday, September 13, 1992

We woke up at 11:00 A.M. and I showered and dressed for the panel discussion. I went downstairs and met Michael Madsen, Mr. Blonde from *Reservoir Dogs*, who was just checking in, and I saw Steve Buscemi, Mr. Pink, wandering around.

As I tried to stuff down a sandwich for lunch, I was introduced to Quentin Tarantino, who said he had heard all about *El Mariachi* and was excited to see it. I told him I'd seen *Reservoir Dogs* at the Telluride Film Festival, and I told him how cool I thought it was. I met Lawrence Bender who had produced it. I told Quentin that he must certainly be a fan of John Woo and the Chinese cinema. He said that he was and that *A Better Tomorrow* was his favorite Woo film. He said he discovered Woo while trying to find Jackie Chan movies in the LA Chinese video stores. I told him that ever since I saw *The Killer*, I figured the new wave of cinema in the US would be made by young filmmakers who were influenced by the frantic, imaginative, hyperaction films made by the Chinese. *Reservoir Dogs* seems to be the first of the bunch. We got on the discussion panel and had a great time. I started realizing how similar a lot of our stories are about how we got started, and how we made our first films, why we made them, and how we pulled them off.

Later, we went to the Miramax party where I met Harvey Weinstein. He told me how much he loved *Mariachi* and that it was a "great fuckin' movie" and that he wished he had seen it first, instead of the "bunch of idiots" working for him. I promised him we'd work together someday.

I actually met Mark Tusk, the guy at Miramax who I had originally sent *Mariachi* to way back when, and who turned it down. He told me how much heat he had taken once it was found out that he was the guy that turned down *Mariachi*. I told him I had never told him how much the movie cost or anything like that because I wanted to see how the movie would be perceived as a movie, and I was also afraid they would give me ten bucks for it if they knew how much it cost.

Monday, September 14, 1992

Interviews, interviews, interviews. Today was the Canadian press and I did a ton of print interviews, television interviews, and even radio programs. I'm really tired now, but the best thing is that people really love the story about the making of the film.

I ran into Lawrence Bender again and he told me he wasn't going to be able to see my movie. I told him they would be having screenings regularly back in Los Angeles.

The hotel finally kicked us out of our cool room.

I got two faxes. One was of the *Chicago Sun-Times* article by Roger Ebert, which came out really good; he wrote all kinds of nice things. The other was from the *LA Times* article on the festival, with only one picture representing all 300 of the movies showing here at the festival. They chose to run the picture of *El Mariachi*. It mentioned three movies in particular. *Hard Boiled*, *El Mariachi*, and *Laws of Gravity*. Mine qualified for what they called, "Most bullets on a budget."

Tuesday, September 15, 1992

Doug Taylor arranged to have a limo take us to the Toronto premiere of *Mariachi*, since this is our big night. I got it all on

videotape. We got to the theater and taped the audience standing in line for the movie. It went around the block. We got
inside, I introduced the film, and we got a great response.
After the show I had a questions and answers that lasted a
good forty-five minutes. People laughed and we had a good
time. Back at the hotel I ran into Quentin Tarantino. We ex-
changed quick stories on how our movies fared, and he told
me he was staying so he could see mine.

Wednesday, September 16, 1992

At 3:15 P.M. we saw *Reservoir Dogs* again; Carlos saw it for
the first time. I met Steve Buscemi afterwards and asked him
to come see *El Mariachi*. I also said hello to Lawrence Bender.
The response was phenomenal again; they're definitely going
to win the Best Feature award at the Festival.

Thursday, September 17, 1992

My movie plays today in the Uptown 1, the 900-seat theater,
right after John Woo's *Hard Boiled!*

At 3:30 P.M. we went to the Uptown 1 and I videotaped Carlos walking beside the huge line of over 900 people waiting to
go see *El Mariachi*. The line went around the block. It's mind
blowing that I couldn't even get the Spanish home video guys
to buy the damn movie, and here we are with a line of over
900 people waiting to see it.

The audience included Quentin Tarantino and Steve Buscemi. The showing went great and the nice thing was that
Steve Buscemi gave me his address and phone number and
told me he wants to be in one of my movies. He wants to send
me a demo tape of a movie he has made. I gave him my mail-
ing address. What an honor.

Quentin had to leave for an interview, but he told Liz and
Carlos that he loved it and that he would tell me so later. A lot
of the audience stuck around to hear the questions and answers and we had a good time talking about the making of the
movie. I gave advice on how to keep the budget low but the
amount of creativity high.

We went back home and ran into Alfonso Arau in the lobby of the hotel. His movie, *Como Agua Para Chocolate (Like Water for Chocolate)*, the movie where we first got the idea to make *El Mariachi*, is having its gala premiere here at the Toronto Film Festival tonight! What a weird coincidence. We told him our little movie *El Mariachi* was here. He was blown away. He said that he thought we were putting it out on video in Mexico. I told him we thought the same thing but somewhere along the way we ended up here. He told me that his was the most expensive movie to come out of Mexico and mine was the cheapest.

Upstairs in the room, Quentin Tarantino dropped by to tell us how much he enjoyed *Mariachi*. He was very encouraging, and then he told me how he's going to be making his new movie called *Pulp Fiction*, and that now that he knows the kind of sick bastard I am he knows I'm going to love it.

I told Doug Taylor I was tired of rabbit food and wanted some Texas style red meat. He took us to a steak house called Barberians, and I ordered an extra thick steak. William Shatner was sitting at the table behind us being rowdy with his buddies, all chowing down on red meat.

Friday, September 18, 1992

As I was checking out at the front desk, Chris Buchanan from Columbia/TriStar home video introduced me to John Turturro. I congratulated John on his film *Mac*, and told him I looked forward to seeing it. As John walked away he shook my hand and remarked, "Good luck with your film." He was cool and I hear his movie is really good, too.

POSTPRODUCTION, TAKE 3

Wednesday, September 23, 1992

Elizabeth has to go back to work, so she won't be going with me to the recruited audience test screening for *El Mariachi*.

They test movies all the time before a movie comes out to get audience reactions, score cards on it, etc. The questions they ask are: Do you like the characters? What do you think of the ending? etc.

Stephanie Allain said that it's in my contract to get two tickets to LA for any screenings. So since Liz can't go it's only fitting that I take along Tommy Nix, since he was there from the beginning and he knows all this movie was supposed to get was a quickie video release. He was the fellow student who was going to be my only crew person on the movie. He'll appreciate how far out of hand it's all gotten. He's never been to LA and I want him to see what it's like to be suddenly propelled into Hollywood after simply making one low-budget movie. He's got his straw cowboy hat and is ready to go.

Sunday, September 27, 1992

I picked up Tommy and we watched some Jackie Chan movies while waiting for the car to take us to the airport. I'm bringing my video camera along and I'm going to be taping his reactions the entire time. Tommy Goes to Hollywood. A car picked us up and took us to the airport where we boarded with our first class tickets.

I told him that Columbia Pictures was spending several thousand dollars for this little trip, so to act cool. We arrived at about 3:00 P.M., we checked into our respective hotel rooms at the Loews Santa Monica Beach Hotel, then went to the Columbia lot in our rental car.

Tuesday, September 29, 1992

Tommy and I raided the movie promo rooms, t-shirts, posters, then we went to the screening room to see a screen test of the new *Mariachi* blowup that was made from the 16mm negative, rather than the one made from the 35mm dupe negative that was shown at the festivals. It looks much better. They are going to have to cut the 16mm negative and make an internegative from that. The other way looked terrible. I told them that if they were going to release it they'd have to make it look as good as it can. The picture quality at the festivals was terribly muddy.

I ran into Lawrence Bender, producer of *Reservoir Dogs*, in the Tram Van. It turns out he and Quentin have an office right here on the lot also, in the Metro building. Danny DeVito is an executive producer on their new movie, *Pulp Fiction*. We said we'd get together sometime this week.

Later that evening Tommy and I went to the *Mariachi* test screening. It was packed. They had recruited 70% Latino audience members and 30% non-Latino. My agent Robert was there and he kept telling me how shocked he was that all the executives were there for the screening. Even Mark Canton and Michael Nathanson, and they sat through the entire movie.

We got a great response, especially considering that the audience didn't know what it was made for, or how it was made. The focus group after the movie said they loved the characters of the Mariachi and especially the Girl. Most said they loved the dog.

Michael Nathanson came up to me and said, "We have to bring the Mariachi back for another movie. It's all there. It's all set up for a new adventure with the same character, it's brilliant. Congratulations."

We went on to Roscoe's Chicken and Waffles later that night with Stephanie Allain and talked about the next step. Releasing the movie. Supposedly, the Sundance Film Festival has invited us to their festival! But in order to show it there we can't show it anywhere else after Toronto. So all these offers from different festivals will have to be turned down. But

Stephanie says that after the Sundance Festival, they are thinking of releasing it in selected theaters.

I asked her if we were going to remake it or not. It seems everyone else wants to release it and then make another movie with the same character. Although I'm pleased the movie has garnered positive reaction, I wouldn't mind shelving this one and remaking it or making something completely different so I can show people what I can really do with a decent budget. I also know I would work harder with just the prior knowledge that it would actually go into theaters.

She said that everyone at the studio is too happy with this movie not to release it. This whole experience is so bizarre I've just got to let it play out. I can't even imagine what my next move should be. I used to be able to trust my instincts. I must have left them in Texas 'cause they're nowhere to be found.

Thursday, October 1, 1992

The meeting with Mark Canton, Steph, Nathanson, and Jerry Greenberg went great. We're having a *Mariachi* distribution meeting on Monday and then they'll let me go write whatever I want. Just to be sure, I'll write two scripts. If they decide to shelve *Mariachi* and remake it, I'll have a remake script ready. If they decide to release *Mariachi* as is after Sundance, then I'll give them a new Mariachi adventure. Kind of like what *For a Few Dollars More* was to *A Fistful of Dollars*. Same character, different adventure.

At the Columbia lot, I ran into Emmanuel Lubezki, the director of photography on *Like Water for Chocolate* who I met back in '91 in Acuña. Emmanuel wants to see *El Mariachi*. I showed him the trailer and he liked it a lot. He asked me how I did the lighting. When I told him about my two aluminum reflectors and 250-watt light bulbs he cracked up.

Monday, October 5, 1992

I went to the lot to attend the distribution meeting but they decided to leave me out of it. So I sat outside in the wings.

After the meeting they told me that they want to release the movie first in San Antonio, Los Angeles, New York, Miami, Chicago, and then if it does well, roll it out from there.

We got on the plane and flew home. I'm anxious to begin writing.

Tuesday, October 6, 1992

I finally bought myself a printer today, and added four megabytes of memory to my PowerBook. Tomorrow, Tommy and I will cruise to San Antonio so I can pick up a new drafting table. I need to set up my lair, because once it's complete I'll lock myself up and not leave until I've created everything I need to get moving onto another movie and get behind the camera again.

Monday, November 9, 1992

Jerry Greenberg told me the bad news. The people conforming my negative screwed up. They weren't watching it closely enough and it got ground up in the gears. About forty feet was destroyed! I asked if it was a crucial scene. He said he thought it was the opening scene. Stephanie called and actually asked if I maybe had any other takes they could use as alternates to the destroyed scenes. "Uh, no. I think that was the whole point remember? Shot everything in one take." She said, she knew but she thought she'd ask to make sure. And then they wonder why I just want to do everything myself. They are going to have to take that scene from the 35mm dupe negative so there will be an obvious picture quality difference during that section of the film.

Tuesday, November 10, 1992

I flew back to LA and George Huang showed me around the *Last Action Hero* set. They're filming around the lot.

I walked by Arnold Schwarzenegger's Humvee and checked it out. (So was everyone else who happened to pass it by.) It's huge. As I passed his trailer I saw him sitting in his chair. His back was to me and he was smoking a big cigar.

I checked out of my hotel and I'm moving into George Huang's apartment. His roommates have all left already and his lease ends later this month. So he says I can crash there on the floor of an empty room for free. I'll save a mint by not staying in a hotel, plus he has a laserdisc player.

Since I'm with Columbia I get passes to all their premieres. Tonight I went to the *Dracula* premiere. To get into the Chinese Mann Theater, you have to go down the red carpet. I actually got my picture taken by four different photographers who said, "Mr. Rodriguez, can we get a picture, please?" That was nice of them. How'd they know who I was? They even got my name right. That's a nice feeling.

The movie was cool, but the party was great. It was at the House of Dracula. I met Gary Oldman and Francis Ford Coppola. I saw Winona Ryder, Larry Fishburne, John Singleton, Barbet Schroeder, even MacGyver was there.

Thursday, November 12, 1992

I moved into my new office in the Myrna Loy building. It has a private bathroom. When George's apartment lease is up I can just sleep in my office, shower at the studio gym, and put all that per diem in the bank.

I went to CFI film lab for a meeting, we discussed the damaged negative and the schedule for getting an answer print. It seems I'm going to be spending a lot more time here. You've got to supervise *everything*. It's true what they say.

Monday, November 16, 1992

I really need to get some serious writing done. I've read so many bad scripts that get bought, I figure I can write my own bad scripts and make a fortune. I was at Columbia by 7:00 A.M., did foley until noon, went to the lab for color correction, and came back for more foley. Foley is when they add sounds like footsteps and prop movements to your soundtrack to fill out the sound. Part of your delivery requirements on a film is to hand over a music and effects–only mix of your movie so that other countries can dub the film. Since a lot of my effects are tied to my dialogue, I have to add extra foley for the foreign sales.

Wednesday, November 18, 1992

Ivy Horta called to say the ratings board is having a problem with *El Mariachi*. It supposedly will get an NC-17 rating. What? Supposedly the big cheese will see it tomorrow, and then we'll know if it's true or not. I reminded her that *Reservoir Dogs* got an R and it was a lot more violent than my movie. She asked me who released *Reservoir Dogs* and I told her it was Miramax. She said that the ratings board loves Miramax so that's why it got the R rating. That made no sense to me, so I told her that Miramax wanted to release *Mariachi* so bad they were willing to pay much more than Columbia did for it, and that maybe I should have gone to Miramax instead. Ivy said she would appeal to the board. I told her the big cheese will probably see it tomorrow and decide that it's fine. There's nothing that bad in it. People like to get themselves all excited for nothing around here.

Wednesday, November 25, 1992

I'm flying home for Thanksgiving. All the kids will be there, even Angela and Patricia who are flying in from New York. Grandma Becky is making her last trip down from Arizona to see us since her cancer has seeped through her bones.

Monday, November 30, 1992

I flew out to LA for the final dub. We found out that our foley editor has been doing a bum job. There is a lot of stuff that was cut *way* out of sync. I got really pissed off. You have to do *everything* yourself in this town. Pathetic. No wonder movies are getting worse and worse while the costs get higher and higher.

Tuesday, December 1, 1992

The *Millimeter* magazine article came out today. I got a lot of calls from people who saw it. Casting Agent Bonnie Timmerman called today. She wanted to see my sister Angela for the Brian De Palma film, *Carlito's Way* starring Al Pacino. I told her Angela would also bring along a copy of my short film "Bedhead" which I wanted her to see as well. Bonnie said she would try and cast me in a movie as well???

Wednesday, December 2, 1992

George Huang came in to visit. We were talking about the costs of the *El Mariachi* blowup, since they basically had to do it twice, not getting it right the first time. I told him the studios waste so much money. I'm glad my share of the video royalties doesn't include any of their expenses and screwups. He said this was nothing. Right now they're trying to figure out what to do with this movie that's been sitting on the shelf called *The Pickle*. I asked him how much that one cost and he said, "Oh, not much . . . about 20." I laughed and told him he had to quit his job *right now*. He's been officially sucked into the business when he says a bad movie didn't cost much, *only* "20 million." He shook his head. He knows he's become jaded. I told him to quit his job and go make his own movie. He won't get any respect around here until he goes out and produces his own pictures. Working for a top level executive is a good stepping stone to move up the corporate ladder, but if he wants to dive into making films, he has to dive into making his own films. He agreed. I have a feeling he's going to take the leap. I can tell he sees how much fun I'm having in here in this Sony mixing room with an automated mixing board and three Oscar-winning mixers doing the final mix on my home movie. He's going to take the leap, I can tell.

(George quit his job a month later, then wrote and directed his first feature *Swimming with Sharks* with Kevin Spacey and Frank Whaley.)

They had to hire an extra foley editor that could check the work of the other foley editor who cut everything out of sync.

I got upset. "Why is it that these union editors are supposed to be the best around, yet we have to hire two of them to do one job. One to fix all the other one's mistakes. How much fucking sense does that make?" No one said anything.

Saturday, December 5, 1992

Some new magazine called *in fashion* called a bunch of young filmmakers together for an interview. I got there and Quentin Tarantino was there, along with Anthony Drazen (*Zebrahead*), Alison Anders, the Hughes Brothers. I gave Quentin a ride home and asked him questions about how he gets through a writing day. I told him I was having trouble staying in the writing groove. He gave me a great tip on writing.

Monday, December 7, 1992

I found out I'm finally going to get my per diem, $10,400 for the rest of my summer, and $5,000 for the last two and a half weeks I was here up until Thanksgiving. I can't believe how much I saved by not staying at the fancy hotels. Right now I'm sleeping in my office. Whenever my agent's assistant asks where I'm staying so they can find me, I tell them I'm staying at the Sony Suites. They say, "Never heard of it." I told them it's new. I have a TV, a VCR, a phone, a couch. I go and work out on the lot gym and I shower in the gym every morning so it's better than a hotel here.

Wednesday, December 9, 1992

I ran into Lawrence Bender, producer of *Reservoir Dogs*. He finally saw *Mariachi* yesterday at a screening here at the lot. He went on and on about it. He said now he knows we're in the same boat as far as the kind of movies we make. He liked how Azul and Domino bought it in the final scene. "That's something you *never* see," he said all excited that someone else likes to kill off his leading characters.

Thursday, December 10, 1992

Steve of the sound department brought us a bottle of Moët Chandon to toast with after the sound mix. The mixers had also brought me a whole banana cream pie from the Apple Pan. After the mix, we gorged on champagne and banana cream pie.

I went to CFI and saw the answer print of *Mariachi*. The color needed correcting and some reels needed hand cleaning. The negative has been handled so much with all the screwups that it's really getting filthy.

Monday, December 14, 1992

I met with Mark Schmuger from the Columbia Publicity Department, he had some one-sheet sketches that were really cool. They were of Mariachi walking down the road where he encounters the turtle. I gotta call Carlos and tell him the poster is going to be just like the photos we took during the turtle scene. The poster will be shot with a wide angle lens and a great Hollywood style blurb: "He wasn't looking for trouble, but trouble came looking for him." Too funny. Goes to show you they can take any home movie and make it a Hollywood movie just by adding a cool poster and tag line.

Tuesday, December 15, 1992

I had dinner with casting director Bonnie Timmerman at Orsos. This is one expensive restaurant. The prices were outrageous and the food portions were tiny. A few weird leaves spread out here and there, that's it. Bonnie pointed out one of the leaves in my salad and told me that it's a weed that she finds in her garden all the time. "I'm eating weeds?" I asked her.

Thursday, December 17, 1992

Early this morning I saw the answer print at CFI. All the reels were from new negatives, because the dirt I saw on the other answer print turned out to be flaws in the hi-con. I watched this mostly cyan print, cringing all the way. We got to the tub scene and I got really upset. This was a scene that looked almost perfect a few days ago and now it was all screwed up again. One step forward, two steps back. No one seemed to know what I was talking about. They told me that it's a common problem in filmmaking, you correct a print but then when you make the new print, the developing chemicals are different, there are so many variables, that it never really comes out consistently the same way. I asked them what the fucking point was if we go through all the trouble of color correcting a print and then it comes back all kinds of different colors. They said that's just the limitations of the film format. What a joke. My $7,000 videotape looked better than this. They agreed.

We had a screening of the new print for the studio executives. I couldn't bring myself to go and sit through it with all the color problems. I walked over later, passing Jersey Films where I could see Quentin Tarantino sitting by his office window writing away furiously on *Pulp Fiction*.

I arrived at the screening just in time to see Mark Canton cutting out early. He remarked on how great it sounded and looked, as did Sid Ganis who was also sneaking out.

Friday, December 18, 1992

I couldn't take it any longer. The soonest they can have another "color-corrected" version for me to see is Tuesday. Every time I see a new "fixed" print it looks worse and worse. They said the "final print" though, wouldn't be ready until Christmas Eve. I'm not hanging around until Christmas to see more lame depressing film prints. I called Stephanie and told her I wanted to go home. She said OK.

I packed as fast as I could, then went to the studio to see the final trailer cut. It was off. The pacing was weird. I asked them if I could take a tape home and recut it. They let me.

Monday, December 21, 1992

I woke up at midnight and I wrote ten pages for my new Mariachi script. It's starting to come together. I should be fin-

ished in time for the January 4 hand-in date. The ten pages I
wrote is a scene with Steve Buscemi telling a story about the
myth of the Mariachi.

Tuesday, December 22, 1992

I ran some errands and once again woke up in the middle
of the night and wrote seven more pages. I edited the rest of
the trailer and sent the package off the next morning.

Thursday, December 24, 1992

They called to tell me that the print still had a way to go
before it would be finished, so it was a good thing I didn't
hang around. Unbelievable. The colorist couldn't account for
the small cuts so he's going to have to do it the old way instead
of with the computer.

Monday, December 28, 1992

Robert Newman called to tell me that Darrell Walker called
about renegotiating the video rights for the movie. He said
that they can't make any money off this movie the way the
deal is now. The reason my video deal is so lucrative Darrell
said, is because they never foresaw releasing *Mariachi* theatrically, which is like a huge ad campaign for the video release.
They gave me a big chunk of video proceeds thinking they
were going to dump it straight to video. I told Robert that I
think we should blow it off. If it was the other way around,
and I came to them and said, "Hey, let's renegotiate! I won't
make any money off of the video sales," they would tell me to
screw off.

Thursday, December 31, 1992

Liz and I ate twelve grapes and walked out the door holding
hands and carrying suitcases throwing twelve pennies according to the Venezuelan tradition. If you do that at midnight on

New Year's Eve, you are guaranteed a lot of money that year, a lot of traveling, and good health.

Friday, January 1, 1993

I went to Tower Records and got the *Dracula* soundtrack. It's really cool. I started writing at about 9:30 P.M., the soundtrack music blasting. I stayed with it until about 3:30 A.M.

Sunday, January 3, 1993

I finished my first scratch draft. (It's too rough to be called a rough draft, so I call it scratch draft.) I printed it out and read it over. It's not bad. Maybe if I keep writing my own scripts the stuff will improve. That would be convenient. The more self-reliant you can be in this business the better off you are.

Monday, January 4, 1993

I'm writing like a dog, but the end is near. I should have spread this out more. I think normal writers write for two to four hours a day. I'm pulling twelve- and thirteen-hour writing days. That can't be good for your brain.

Steph called and said she's pressuring me for the script because they have to decide who gets a movie made and who doesn't at this week's meeting. I told her it was on its way. Damn. Gotta get it done.

Tuesday, January 5, 1993

I wrote all day again. The script is in its rough draft stage. It has a ways to go, but I think it's readable. At 5:00 P.M. Liz started reading it. I haven't been this nervous since the first time I showed her *Mariachi*. If she doesn't like the script, it's not like there's a whole hell of a lot I can do before tomorrow. I need to send it off.

Liz finished the script. She told me she loved it and that as excited as she was to sit down and read it, it was still far better than she had expected. Whew. I know it needs a lot of work, but it's good enough to go. I printed out a copy and I dropped it off at Federal Express five minutes before closing.

I feel dead. Although the script needs more work, sending it off FedEx gives a certain closure to the process where I can finally feel like I'm done. On the way home I drove straight through a red light, dazed. My brain is completely fried. I guess that when you've been writing such long hours when you're finally done you feel completely dead, completely spent. Your body feels fine but your mind is numb. I couldn't sleep very well, nodding off somewhere around 2:00 A.M.

Wednesday, January 6, 1993

Steph called to say she's read up through page fifteen and that she loved the opening scene. She will finish the rest tonight and call me tomorrow.

She said that there is some bad news. *Mariachi* can't be shown 1:66 in all theaters, and that most theaters are only equipped for 1:85, meaning the top and bottom of the screen will be cut off some. Wonderful.

Thursday, January 7, 1993

Steph called and said she loved the script.

George Huang called to say that they're all going up to Sundance, but they won't be able to see my film, because all five showings are sold out. Cool.

Monday, January 11, 1993

My old film teacher Steve Mims joined Elizabeth and me at the Dobie theater, where we screened a fresh print of *El Mariachi* that Columbia sent down for me to check. Mims said he really liked it. He called it "pure cinema." He told me that it was perfect, and that you just don't see movies like that anymore, too much emphasis is on the dialogue. The print was still screwed up, though. The color went off several times and washed out bright only in places that were never a problem before. I don't get it. The only place we'll ever get the color right is on video. That makes sense doesn't it?

Steph called and told me the absolute deadline for the first draft script would be Thursday. I told her I could do that.

David and Robert called to tell me they have to receive the script first so they can send it to Columbia. I told them I would send them a copy tomorrow to read over and give suggestions on before turning in the final copy Thursday.

I got a call from Mark Gill, who called to tell me that Austin has been set for an opening that will include a run in San Jose and San Francisco instead of Sacramento. That's good. Originally they weren't going to open in Austin, only in San Antonio and Houston. I told them it was a mistake to ignore Austin, that the movie could do great here. Even though I was born in San Antonio, Austin claims me as one of their own, and the movie would do better here than in San Antonio. So now we'll get an Austin opening. Cool. (As it turned out I was right. Austin did outgross San Antonio.)

I revised the script and sent it to David Wirtschafter. Liz and I barely made it to Federal Express again. It was already closed and the lights were off but Elizabeth banged away on the door until they turned the lights back on, reopened, and sent our package off. I think I'm destined to be one of those last minute kind of guys. That's terrible. I need to work on that.

Tuesday, January 12, 1993

Doug Taylor and Andre Carraco called to tell me that the *Vogue* magazine piece will include a photo by Annie Lebowitz of independent filmmakers and I'll be included.

Mark Wyman called to say he attended an AFI panel discussion on Hollywood, and someone said that you couldn't make a movie for two cents these days, and Jeffrey Katzenberg butted in and said, "Correction, Mark Canton has a film on his hands that was made for $7,500." Mark Canton then butted in and said, "Correction . . . $7,000."

Wednesday, January 13, 1993

Robert Newman called and said the script was fabulous, congratulations. He said it was hard and violent and that if I made it, and even if it didn't make a dime, I'd work forever just off the action alone. Later both he and David called and they gave me their thoughts and comments, all very positive.

Mark Gill called to tell me my planned promotional schedule for February. In a word, hectic.

SUNDANCING

Thursday, January 21, 1993

My wife Elizabeth and I arrived in Park City, Utah at 4:30 P.M. We went to the Z Place to pick up our film festival packet including tickets to events and an itinerary, but it won't be available until tomorrow.

My agent, Robert Newman, crashed the town. He asked me if I thought I'd win. I told him quite seriously that I was just happy to be here and that my movie would be sitting on a shelf right now if it was up to me, so I'm not expecting anything. I told him he should just be happy we're here, too. Anything else is gravy.

Friday, January 22, 1993

Tonight was our first screening. It was in the Prospector Square theater, 400 seats. While I tried to prepare my opening speech, I was told by a staff member that supposedly ours was the only movie to sell out all six of its screenings and that the early word is that *Mariachi* will be the sleeper hit of the festival. I found that odd, since tonight is the first screening.

The place was packed. I gave a speech lasting about ten minutes, filling in the audience on how this movie came to be. It takes a while to explain because it's a bizarre and complex tale. I wanted them to realize that had I known all these people were going to see my experimental film, that I would have spent more money. I told them how I shot the movie silent, how I saved money by writing the script around things I already had access to: a pit bull, a motorcycle, two bars, a ranch, a turtle. I told them that I also saved money by making myself shoot only one take of every shot. This brought on very audible gasps. I told them, "In all honesty people, this is an action film. How many takes do you need of a guy running down the street or kicking open a door? You get it in one take, even if the performance isn't great, you get the idea, and you move on." They laughed. I encouraged them to stay for the question and answer section afterward, since the nice thing about making a movie all by yourself is that if anyone has a question about the writing, the directing, the camerawork, the editing, the sound, whatever, I did all those things, so I can answer all those questions in layman's terms because I'm not the most technical person either.

The screening went great; people laughed at all the right places and more than half actually stayed for the questions and answers. We had a great time. In fact, the questions and answers went on for over a half an hour and we were thrown out to make room for the next showing at 10:15 P.M. Best of all, again, people were really inspired to go out and make their own films.

After the questions and answers, a woman from Kodak came up to me, handed me her card, and said, "I loved your movie and I know from your speech that you bought all of your film from us at full price. I just wanted to say that I could have saved you a lot of money. We give discounts to independent filmmakers." I accepted her card, now that it is completely useless to me, and I asked her how I was supposed to know about this. She said, "Oh, we don't advertise it." Wonderful.

Saturday, January 23, 1993

We went to the Barking Frog to have dinner with a bunch of ICM talent agents. These guys went on and on about how they waited forever at the rental car place for a sports car with a cassette player to come in. One agent said he waited the extra hour to get the four-wheel drive with a CD player. "I'm not listening to any of this local hillbilly music, I need my Nirvana," he said.

They asked where I was staying. I told them the Olympia Hotel, but supposedly the festival wanted to put us in a semi-private condo with three other filmmakers. Being protective fathers, they said, "What? No man, that's not your crowd! Backstabbers would come after you, you've got a distributor and a deal; they wouldn't like that. Keep your script hidden. I don't want any of those guys stealing your ideas. Hey, next week there'll be about twelve of us here from ICM, we'll all go out and have buffalo steaks, OK?" I said, "Sure." These guys are really funny.

Sunday, January 24, 1993

I had another film screening tonight that went well. Someone asked how I did the sound. I told them that sometimes it's good to have less money and resources because you're forced to be creative. I told them that we had actually shot the movie silent. The camera was nonsync, and so noisy we couldn't even record sound at the same time. So I would shoot an entire scene silent, then put the camera aside, strap on the sound equipment, and I would become the sound man. I used a Marantz tape recorder, just like the one used in Film Production I at UT. I had a Radio Shack microphone. Since the camera was off I could bring the microphone in really close up and get good recording levels. I taped the dialogue and all sound effects wild, by having the actors say their lines again and re-enact the scene. Later I synced all the sound up by hand. Since I used nonactors, a lot of the time their lines would sync right up since they were talking in their own beat and rhythm. Where they didn't sync up, I would cut away. Someone in the audience said I had a great cutting style, the picture was always cutting even during the dialogue, so the dialogue scenes seemed just as fast as the action scenes! I explained that it was a necessity more than a style, I *had* to cut away because the actors ran out of sync! Of course, from now on that will be part of my style in future films, but I never would have discovered that if I had more money for sync sound. Low-budget movies put a wall in front of you and only creativity will allow you to figure out how to get around that wall. The less money and/or resources you have, the more you are forced to be creative. And what is a movie, anyway? A completely creative endeavor. Anything you can do to get away from the things that aren't important, the better chance you have of being truly creative.

Monday, January 25, 1993

I went skiing for the first time today. Actually, all I did was fall.

I have to do a "Twenty Somethings" panel discussion on Thursday. Among the other filmmakers attending will be none other than Jennifer Lynch, David Lynch's daughter, who has a movie here called *Boxing Helena*.

I went to the Z Place for an interview with Donna Parker from the *Hollywood Reporter*. She came in saying that she's heard several filmmakers around the festival saying that I'm lying and that there's no way you can make a movie for $7,000 in 35mm and have it shown in the festival. I told her the whole story, cleared up the fact that it was shot on 16mm, *not* on 35mm, and that my finished tape that got me representation at ICM, one of the biggest talent agencies in the world, and a writing/directing deal at Columbia Pictures was made for $7,000. You transfer your negative straight to videotape, and you can take the tape to distributors instead of making a 16mm film print. I told her that a 16mm film print would have cost me over $20,000. My movie has over 2,000 cuts in it, and that's not cheap to conform. In fact if you compare my budget dollar for dollar with two other recent low budget indies, *Laws of Gravity* and *The Living End*, you can see that where those guys spent more money was on rented film and lighting equipment, and they made a 16mm film print, which is an expensive process. They made the print to show to distributors. But when a distributor chooses to buy your film, they pay for a whole new 35mm blowup anyway, so if you don't have the money, the lower cost option is transferring to video. It's more convenient to watch a tape; and if they want your movie, the distributor will pay for all the prints and blowup costs. That's their job, anyway. She then asked, "But how did you feed the crew?" I told her that people don't realize that I had no crew. If you want to do a movie for nothing you have to get rid of the crew, because even if they work for free, you have to feed them and it adds up. I told her that the main reason those people don't believe it can be done is because they haven't heard the whole story and gotten the facts straight, because it actually makes sense when you know how it was done. Donna finished the interview, excited and enlightened she said, "This'll make a great feature story!"

Wednesday, January 27, 1993

My wife realized how boring my life of interviews is, so she hit the slopes.

I got a call from Columbia and they are gonna FedEx the finished movie poster, which they claim is "fantastic." I've yet to see it, and through the little experience I've gotten working for a studio I've found that whenever they say something is "fantastic" and that "everyone loves it" you know you're dead. So I'm a little nervous.

Two of my actors, Carlos Gallardo (El Mariachi) and Peter Marquardt (Moco) will be flying in later today. Peter has yet to see himself on the big screen so this should be fun. There's an *Entertainment Weekly* party being thrown tonight that I'll try to sneak them in to.

Thursday, January 28, 1993

I didn't get much sleep again. Had to get up early and go to the local radio station for an NPR interview. It was fun because the guy interviewing me interviewed me once before in Toronto. He asked why it was that suddenly low-budget has a different meaning. Roger Corman would make movies for $30,000 and people would say it looked like he spent $15,000. Doesn't low-budget mean low quality?

I responded that I was a filmmaker who never thought he'd make it in the movie business, simply because I was led to believe that you needed at least $100,000, a limited partnership, and rented film and lighting equipment to make a feature film. I didn't want to do that. But I wanted to make movies, so I made movies for myself. I was never doing it to get rich and famous because I knew that was impossible, especially because I didn't know anybody in the business, and we all know how important contacts are. After I made *Mariachi*, within two weeks of Hollywood seeing my movie I had more contacts than I knew what to do with. All those years I had been making movies because I loved movies, and that's what made all the difference. If you're doing it because you love it you can succeed because you'll work harder than anyone else around you, take on challenges no one else would dare take, and come up with methods no one else would discover, especially when their prime drive is fame and fortune. All that will follow later if you really love what you do. Because your work will speak for itself.

I came back to the hotel and picked up a package waiting for me: the movie poster for *El Mariachi*. Carlos, Peter, and I videotaped the event of opening the posters for the first time. The poster was fantastic. I think this is finally hitting us. It's a strange feeling seeing your name on a real movie poster, alongside the Columbia logo, the Dolby Stereo logo, and that Rated R thing.

I was interviewed by Peter Travers of *Rolling Stone*. He loved the story of the making of the movie, and loved the movie even more.

I went to the panel discussion on "Twenty Somethings." John Pierson was the moderator. The highlight was when an audience member asked the big question: "No one ever thought Michael Lehman (*Heathers*) would run off and make a seventy-million-dollar Bruce Willis film, so what if you were asked by Joel Silver to direct the fifty-million-dollar *Lethal Weapon 4*? Would you take it?" We went down the line, everyone saying they wouldn't take it. You could feel the "yeah right" vibes coming from the audience. So when it came to me I said, "Damn right I'd take it!" Cheers from the audience. That's what they wanted to hear. But I added, "The studio would give me a fifty-million-dollar budget, but I would really make it for one million, and I bet you the studio would never know the difference. I'd then take the rest of the forty-nine million and I'd save a country with it. I'd also kill off Murtaugh and Riggs in the first five minutes, and let two great out-of-work actors carry the rest of the film." Big laughs, great audience. At fifteen bucks a ticket for these panels you've got to try and give them their money's worth.

Friday, January 29, 1993

We got back to the hotel to get ready for the biggest screening yet: a sold out audience of 600 people. I gave a long opening speech. The staff was in the back waving flashlights to signal me to speed it up. But I didn't want to. The audience was having a great time hearing how we put the film together, how confused I was when Columbia bought my home movie, slapped their logo in front (which costs more than my whole movie), and now they're going to release it in over sixty theaters nationwide on February 26. I told them I didn't have a crew, because I made this movie to learn, so I wanted to do everything myself and make all the mistakes myself. (You'd be surprised how easygoing you are after you make a mistake and there is no one around to see it. You accept your error and move on. Had a crew member made the mistake you'd be yelling at him the rest of the shoot.) Without a crew there is no one to feed and there is no one contributing their ideas, their two cents, allowing you to be a very decisive director. That speeds up the production, which works great because creatively your mind races anyway. If you can keep up with that you can do really great work. It's the waiting that can kill creativity. I also asked the audience to please vote if they liked the movie, because I truly couldn't think of anything funnier than seeing this movie win something.

Outside the Z Place I ran into none other than Steve Buscemi and Seymour Cassel. Steve Buscemi said he had heard that my new script has a character named after him. I told him it was true, I had written the part with him in mind. He asked me to please send it to him. I will. Seymour Cassel said he heard I gave a twenty-minute introduction to my movie. I told him it was more like fifteen minutes. "That's good," he said, "only I give twenty-minute speeches before a movie." Seymour and Steve were in last year's winning film *In the Soup*, and Seymour is the Master of Ceremonies this year.

Saturday, January 30, 1993

I didn't get much sleep again. I keep waking up at 5:00 A.M. even though I'm not a morning person. I stared at the ceiling and tried to think about the future. My mind was blank for hours until my wife woke up.

I did a couple of interviews, one for HBO, and one for . . . who knows.

I attended the last screening of *El Mariachi*, unless we win something, then they'll show it on Sunday.

The response to the screening was great. Afterwards, many encouraged filmmakers came up and told me they were going to forget film school and spend that money on making movies.

I ran into Seymour Cassel again at the awards presentation. He saw my movie this morning. He said he loved the movie but not to expect to win anything because it's all predetermined. Fixed. He knows because it happened to him last year.

Tim Roth was sitting behind us and wished us luck.

Elizabeth was videotaping just in case. Seymour Cassel announced, "And the Audience Award prize for a dramatic film goes to: *El* . . ."

The cheers began, Carlos and I leapt to our feet . . . *"Mariachi."*

We walked dreamily up to the stage and I was handed a glass plaque. Carlos took the mike first. He said, "Gracias a mi familia, gracias a toda la gente que trabajó en la película, y gracias a ustedes. Thank You."

Since I was the filmmaker giving the longest speeches before each screening I figured I'd keep this one short, and focus it on independent filmmaking rather than thanking the crew I never had. I wished I'd had prepared something just in case.

I simply said, "If by giving us this award you wanted to encourage independent filmmaking, you did that. Because when the word hits the streets that we won the Audience Award at the Sundance Film Festival, filmmakers all over the country are going to pick up cameras and make their own movies. So if you find that at next year's festival you have more entries than you know what to do with, it's your own fault. Thank you." As we left the stage they snatched the plaque away from us. "For engraving," they assured us. We sat down.

Past winners of this award were *sex, lies, and videotape* and *Waterdance*. The next best thing to happen was when Judy Irola won the cinematography award for *Ambush of Ghosts*.

Her acceptance speech was, "This is a great honor, especially since I just saw *El Mariachi* this morning which I think was one of the most beautifully shot films I've ever seen." That was too nice of her to say at the podium, especially since I hadn't even met her.

We hit the hotel to call our families, to call our friends.

Sunday, January 31, 1993

I woke up early once again. I realized we had won the Audience Award. It didn't seem that important for me to win a few days ago but suddenly I'm really glad we did.

We barely caught our plane in Salt Lake City. After trying to get comfortable for a much needed nap, my wife turned to me and said, "I forgot to tell you. There was this guy at the party who told me to tell you how sick he felt after hearing you speak. He had been to Sundance three times and had attended UCLA for three years, spending about $20,000 per semester as an out-of-state student, and he said hearing you made him realize how much fresher and experimental his style was before he attended film school. He said this is the first time in three years attending Sundance that he's felt inspired to leave LA, go back home, and make his own movie." With that said I finally fell asleep.

EL MARIACHI: THE RELEASE

Monday, February 1, 1993

Today I was running around with a million things to do before leaving on the publicity tour. Bills, paperwork, plus the *Austin Chronicle* had asked for an excerpt from my diary pertaining to the Sundance festival. They want to print it as a cover story.

Peter Marquardt came into town and dropped off the pictures from the Sundance trip. He told me that he and Carlos had gone to the Sports Bar in Park City to watch the Super Bowl yesterday, and that people were asking them for autographs. He had a great time.

People called to tell us we were on CNN last night but I missed it.

Tuesday, February 2, 1993

Elizabeth and I flew to New York and Columbia checked us into the Parker Meridien Hotel. I called my sister Patricia who lives in New York and she told me that they were talking about me on the Howard Stern Show this morning. Howard Stern had been reading the news on the air and had said, "Hey look at this, some kid sold his body to science, made a movie, and now he's rich and famous."

I think I'll call in myself and talk to Howard. It would be a great way to start the publicity tour. If I can survive an interview with Howard Stern, the rest of the interviews will be a cakewalk.

Wednesday, February 3, 1993

I called the Howard Stern Show and they told me that they want me to call tomorrow at 7:30 A.M.

I went to the Columbia offices here in New York and had interviews all day, including a CNN interview at the end of the day. Everything went well.

Thursday, February 4, 1993

I woke up at 7:00 A.M. to the sound of Howard Stern on the radio and Robin asking him, "Hey, aren't we going to talk to that kid that made the $7,000 movie?" Howard said they would. I got on the air and it was as if someone had sedated him. The interview went great, we made good jokes, and I got the word out there to everybody. He didn't even tear me to pieces. I told them all about the medical experiments and then Robin said something nice at the end of the interview after I hung up, she said, "Imagine what he'd go through. All that just to make a film."

After Howard Stern, I went to the Columbia offices for more interviews. One guy from the *Daily News* came in and admitted he was somewhat cynical about the whole thing. Fortunately, I brought along my show-and-tell videotape that had an edited scene from the movie along with my raw footage so I could demonstrate how to get several camera setups in one take. He was ecstatic. "I came in here wondering how you shot a movie for so little, and now you're showing me and it makes perfect sense." I gave the same little low budget film-making course to all of the interviewers. It really helped them understand the "making of" story a lot more.

I gave a phone interview to the *Miami Herald* about *El Mariachi.* I'll be attending the Miami Film Festival this weekend.

Friday, February 5, 1993

Mara Buxbaum, from the Columbia Publicity Department in New York, set up a phone interview with Daniel Kellison, a segment producer for David Letterman. Daniel asked me a bunch of questions, and was laughing at my whole story, from the research hospital on through the meetings with studio heads. He told me he'd try and bring me on for a spot on "Late Night with David Letterman," and that he'd call me back.

Liz and I were then flown to Miami. We went to the Miami Film Festival Opening Night Party later that night. Supposedly they are going to show *Mariachi* in a huge renovated 1,500-seat movie theater. I spoke with Nat Chediak, the Miami Film Festival Director who I met originally at Telluride. He was the guy that wanted me to bring the film to this festival along with the pit bull, H.B. He was a little disappointed that I didn't have the dog with me.

Sunday, February 7, 1993

The theater was packed with over 1,500 people. The movie got a great response. I called Carlos Gallardo and told him how it went. He pointed out that we've completely switched roles. Originally I wanted to stay behind the camera and make my movies and let him do all the publicity and be the actor out in front, the one who is seen and recognized. But now he's the behind-the-scenes guy and likes it that way, whereas I have to go and do all the interviews and all the selling. I can't say I mind, since the response has been so positive, but I can imagine the curse that this could be if your movie isn't well received.

Monday, February 8, 1993

Next stop on the promo tour was Albuquerque, New Mexico.

I did an interview on live TV with Ted Dawson, and he told me a funny story about how one day he was told to cover the sports arena because they were filming a movie about boxing and there were supposed to be a bunch of heavyweights there. When he got there, no one was there and when they asked if he wanted to be in the movie, he said no. He went back to the station and told the TV audience that there was a terrible movie being filmed at the arena. The movie turned out to be *Rocky*. So he understood that you can't judge a film by the size of the budget or the size of the film crew. Means nothing.

We went back to the hotel and I had a press conference with local high school students.

We flew back to L.A.

Wednesday, February 10, 1993

We had the Annie Lebowitz shoot today for the *Vogue* article. She was so cool. I don't know what I expected, but I didn't expect her to be so cool. I had my video camera and I got lots of videotape of the whole thing. Alexander Rockwell was there, so was Alison Anders, Rob Weiss, Rick Linklater, Greg Araki, Stacy Cochran, Todd Haynes, and Carl Franklin. We shot in a white wall studio, in a hotel room, and in a movie theater.

Tuesday, February 16, 1993

Liz and I were flown to San Francisco for more publicity. I got a call from producer John Watson and he said, "We haven't talked to you since you won the Audience Award at Sundance. Just wait till they turn on you, believe me, no one ever sees it coming. Kevin Costner never saw it coming and I warned him after he won the Oscar. I told him they were going to turn on him and sure enough, they just gave Costner worst movie, worst actor, and worst haircut award in the Raspberry Awards for *The Bodyguard*. You'll get your backlash next." Nothing like a dose of hard reality when you're just starting to build some confidence.

Wednesday, February 17, 1993

We did a few Univision and Telemundo interviews at the press conference at Acapulco restaurant. I had to convince many of the interviewers that we really did make the film for $7,000. I didn't have a TV around or I'd have shown them my videotape demo that I usually show doubting interviewers. It's such an easy concept that most people tend to overlook it completely. Once explained it makes perfect sense.

At ICM I made copies of my Sundance diary that was printed in the *Austin Chronicle*. It came out pretty good, so I gave ICM the copies of the article so they can send it to publishers for a possible book on the making of *El Mariachi*.

Thursday, February 18, 1993

After the interviews we had to get in a car and drive to Sunset Boulevard for the premiere screening of *El Mariachi* that the Grammys were throwing as a part of their weeklong celebration of movies about music leading up to next week's Grammy awards here in LA. They are paying for this premiere.

It was pouring rain and hail outside. The 405 freeway was closed off because the mountain was falling down. Our car was forty-five minutes late arriving to pick us up because of the weather. We barely got to the screening on time. I didn't think anyone was going to be there, since I barely knew about it myself. Outside the Directors Guild theater were those rotating movie premiere flashing arc lights, and inside the lobby of the building was a small red carpet and Mariachis playing music. It was great. A line of photographers were shooting photos of Carlos and me with the group of Mariachis. HBO and Galavision interviewed us. It was fun, but we were so late in arriving, everyone who showed was already in their seats. I was surprised who showed up. I saw Paul Rodriguez and Tony Plana. They said they were there to cheer us on. It was cool having them there for support. Even Cheech Marin showed up. I told him I wanted him to be in my next movie and he gave me his address and phone number and invited my wife and I to visit him at his Malibu home. All there was time for was a brief introduction. People had a good time watching the movie, and I came out immediately and got some pictures taken in front of our poster with Barbet Schroeder. He told me how much he liked the film. The whole thing was like a bizarre dream. Especially when I realized this is the same theater where I attended *The Player* premiere almost a year ago.

Friday, February 19, 1993

I had a great interview with Juan Rodriguez of the newspaper *La Opinion*. He has already written a story on the *Mariachi* phenomenon. He said what he couldn't believe was the fact that here he was watching a film released by a major studio that was in Spanish with English subtitles, and not the other way around!

Tuesday, February 23, 1993

Did a few radio shows. I had to do a phone interview with Joel Siegel from "Good Morning America," who saw the movie and said he loved it. He asked a bunch of questions for his review later in the week.

Thursday, February 25, 1993

"Entertainment Tonight" came over to my apartment today to shoot a kind of "Day in the Life" sort of thing. They are actually filming me *right now*, as I type this in. I'm supposed to look like I'm working. This is getting really scary.

I flew to New York and checked into the Essex House hotel. ABC arrived for the pretaping of the interview for, of all things, the Person of the Week with Peter Jennings. It'll air tomorrow. I can't believe this. They have today and tomorrow morning to gather up the story for the Person of the Week segment. They are flying to Texas to film the research hospital I was checked into when I wrote the movie and they are interviewing Peter Marquardt who is actually back inside the research hospital this month trying to earn some more dough. They are also compiling some of my old short films and interviewing Peter Travers from *Rolling Stone* magazine, my agent Robert Newman, all kinds of stuff. I was sleepy but it went well. I'm going to be on the David Letterman show tomorrow so I did another preinterview with producer Daniel Kellison, who said he wished we could make my appearance on the show two segments long instead of just one. He said David Letterman has been talking about this all week and that he's anxious to have me on the show because he hates big-budget movies.

We went to PBS channel 13 around 11:00 P.M. and I met writers Richard Price (*Clockers, The Wanderers, Sea of Love*), Oscar Hijuelos (*Mambo Kings*), and director Sidney Lumet.

They were finishing up a show with Charlie Rose, and then I was on next. It was really cool walking into a green room and seeing all these guys in there hanging out after their taping. They all wished me luck.

I talked with Charlie Rose for the "Charlie Rose Show," and it was a lot of fun, mainly because it was a longer segment and we got to talk for a full fifteen minutes. I got the entire story out in a way that finally made sense. It's probably the best TV interview so far, because the other ones are so short everything is reduced to a tiny sound bite that makes no sense. "Seven thousand dollars, no crew . . . what?" This way I could explain the whole process. Charlie seemed genuinely interested and had great questions and we laughed the whole time.

Friday, February 26, 1993

Today I woke up and experienced a day to end all days. These are the kinds of days you start a diary for in the first place. If I never have a day like this again, it would be all right, because now it's in the diary and I'll never forget it. Briefly, it went something like this.

Woke up next to Elizabeth in my New York hotel room. It was cold outside as they drove us to NBC for the "Today Show" taping. On the way I read two really good reviews for the movie in the *New York Times* and in the *New York Post*. *El Mariachi* opened in ninety theaters today across the country.

On the "Today Show" I was interviewed by Bryant Gumbel, who had seen the movie earlier that week. Incredibly, he was very nice to me the whole time. By the end of the interview he was smiling, and was extremely congratulatory.

After the interview I went downstairs and bought some "Late Night with David Letterman" T-shirts since he's leaving for CBS later this year and will have to change the name to "Late Show with David Letterman."

I had a preinterview with producer Lisa Freed from NBC's "Dateline." They want to do a full twelve-minute story on me for "Dateline"!

As I ran around town doing a few other interviews, the

World Trade Center *blew up* a few blocks away. Some terrorist attack, supposedly.

"World News Tonight" with Peter Jennings aired, and I saw the story they put together for the ending piece of the show, the Person of the Week segment. It came out incredible. I can't believe they put all of that together in a day and a half. It had clips of my home movies, interviews, shots of the research hospital in Austin where I was a human lab rat, all sorts of stuff.

I went back to the NBC building for the taping of David Letterman. There were a couple of older guys, autograph collectors, staking out the lobby saying "Mr. Rodriguez! Mr. Rodriguez!" So I signed their autograph books. One of them had a photo of me, I don't know where the hell he got it. I don't even have photos of me.

Up at the Letterman show, Daniel Kellison showed me to the dressing room and gave us souvenir Late Night baseball caps and shirts. My sisters Angela and Patricia got tickets for tonight's show and had presents waiting for me in the dressing room. I went to the green room and met Martin Short and Tom Jones. I almost got bumped from the show because Tom Jones was going to sing another song, unplanned. No one knew how to get him off the set until finally during the commercial break Letterman said into the microphone, "Somebody get Tom a cab, so he can go home." Tom got the hint and got off the stage.

Daniel Kellison gave me the questions David Letterman was going to ask me. Maybe. He told me the realities of the show, being that since this is essentially a comedy show, they have to focus on the comedic aspects of my story. That's why he preinterviews me, selects the funniest stories, makes questions for David to ask to sort of lead me into the funniest stories, and we go from there. He said David might stray from the questions completely, but if it looks like I might get stuck talking about something that isn't very funny, to steer back to the funny stories. Since the show was running long, my segment is being cut from eight minutes to four minutes, so Daniel told me to talk fast and remember my answers.

I went out for my little four minutes of fame. Letterman

doesn't meet his guests beforehand so I met him on stage. It was incredible. Paul Shaffer and his band play so loud during commercial breaks, it's like being at a rock concert. You never get the feeling that they're playing that loud when you watch it on TV. Everyone is pumped up throughout the show and Letterman is a wild man, slamming the desk to the beat and pumping fake snow around the set during the breaks and it was wonderful. They must have the *applause* signs up because the audience cheer really loud when the guests come out. I sat down to talk and I realized I was going to be all over the country on David Letterman and I could feel my heart pounding out of my chest. I wondered if I was going to make it. I've never been more nervous. I struggled to say all my jokes on cue and since we were short on time we ran through the lines. We sounded really smart, though, because David was asking questions right on top of my answers and I was answering his questions before he even finished asking them. It really does pay to have what you're going to say worked out in advance. We talked mostly about the research hospital and Letterman and I wished Peter Marquardt good luck since I told Letterman that Peter was in fact watching the show from the hospital since he's back in there earning money.

Later I talked to Peter and he said everyone knew who he was in the hospital, and that all of his fellow lab rats were watching Letterman and they all cheered when we mentioned him. He said that people were coming up to him and saying, Hey! You're that guy! What're you doing in here? Aren't you famous? He said there was another Robert Rodriguez who was in there who said he had been getting calls recently from *Rolling Stone*.

My family called to say they saw the Peter Jennings spot and that it made them all cry. They said the phone's been ringing off the hook from old friends they haven't heard from in years that saw the show.

I got back to the hotel at about 8:00 P.M. Dead tired. Tomorrow I fly back to San Antonio for a screening and party. Tonight Liz and I are just going to relax, watch the airing of the Letterman show, and order room service.

As soon as I laid down I turned on the TV and "Siskel and

Ebert" was just ending. They were doing a recap of the movies they reviewed and they said, "Two Thumbs Up for *El Mariachi*!"

With that I laid back in the bed and said, "What a day. This is a day to end all days. I can't believe it. It's gonna be all downhill from here on out." It has to be. Doesn't it?

EPILOGUE: THE CURSE OF *EL MARIACHI*

Mariachi opened with a bang and fell off quietly. It did much better than I had imagined, fueled mainly by the wonderful ad campaign that Columbia put out with the film. How do you sell a Spanish language movie to mainstream America without calling it an art film? I never thought Columbia could sell the movie the way it was. But then again, they probably never thought I could make this movie the way I did either, so we both had something to prove. And they did it.

Later in the year *El Mariachi* was released on videotape, selling over 1.5 million dollars worth of videos. I was told that we'd sell more videotapes if the video stores were offered a dubbed version of the movie as well as the subtitled, because a lot of people hate subtitles. I figured I'd rather people see the movie than not, so we dubbed an English version and sold twice as many cassettes. The subtitled version is obviously the better version, but the dubbed copies made the movie available to more people.

A laserdisc was also released in a Special Collector's Deluxe Widescreen Edition, which is funny because the movie was shot on 16mm so there was no wide screen. When you play the laserdisc you see two really thin black bars at the top and bottom of the screen. I included my short film "Bedhead" at the end of the disc, and added a running voice commentary throughout *El Mariachi* on the laserdisc's alternate soundtrack. That allows me to talk to the viewers throughout the movie on a separate soundtrack and tell them how we actually made the film shot for shot. A low-budget filmmaking show-and-tell seminar, all in one package.

It was strange finally holding my own video box cover for *El Mariachi* in my hand. Two years ago I remember part of my motivation for making *Mariachi* in the first place was so I could have my own videotape of it sitting on my shelf with cool cover art so I could show people what I had done with my summer of 1991. Now I have a video box cover that has *great* cover art, critics' reviews on it, including the two thumbs up from Siskel and Ebert, a blurb about winning the Sundance Audience Award, the Columbia logo, and even a Surround Sound (?) Dolby Stereo logo! It's too much.

But just when I thought I'd seen the last of the *Mariachi* publicity blitz, it started all over again when the movie went overseas in mid-1993. I got to see the world anyway and *Mariachi* turned out to be my international ticket.

Going on an international publicity tour is the best way to travel because you get to visit different countries not as a tourist but as a guest, people actually wanting to talk to you about your film, eager to see what you're all about. It's incredible, because I never would have entertained the idea that *El Mariachi* was going to end up being my breakthrough film that would later be released theatrically not only in the US and Canada, but in Australia, Spain, France, England, Scotland, Germany, Norway, Italy, South America, Mexico. It even made it to the Holy Land, playing the Jerusalem Film Festival.

Just weeks before Alfonso Arau's movie *Like Water for Chocolate* went on to becoming the highest grossing foreign film of all time, I ran into him at the Independent Feature Project's Spirit Awards, sort of an Academy Awards for independent films. We congratulated each other on how far we'd come since we first met back on the set of his film in that little border town where we both shot our films a month apart from each other.

Even though I shot *Mariachi* in '91 and sold it in '92, at the Spirit Awards of '94, *Mariachi* ended up winning Best First Feature of '93. Figure that one out. When I'd tell people who were there from the beginning, people like Tommy Nix, they'd say "You're still getting awards for that movie? Hasn't its time passed?"

I guess the Mariachi will always live on as long as there are video stores. Actually it's kind of found new life already in schools. I have a lot of high school Spanish teachers telling me that they show the movie in class to help teach Spanish to their students in a fun way. They say everyone speaks very clearly in the movie and since the film is so visual, they can make out what people are saying by context. So I guess *Maria-chi* can be considered an educational film.

The release of *El Mariachi* meant that I wasn't going to be able to get behind the camera for a long while. But once I finally started shooting again in January 1994, I didn't stop. I wrote, directed, and edited three movies in 1994, and then directed and edited another in the summer of 1995. The first was an obscure little movie entitled *Roadracers*. It's a cool, fun little 50s movie like *Grease* or "Happy Days," but where everyone dies at the end. I wrote, directed, shot, and edited it for Showtime as a chance to warm up with 35mm before making a bigger budget film. I took the assignment because it offered complete creative freedom and the chance for me to finally see what it is a Hollywood film crew does (or doesn't do). I learned an incredible amount. The best thing I learned was that I could continue shooting in my *Mariachi* style and get great results, even in Hollywood. We had a one million dollar budget and thirteen days to shoot the ninety-five-minute *Roadracers*. And in those thirteen days I was able to get an unheard of 586 camera setups. In one day alone we got seventy-eight single camera setups, all single camera. It's unheard of in this town, but shooting *Mariachi*-style, we got it done and the movie came out looking like a real movie as opposed to a cable movie. I was very proud and even more excited to run out and tell young filmmakers out there that if you're willing to work hard and break rules you can have a blast and make good pictures to boot.

Later that year I went on to the next step of returning to Mexico to shoot another Mariachi adventure titled *Pistolero*, later retitled *Desperado* by the studio. This time with a seven-million dollar budget. (I just added a few zeros to the original *Mariachi* budget.) The main reason was that I wanted to make a modestly budgeted Hollywood picture with a Latino action hero, something I'd always wanted to see in movies since I was a kid. I wrote, directed, edited; I was even the Steadicam operator. It was a battle with the studio for them to let me edit my own movie. The reason? They just weren't used to having a director edit his own picture. Gotta break those rules.

A week after wrapping *Desperado*, and during my editing

period, I ran off and wrote, directed, and edited a segment of the movie *Four Rooms* with codirectors Quentin Tarantino, Alex Rockwell, and Alison Anders. Then in the spring of '95, while I was mixing *Four Rooms* and *Desperado* in adjacent mixing rooms on the Fox lot, I began preparing to direct the Tarantino scripted action/horror film *From Dusk Till Dawn*. Why shoot nonstop? Usually you are so scrutinized on your second film that you freak out and fumble. I knew people would be watching for that sophomore slump, so I figured that instead of making one film and putting all the eggs in one basket, I would simply confuse the marketplace by putting out four films quickly. No one would be able to figure out which was the second, third, fourth, or fifth. I also wanted to get the moviemaking experience I missed out on by not making my low-budget *Mariachi* trilogy as originally planned.

As for the Curse of *El Mariachi*? Well, so far there's been no real curse, it just sounded like a cool chapter title.

El Mariachi actually turned out more mythical than I ever imagined. And that little taste of glory after years of hard work was a lot closer than I was ever led to believe. That's why I submitted this book to be published. There are a lot of people out there just waiting to be inspired, people who know they are creative and talented yet all they ever hear is that success in this business is the impossible dream. When I found what a pleasant, attainable, and rewarding challenge filmmaking can be I wanted nothing more than to stand on a mountain and scream the news, because this is exactly the kind of story *I* would have loved to have heard a few years ago, instead of all the negative stories we usually hear all the time.

Good luck to you in following whatever passion you have. You will most probably succeed in attaining it. And if you don't, you'll find that if it's really your passion you are following then you will find enormous fulfillment and incredible satisfaction from at least trying. Thank you for your time, and I hope someday I can meet you in person. Until then . . . good luck and God bless.

APPENDIX 1:

The Ten-Minute Film School

Fellow Filmmaker:

So you want to be a filmmaker? First step to being a film-maker is stop saying you want to be a filmmaker. It took me forever to be able to tell anyone I was a filmmaker and keep a straight face until I was well on my way. But the truth was I had been a filmmaker ever since the day I had closed my eyes and pictured myself making movies. The rest was inevitable. So you don't want to be a filmmaker, you *are* a filmmaker. Go make yourself a business card. Next.

Now what about all the basic technical knowledge you need to actually make a film? I think some famous filmmaker once said that all the technical stuff you need to know in order to make movies can be learned in a week. He was being generous.

You can learn it in ten minutes.

With the following information you can embark on making your own cool movies, all by yourself without a film crew (and trust me there are extreme benefits to being able to walk into this business and be completely self-sufficient. It scares people. Be scary).

It's good to be self-sufficient in a business where people are used to relying on other people in order to get anything done. Because then people realize you can run off and make your own great film without them, and they let you have your way. That's why you need to be educated in all areas of production. If for no other reason, so no one can take advantage of you or give you false information.

I knew even less than this when I started shooting *El Mariachi* and I did just fine by it so you should do great. Most of this

I actually learned while I was shooting. But I'm handing it over to you now, a gift from me to you for buying my book.

Here we go . . .

THE ROBERT RODRIGUEZ TEN-MINUTE FILM COURSE

The first lesson in this filmmaking school of thought is that it's not your wallet that makes the movie, no matter what they tell you in school or in Hollywood. Think about it. Any monkey can tap himself out financially while making a movie. The idea is to tap yourself out creatively first.

What is a movie anyway? It's simply a creative endeavor. The more creativity you can apply to solving your problems the better the movie can be. Problems come up all the time no matter how big a budget you have. But on a big-budget movie, a problem arises and since a movie studio's pockets are deep, money is readily available. So, the problem isn't usually solved creatively, instead the problem is washed away quickly with the money hose.

But when you don't have money and are working self-sufficiently, your problem-solving skills are challenged, your creativity has to work, and you fix the problem creatively. And that can make all the difference between something fresh and different and something processed and stale.

The most important and useful thing you need to be a filmmaker is "experience in movies," as opposed to "movie experience." There's a difference. They always tell you in film school and in Hollywood that in order to be a filmmaker you need to get "movie experience" so you can work your way up in the business. The reasoning being that by working on other films, even as a production assistant, you get to see firsthand how others make movies. Now, that's exactly the kind of experience you *don't* need. You don't want to learn how other people make movies, especially real Hollywood movies, because nine times out of ten their methods are wasteful and inefficient. You don't need to learn that!

"Experience in movies," on the other hand is where you yourself get a borrowed video camera or other recording device and record images then manipulate those images in some kind of editing atmosphere. Whether you use old ¾″ video editing systems, VCR to VCR, or even computer editing. Whatever you can get your hands on. The idea is to experience creating your own images and/or stories no matter how crude they are and then manipulating them through editing.

I think that everyone has at least a dozen or so bad movies in them; the sooner you get them out the better off you are. Better to make them in an inexpensive platform such as video so that you're not broke after teaching yourself and so that you can produce as much as you can as quickly as you can. There is nothing better than getting into a creative groove. If you can start and complete a project in a week on video because it's inexpensive, then do that. It's better than dragging out a movie on something more expensive like 16mm that you can only work on every other week or month because you financially tap yourself out. The experience of making your own experiments your way, will give you the necessary confidence and experience before tackling your dream project. And if you do it all yourself, you'll be even more confident because there is nothing that feels better than knowing you are completely self-sufficient and that you won't have to waste your time trying to convince a slew of people to help you out.

During my short stint in film school I saw what happened to the students who didn't get the "experience in movies" that I'm talking about. When some of us got into the film class, we had already been noodling around on borrowed video cameras and editing short meaningless movies. However, most of the other students had not. They figured everything they needed to learn they'd learn from the teacher and they were wrong. There's no way you can go into a class and expect to learn all the technical aspects of making a film, plus how to tell a story, then how to effectively construct that story through editing later. There is too much to learn. You have to introduce yourself to it at your own pace in your own way beforehand. Think of it as research and studying before the big test. If you walk in for a test on the day, having not done some homework or studying on your own, you'll get clobbered. As much as that makes sense many students hadn't done anything yet. So, understandably, they made their first films in the film class and spent about $1,000 on their projects since it was 16mm and the projects came out lame, because they were trying to learn everything at once and expected the results to be better. I talked to a few of these students who all semester had been talking about how much they wanted to be directors, then they made their film and it's less than they expected and so they got discouraged. They gave up and said "I don't want to be a director anymore, I don't think that's my bag. What I really want to do is produce!"

You see? First of all, this is where producers come from. Second, they wouldn't have been so discouraged and given up so easily if they had just kept going. My first fifteen or twenty short video movies were unwatchable, but I learned a lot from them and I kept making them because I enjoyed the process more than the result. Third, the more experience you give yourself the better prepared you are for the next project. If you want to be a rock star, do you go to rock star school and expect to come out like Jimi Hendrix after a few short classes? Of course not. Don't be lazy, you know the drill. You have to lock yourself in your garage and practice till your fingers bleed.

And it's actually better if you learn movies on your own, without formal training—otherwise your movies will be too formal. Now, you may hear all the time that you need to learn the rules so you can break the rules. Don't bother. I've found it more effective to ignore everything and question everything because it can all be rethought and improved, and in the end the only techniques worth knowing are the ones you invent yourself.

The theory that nowadays you can learn filmmaking by shooting on home video makes a lot of filmmakers nervous, of course, for it suggests that any imaginative person out there right now can get a hold of a video camera and can teach himself how to make great imaginative movies, meaning there would be more competition in an already competitive market. But it's true. And they should be afraid. They should be *very* afraid.

WRITING THE SCREENPLAY

When learning to write screenplays, it's best to start with original material, rather than adapting someone else's work. You should also try and learn without taking a writing partner or partners. The experience is much more rewarding and you'll learn a lot more. It's scarier, of course, because if you fail there's no one else to blame, and the work load is enormous and the only person you have to bounce ideas off of is you. But what you want is to be as self-sufficient as possible, because no matter how many people you drag in with you to create that safety-in-numbers feeling you're going for by bringing in the brigade, at some point it's going to be all up to you and you need to be prepared for that.

I think the same can be applied to filmmaking. Although filmmaking is known as a collaborative art, it doesn't have to be. There's certainly no rule that says it has to be, and if there is then by all means break it, because the experience you get and the confidence level you will have after tackling a film solo will be greater than any collaboration you can go into. Since you are in the beginning stages, you don't want too many partners. If your movie is good, you'll wonder if it was the other people that made it good; and if it's bad, it's too easy to use your partners as the scapegoats and you'll never learn anything that way.

If you're still thinking you may need to go to film school to learn some more, forget film school! Take that $20,000+ you were planning on spending on UCLA or New York University Film School and put it right back in your pocket. They can't teach you how to tell a story in film school, and even if they did, you wouldn't want to learn it from them anyway. They also won't teach you how to make a good low-budget movie all by yourself, with very little money. They teach you how to make big movies, with a big crew so that when you graduate after spending $20,000+ on your diploma, you can go to Hollywood and get a job pulling cables on someone's else's big movie.

The biggest mistake you can make is trying to make a low-budget movie using techniques of the big budget movie that you are taught in school. When you have a big budget and a lot of equipment you'll find that a film crew comes in real handy. But until then, they're dead weight.

The advantage of shooting *Mariachi*-style is that there are never any budget problems because there's no budget! There are no crew mutinies or catering problems because there's no crew and no food to feed them! There's no equipment or light problems because the quantity of equipment and lights are minimal. But then again you don't have to shoot *Mariachi*-style to make a low-budget, highly creative movie. Question everything, make your own rule book and invent your own methods. I've talked to people that are making their own no-budget movies and their inventiveness is inspiring. There's a million different ways to achieve the same result, so find what works for you and do it.

BE YOUR OWN DIRECTOR OF PHOTOGRAPHY

How do you go about shooting a movie? What equipment do you need? I started off with a borrowed 16mm camera I knew nothing about, but in a few minutes I learned everything I needed to know simply by making some calls to companies that dealt in used camera equipment.

Choose your weapon, whether it be video, 16mm, Super 16, 35mm, Super 8, Hi-8. None is better than the other. What your project is and what you expect to achieve will determine what you are going to use. It may also depend on what is most easily available to you. I talk to aspiring filmmakers who waste so much time asking people what kind of camera or format they should shoot on and blah blah blah. Grab the camera you can get your hands on fastest and start shooting with it. Everything else will fall into place. Otherwise you'll never get started, and that's the most important step to achieving anything: The first step. So take it and go.

I had my old trusty Sekonic light meter that I had bought a few years back at the photo shop where I used to work. It was still in great shape, so for light readings, all you do is set your film speed into the dial. If you're shooting outdoors, you'll use an outdoor film with a lower ASA, 64 maybe. So you dial in 64, hold the meter up against your actor's face, and aim the little white dome towards your camera. Now press the meter button and read off the number it gives you. Cool. Now, roll that number into your camera iris on your lens and you have your F-stop. What's an F-stop? Who cares what an F-stop is? Don't worry about the F-stop. I never did. Just do what the meter tells you; the meter is your friend. Just take that magic number that the meter whispers in your ear and set your lens to that number. Bingo. You've just become your own director of photography. Congratulations. Put your name on the credits as such. I did. If you overexpose your negative a little, don't sweat it. You'll get a denser negative with richer blacks and more saturated colors. You're clear.

Speaking of light meters, what about indoor lights? I decided to light all my interiors with practical light bulbs, or photofloods, and use a faster speed film. These are regular size light bulbs that fit in regular lamp sockets, but that give off light at 3200° Kelvin so it registers as white light. It'll give your film a natural, gritty feel. For a long while, before the concept of no-budget feature filmmaking came into practice, aspiring filmmakers would make short films or simply trailers for their scripts in order to get attention and they would pour a lot of money into these short films and try and make them look as Hollywood slick as they could, to show they could be competitive. That's not a great idea. No matter how hard they tried, with their limited funds they could never make their demo as slick as Hollywood. They'd come off looking like cheaper imitations. So go the opposite way. Why try and make a slick-looking film when you have no money? Don't even try. Make a movie that Hollywood could never make no matter how much money they have. Tell a story they'd never risk, or make a movie that goes for the throat the way they'd never do, because they are too mainstream. Fill your film with great ideas, which they can't come up with no matter how much money they have. They can't make their movies more creative with money. Only more expensive. The creative person with limitless imagination and no money can make a better film than the talentless mogul with the limitless checkbook every time. Take advantage of your disadvantages, feature the few assets you may have, and work harder than anyone else around you. When given an opportunity, deliver excellence and never quit.

OK. Back to shooting your movie. Hold the camera and look at your actor through your lens. No camera stand? Good. There's nothing worse than having a decent camera stand when shooting a low-budget movie. Because a decent camera stand will get you nowhere. A great camera stand will probably work wonders. I don't know, I've never used one. But I know what a decent camera stand will do for you: nothing. It will make you want to lock the camera down so what you end up with is a stiff-looking movie that looks dead.

The answer? A *shitty* camera stand. The one I had on *Mariachi* wasn't even for film cameras. It was a still camera tripod, one of those wimpy ones. No fluid head, no nothing. I put my film camera on and it barely held it up. Mine broke by the end of the shoot. I used it for close-ups during dialogue scenes. All my dialogue scenes were shot with the camera locked down. You don't need a fancy tripod for that. And since the stand was so useless for panning or tilting, it actually freed me up to take the camera off the stand and run around handheld, and shoot documentary style. It gave the movie more energy.

So put some energy in your movie! Energy is good, energy adds production value, makes your movie look more expensive. You can't believe the number of people, professionals and non, that told me how expensive my movie looked just because the camera was constantly moving. Of course, I was moving the camera! If I tried to stand still with the camera and try and hold it steady with my arms it would still move around a little as I breathed. So if it's gonna move a little anyway, why not move it a lot? Make it look like you've got a dolly, a Steadicam, or a crane, something expensive.

OK, so you're looking at your actor through your camera. You're not locked down on a stand so you're in a great position to get a great shot because . . . what do you see? You're the audience now, looking through the lens at the actor. Is this the most interesting angle you can be watching this movie from? Move the camera and see what the scene looks like now if you squat, and shoot from a lower angle, looking up at your actor. Move in closer, do you really need to see the lack of production design on your set? Move in close and fill the frame with an interesting-looking actor. The interesting human will always beat out the uninteresting set. How's this angle? Is it interesting but not too distracting? Good. Again this is one way to do it. Question everything and find what's best for you.

Now before shooting anything, you should really watch your movie in your head. Play it out in your head, watching it while imagining the actors and angles you've chosen. Picture the scene. See what cuts you'd make if you were editing it together. Would you stay on one actor the whole time, or would you cut midscene to something else? Watch the movie in your head; then when you think you've seen something interesting, get out a piece of paper and make your shot list. List each shot you need to make the scene work. Don't overdo it, just follow your instincts. On a low-budget, shoot-from-the-hip kind of movie your instincts are all you've got, so start learning to trust them. Trust your instincts and your light meter. I wasn't smart enough to figure out how to do everything I needed to do on *El Mariachi*. So I had no choice but to trust my instincts and they served me well.

After you've made your shot list, go through it. Read the shots you've written and watch them in your head, as if it's a cut movie. Are you missing any shots? Watch it again. What shots do you see in the movie that you're watching in your head which are not written down. Write those down. Now keep that shot list handy because now with your list you can concentrate on one shot at a time. All you have to do now is get each shot and cross it off the list. When your list is completely crossed off you're done for the day. Congratulations.

Note: If it seems that I'm oversimplifying even these basic aspects of filmmaking, I'm not! I think it's best not to concentrate your energy on all the pain-in-the-ass details that aren't that important at this point in your career. I'm telling you what you need to know in order to get by, so you can free yourself up to concentrate on what's really important: the pacing, the characters, the story. No one will ever care that your movie has great F-stops. Is the story compelling? Are the characters interesting? When it's all over, those are the only things that will really matter. And all the rest will be forgiven.

You should learn every aspect of the filmmaking process no matter what area in film you think you want to go into. If you work each job yourself you'll have a better sense of what you really want to do. Later on, if you're directing a movie, you'll know the needs of the sound recordist, the camera operator, etc. because you would have done all that before.

On one movie I was shooting with a film crew, we were consistently getting an unheard-of number of camera setups per twelve-hour day. One day we got as many as seventy-eight setups in one thirteen-hour day with a single camera. Now I could never push a crew to get that many setups by sitting in a director's chair and barking "faster faster!" at them. They'd have told me to fuck off. But what I did was simply pick up the camera and begin shooting my shot list, as quickly as I felt I could go and get the shots correctly. My crew saw me with the camera getting the shots and would work right alongside me. Had I asked them to do it alone, they'd have called me crazy and left. The fact that I was shooting made it easier to get cooperation and to work together, because they knew that if I could do it, they could do it. So without any complaining or anyone dropping dead, we were able to move fast and get everything quickly. The actors had a great time because they were constantly acting, and we shot so many scenes that day they were never stuck in a groove, repeating the same two lines for five takes. They actually got to rip through their scenes, maintaining an energy and spontaneity they could never display if the movie was shot at a slower pace for more shooting days. The energy would have been killed.

Why is it that when you see movies in a theater today, they seem for the most part big and lifeless? The reason is because the energy was killed before the cameras ever ran. By moving slowly you suck the energy and momentum from not only the actors, but the movie as well. The movie will only last about an hour and a half anyway. Why take three months to film something that will last ninety minutes? The faster you move, the less your movie will cost. And the shooting environment will be more conducive to creativity and imagination, not to mention the fact that your movie will have a level of energy that a big, fat, slow Hollywood production could never match, no matter how much money they spend.

So don't think that in order to make movies you have to make them Hollywood-style. Their way is so slow and expensive that you'll find yourself falling asleep on the set and forgetting to say "action."

With the advances in film technology, you can shoot your movie entirely in available light, or with a few practicals. That's what I used on *El Mariachi*.

CUTTING YOUR MOVIE

Usually when editing on video you would transfer to digital tape or 1", and then make a dub onto ¾" and do an off-line edit. Later, you conform the 1" using the matching SMPTE numbers printed on the videotape. That's fine if you're rich, otherwise you can do something like what I got away with on *Mariachi*. I simply cut off-line or ¾", no numbers. I did it without numbers 'cause I never foresaw conforming anything. I was going to go straight to the video market and sell my off-line ¾" as the master tape.

But what this will do is give you an inexpensive rough cut of your movie to show around, where maybe an interested distributor, of films or of videos can buy your film and pay for the finishing costs. Now this is different from what film schools or books on filmmaking would teach you. They'd all tell you to take your 16mm footage, edit a work print, get it conformed, make answer prints, then set up screenings for distributors or send the answer prints to festivals. Which isn't a bad idea if you're a millionaire. For the rest of us there are smarter, enormously less expensive ways to achieve the same results. To make an answer print off of a conformed negative to *Mariachi* would have cost me at least another $20,000. And what would have happened? I would have shown it to a studio or distributor and they would have bought it then paid for a 35mm blowup and stereo sound mix so theaters would play it. That's their job. So why show them an expensive film print when you can show them the movie on inexpensive video? They still have to blow it up to 35mm anyway. Let them eat the costs; it's their job to do so. Take advantage of new technologies, plus rethink and question all the old methods. There are better ways to do things and you can figure them out.

Some people say that cutting on film itself rather than video or computer gives the filmmaker a much closer relationship to the film by allowing hand manipulation of the images, as opposed to pushing electronic buttons to cut your film. If you like the sound of that, do yourself a favor and take some film home at night and fondle it all you want. But when it comes time to cut your movie use a video or computer system. Cutting on film is the slowest most absurd way to cut a film in my opinion. It takes forever to do anything. Cutting on a crappy off-line video system is faster and that's pretty cumbersome. When you're cutting your own movie, the movie you've lived and breathed since forever, the ideas you get on how to put it together come so fast that cutting on film only slows down that momentum—the waiting and the time consumed kills you creatively. It kills me, anyway. I've found that video editing is much more conducive to the way you think, and you can cut a scene almost as fast as you can see it play in your head.

I didn't mention sound. I shot my movie silent, recording all the sound on location wild, then syncing it later by hand. Now they would never teach you how to do this in film school because it's too much work. They'd rather teach you how to do it the right way. Which is a more expensive way. The bottom line is that there is no one way to do things. Invent whatever works for you. After finishing *Mariachi* I heard some kids talking about a movie they were shooting with a quiet camera, and even though they didn't have a Nagra, they recorded all their sound digitally using a Hi-8 camera. Cool idea. The Hi-8 has digital sound. They can transfer that over later and have great sound. Others I met were recording their sound right into their computer hard drive and editing digitally using a sound editing program like Protools. Make up your own way.

So why do most movies cost so much? One of the main reasons is that they take too long to shoot them. There is a lack of decision making before a movie and people go in and take five months to shoot something that is going to last about an hour and a half on the screen. On most movies, I don't see why someone would need more than fourteen days to shoot them. When you're spending at least fifty grand a day, you'd think a cost-conscious director would get the most he can in one day.

Every time someone talks about shooting movies don't they say the same thing? They say "it's the waiting . . . the waiting." Everyone waits. I'm telling you, waiting is bad. Waiting is your enemy. Waiting will kill your creativity, and it will kill your energy.

So, how do you shoot fast? Rehearse it until you think you've got it, shoot it, then forget it. Move on. Keep in mind that your movie will be made up of many parts, and pouring a lot of detail and painful retakes into each tiny moment is a waste of your time and money. It's the overall effect you're looking for. Get used to the idea that you'll have to live with the first or second take and make it work later in the editing room. If you've planned your shots carefully you'll find you'll have all you need when you get to the cutting stage. Again, follow your instincts. The great thing about operating your own camera is that you know when you've got the shot. By looking into the lens while the action is going you are seeing what your movie will look like on the screen. You can't get that sense from a video monitor or anything else.

Enough schooling. Get your ass out there and make a movie because I'm telling you, Hollywood is ripe for the taking. There are so many creative people out there itching to make something, but they're too negative in thinking they'll never get anywhere or it'll never happen. I know all that stuff because I believed the same thing for too long. So get on with it and call me when you're done. You make the movie, and I'll bring the popcorn. Until then . . . all the best.

Work hard and be scary,

Robert Rodriguez

APPENDIX 2:

EL MARIACHI

THE ORIGINAL SCREENPLAY

This is the screenplay I wrote while in the research hospital. I had been viewing videotapes Carlos Gallardo had been sending me of the locations so that I could visualize the layout and write for certain set-pieces, which would speed up the preproduction process since we wouldn't have to find anything the script specified. We'd already have it.

The script came out to be only forty-five pages long, so I was afraid the movie would be too short. But every time I sat down, closed my eyes and visualized the movie from beginning to end with a stopwatch it came out to over eighty minutes. So I hoped that I had simply misformatted my script and that it would be long enough. I wrote in a few safety devices though that would allow me to seamlessly add lots of extra running time if needed through voice over black, and most effectively through the dream sequences. At the end of a roll of film we would spend the last 10 feet or so shooting miscellaneous dream sequence imagery and generic weird stuff so that if the movie came up short (we needed it to be ninety minutes to sell to the Spanish market) then I could cut extended dream sequences to pad out the film. There is only one sequence scripted, the others were to be improvised and built in the editing room.

As for the main set pieces and props, including the guitar and case, the guns lent by the cops, the pit bull, the schoolbus, turtle, the vehicles owned by our cast, ranches, bars and hotel . . . we knew these things were all available to us beforehad so that's why they are specified in the script.

I'm proud of this, my first screenplay, and know that if you really want to write one, the best way is find an idea that excites you, no matter how small (mine was simply the guy with the guitar case full of guns). All you have to do is use that excitement to sit down and start banging it out and not stop until you're done.

FADE IN

SCENE ONE ACT ONE
A JAIL IN MEXICO EXT DAY

1   It's an early Friday morning and a patrol car drives up
2   an unpaved road and parks next to a gutted police car
on cinder blocks. The camera pans with the officer as he
exits his car and walks up a ramp leading to the baby
blue JAIL HOUSE. He is carrying a greasy bag of fast
food. (Establishing shot)

**I specified a police car on cinder blocks and the color of the building only
because I had already seen the jail we were going to use before I had written
the script and it had a gutted car outside on blocks and was painted baby blue.
Not that I would ever paint a jail baby blue for purposes of a movie. I just take
what I can get. If it was puke green or lemon yellow I also would have used it
as was.**

JAIL LOBBY INT DAY

3   The officer enters the lobby, tosses the bag of food to
4   his partner who is sitting at a desk. He grabs a tin cup
5   and walks over to barred entrance of Block A. Twenty or
so criminals, from drunks to drug dealers, are sleeping
peacefully in their cell on Block A. The officer rattles the
tin cup between the entrance bars.

JAIL CELLS INT DAY

6   The inmates stir, rubbing their dirty faces and trying to
7   sit up. The camera dollies slowly down the narrow hall-
8   way of the block which has three cells: Two small ones
9   side by side, and one bigger cell that faces the block
entrance. The sound of scribbling and business dealing
can be heard from inside the big cell. It is AZUL jotting
into a business ledger while chatting on his cellular
phone. His cell is equipped with a small desk and a refrigerator. He hangs up the phone and continues
writing.

JAIL LOBBY INT DAY

10   The officer with the tin cup sits in a couch across from
11   his partner, who is now eating, and reads a magazine.

**The "officers" were played by the real guards of the jail so that we wouldn't
have to rent uniforms or find actors. Since this was a real jail, they were there
already. There was a female guard and a male guard. I let the female guard
do the main stuff because she was the only one wearing her full uniform that
day. The other guy was slacking off in a regular shirt so he got the supporting
role. There was no food in the scene as the script specified because on the
day, we were too cheap too buy food.**

JAIL CELLS INT DAY

12   Azul picks up his phone and makes another call. He
13   talks business. In the other cells, prisoners are getting
14   up and looking around. Azul hangs up the phone and
      writes.

EL MOCO'S RANCH EXT DAY

15   A gorgeous, bikini-clad babe struts slowly into a tightly
16   framed glamour shot. She pauses, takes a deep breath,
17   then dives a 'perfect ten' dive into a house-side moat.
      She swims long, slow-motion strokes around the moat
      as the camera tracks alongside her, lovingly admiring
      her tan lines and hydrodynamic build. She slides out of
      the water and walks up a cobble stone walk, dripping as
      she passes a seated gentleman in a white suit. His face
      is unrevealed. As she enters the house, he sets his drink
      down by a phone. He lifts up the receiver and dials.

**I got the idea for the following scene from a real event that I had read about
in the San Antonio newspaper. In Matamoros, a Mexican border town, a drug
dealer was running his business from his cell with a cellular phone. When a
rival gang sent a hitman in to kill him, he had armed body guards in there with
him that shot up the place, burned some of the inmates that belonged to the
rival gang, and impaled the hitman on a post outside the jail. Of course, I knew
we didn't have the time or the money to stage such an elaborate sequence. In
the real story over seventeen men were killed. We would have had to have
found a bigger jail and cast more people. As you can see, I simplified the**

action considerably. I just thought the basic idea would be cool for the opening of a movie.

JAIL CELLS INT DAY

19 Azul's phone rings. He looks up at it startled, as if no one has ever called him before. He glances at his watch, and then back at the phone, hesitating to answer it. He looks around the cell block as if someone might be playing a trick on him. Finally he answers it, pausing before saying hello. It is El Moco.

MOCO

20 Good morning, Azul. Do you know who this is?

AZUL

21 Moco . . . What the hell do you want after all these years?

EL MOCO'S RANCH EXT DAY

22 MOCO is sitting on his porch drinking tequila.

23 MOCO

We've got a lot to talk about. I'm just a few towns away with a whole new gang. I heard you were nearby so I thought I'd give you a call, amigo.

AZUL

24 That's sweet of you, asshole. I don't suppose you could get me out of here, and then maybe hand me over my share of our money.

MOCO

25 Yes, I figured you'd want your money, my friend. That is why I have called you. I heard you were getting out soon, and figured I should deal with our situation. But do you

really need me to help you get out? From what
I hear, you are running quite a business out of
your cell with a phone and some loyal men. It
keeps you well protected I hear. Not a bad idea.
I may try that myself sometime.

AZUL

26   I could stay in here and earn peanuts compared to what you owe me if I were to get out.
So, yes, I want you to help me . . . my friend.

MOCO

27   Soon my friend, soon. I'm sending some people in a few days to get you.

AZUL

28   Really? Well, that's more like it. Just like the
Moco I used to know.

29   Azul is walking towards his window at the sound of a
truck racing in.

MOCO

30   Just hang in there my friend. I won't forget
that you have been a big part of our success.
What's wrong?

JAIL EXT DAY

31   A large truck drives up to the jail, parking beside the
32   police car. Two tall, well-dressed men step out. They
reach into the cab and pull out machine guns. They walk
briskly towards the jail.

**Most of the dialogue was written in English. I write faster in English and knew
that Carlos and I could translate it to colloquial Spanish in preproduction.**

AZUL IN CELL INT DAY

33   Azul walks to his toilet and stands on it to see out his
barred window.

> AZUL
>
> There's something going on outside. Is this a double surprise? Are you getting me out today, Moco?

There is no response from Moco.

JAIL INT DAY

34 The guard reading the magazine stands when he sees
35 someone approaching the door.

JAIL EXT DAY

36 Close tracking shot of guns as tall men open the door and enter the jail.

AZUL IN JAIL CELL INT DAY

37 Azul looks out of the jail cell suspiciously. Peering down
38 the hall, he sees the guys with the guns. He hides be-
39 hind the wall, peering out to see what happens next.

JAIL LOBBY INT DAY

40 The tall men walk right up to the guard, and hand him
41 a huge wad of money. The guard tosses the money to his partner (still eating), then turns to unlock the block entrance bars.

42 ## AZUL IN CELL INT DAY

Azul puts the receiver back up to his mouth.

> AZUL
>
> There are two men here with guns. Did you send them?

43 ## EL MOCO'S RANCH EXT DAY

Moco, glancing at his watch, hangs up.

AZUL IN JAIL CELL INT DAY

44 Azul hangs up the phone and kicks his bodyguard
45 awake. The bodyguard gets up and peers out the bars
    as Azul hides in a corner.

TALL MEN IN HALL INT DAY

46 The tall men walk steady and alert, ready to kill. They
47 enter Azul's block and scope out the cells.

48 The bodyguard, seeing the tall men, retrieves his shot-
49 gun from under his mattress and grabs his machete
50 from under the sink. He stands ready to fight.
51
52 The tall men move slowly towards the big cell, some-
53 what cautious. They see the bodyguard a second too
54 late, for he sticks the shotgun between the bars, and
55 shoots one of them before they can react. The shot one
56 stumbles back into his buddy's arms. Azul's bodyguard,
57 amused by all this, opens his cell door effortlessly, and
58 walks out as if to greet them. The tall men hear the
59 sound of the other cells opening so they turn around.
60 The other prisoners on the block begin exiting their
    cells, carrying guns and Molotov cocktails. The tall man
    drops his gun. Finally, Azul exits his cell carrying his
    phone. The bodyguard forces the tall men into an empty
    cell, closing and locking the door.
    Azul presses the # button on his phone. Moco's phone
    number is automatically redialed.

61 Moco answers.

I just noticed the numbers on the left side of the script. I didn't know how to
format a script so that's my own way of keeping track of how many shots I
thought I was going to need to tell the story. To this day I always write down
the number of shots I think I'll need, only now I multiply that number by three,
because inevitably I end up shooting three times as many shots as I think I
need.

62   AZUL

I'm still here Moco. And so are your little friends. But not for long. They have something they want to scream to you. Listen close, because you're going to repeat it to me when I come to visit you.

63 <u>TALL MEN IN CELL INT DAY</u>

64 The cellmates throw their Molotov cocktails into the cell. Moco hears the men screaming as they burn to death. Azul is holding the phone at arm's length into the cell.

65 <u>JAIL LOBBY INT DAY</u>

66 The guards exchange glances when they hear the screaming, they smile and shrug, then go back to what they were doing. As Azul and his bodyguard exit the block, the guard with the magazine stands up as if to stop them, but Azul tosses him a wad of money and the guard sits back down to count it.

<u>JAIL EXT DAY</u>

67 A blue truck races towards the jail. (crane shot?)

Notice I added the question if we would use a crane shot. This refers to a crane the local electricians had. We wanted to use it for at least one shot early in the movie so that when the Spanish distributors saw the film they'd think we spent money on renting a real movie crane, which would raise our production value. We were always thinking of ways to make the movie *look* more expensive.

68 Azul exits the jail carrying a shotgun. His bodyguards get inside the tall men's truck and start it. Azul waits patiently for his blue truck.

69 As the blue truck pulls up, two little ratlike vatos exit
70 the blue truck, one handing Azul a guitar case. Azul
71 tosses it onto the hood. The bodyguards wave as they

drive away. Azul waves back. He opens the case, revealing an arsenal of weaponry. Azul notices one piece is missing. One rat quickly pulls the missing weapon from his jacket and replaces it in the case. Azul is unamused. He grabs his MAC-10 machine gun from the guitar case and aims it at the thieving rat's head.

72   Suddenly, the guard bolts out of the jail waving the wad of money, as if complaining.

Azul turns his MAC-10 onto the guard instead. A few
73   blasts later Azul and his rats pack up and go as the
74   guard twitches helplessly on the ground, still clutching
75   the money in his bloody hand.

SCENE TWO ACT ONE
(credits sequence)
<u>AZUL/MARIACHI ON HIGHWAY EXT DAY</u>

1   The blue truck barrels down the highway and the camera pans with truck as it passes a hitchhiker, MARIACHI, standing in the sun with a thumb in the air. The truck passes him up so he continues walking. Mariachi is carrying a guitar case in one hand and a black jacket in the other. He is wearing a white T-shirt, black pants. The camera pans to a sign that reads "ACUÑA 18 miles."

The sign that said 18 miles was written into the script again, because it existed already. We had to drive 18 miles out of town for these shots. In a real movie you would just pay someone to make you a sign and put it anywhere you want. Again, we were too cheap for that and had to settle for the real thing.

SCENE THREE ACT ONE
<u>MAIN STREET EXT DAY</u>

1   Mariachi is walking around downtown Acuña. He no-
2   tices a bar across the street and, liking the way it looks,
3   he puts on his jacket and crosses over to it. He stops to

4   read a sign on the building that says "MEMBERS AND
NON-MEMBERS ONLY." He prays silently to himself before confidently walking inside.

5   <u>CORONA CLUB INT DAY</u>

6   Mariachi enters the club, greeting the patrons as he
7   makes his way to the bar. No one seems to greet him
8   back. He sits on a barstool near some other drinkers,
9   laying his guitar case down lovingly beneath his stool.
He looks around the place, as if sizing it up.

10   BARTENDER
What do you want to drink?

11   MARIACHI
Refresco.

12   The other drinkers stare at him.

13   Glancing around the room, Mariachi notices a small,
14   table-shaped object draped with a cloth in one corner of
the room.

15   Sitting directly behind him are four mean-looking
dudes. Mariachi is served his drink.

16   MARIACHI
No hay musica?

17   BARTENDER
(cleaning a glass) Why?

                            MARIACHI
18   I'm a mariachi. A good one. I play beautiful
ballads, old classic ballads, on an old-fash-
ioned guitarra.

                            BARTENDER
19   So what?

MARIACHI

20   I could add a little class to this place. I work for
fairly cheap, I live mostly off tips. But I need
steady work, and I can guarantee bringing in
more customers.

21   BARTENDER
(nodding) Tell me, why would I need one little
guitar player when I've already got a full band?

22   Mariachi gives him a silent ''what?'' look.
23   The bartender motions to a young man sitting near the
small draped table.

24   The young man removes the drape revealing a key-
25   board. Puts on his mariachi hat, dips his fingers into his
26   shot glass and rubs his fingers together (as if warming
27   up for a big show). He hits a few switches in extreme
28   close-up as . . .
29
30   . . . Mariachi adjusts himself in his seat.
31
32   The young man gently taps one switch and the keyboard
33   sounds like an accordion, pulsing out a beat. He then
34   presses another switch and a horn section swells to a
35   crescendo and waltzes the familiar riffs. He adds the
36   strings and horn accents by banging on the keys. He
sounds awful.

Mariachi grimaces slightly then turns back to bartender
who seems to enjoy it.

The keyboard mariachi finishes his song, and sits back
down.

**We were almost out of film the day we shot this scene. We had waited all day
for this kid to show up. He was the only kid in town with a keyboard, so we
had to use him. The idea was that if you brought us a prop we needed, we put**

you in the movie. Since the film was running out I decided to shoot it at a slower speed to conserve film. 16fps instead of 24fps. It added a slight comical touch to have him sped up, but the reason it was shot that way was economical rather than creative.

37   BARTENDER
    (nodding with satisfaction) There you see? Either I can pay one guy to sound like a full mariachi band . . .

38   Mariachi picks up his guitar and lays some money next to his full drink. He looks disappointed.

39   BARTENDER
    . . . or I could spend the same money and only get one little guitar player. . . . Understand?

40   MARIACHI
    (walking away) Thank you, sir.

41   BARTENDER
    You want to earn a living? Get a real musical instrument!

42   The bartender picks up the bottle of soda pop Mariachi
43   left behind and offers it to the other men at the table.
44   They say no, pay, and leave. The bartender offers it to the mean dudes at the table.

45   They all shake their heads no.

46   The bartender shrugs and dumps it.

SCENE FOUR ACT ONE
MARIACHI OUTSIDE CORONA CLUB EXT DAY

1   Mariachi walks out and looks up and down the street.
2   He decides to walk south.

3   As he walks down the sidewalk, the camera pans into a
4   close-up of another guitar case that is moving towards

the Corona Club. The camera falls back a little revealing the backside of Azul, dressed also in black. Azul walks into the bar.

AZUL CORONA CLUB INT DAY

5   Azul enters the bar, and notices to his left the table with
6   four mean-looking dudes, drinking and eating chips and salsa.

7   The oldest one, with his back to Azul, takes a sip from
8   his mixed drink, then stands and excuses himself to the restroom.

OLD MEAN DUDE IN BATHROOM INT DAY

9   The old mean dude walks into the first stall and sits
10   down.

AZUL CORONA CLUB INT DAY

11   The three remaining mean dudes notice Azul's guitar
12   case. So does the bartender. They all look at each other
13   and laugh.

BARTENDER
14   *(laughing and rolling his eyes)* What the hell is
         this, *mariachi day?* There is no work for you
         here!

15   Azul walks towards the mean dudes' table. Their laugh-
16   ter quiets down a bit as Azul stands before them. The
17   bartender stops smiling.

AZUL
18   Bartender . . . one beer.

19   The bartender nods and grabs a frosty glass. He begins
     to fill it up at the tap.

AZUL

(without looking at him) In a bottle, wey.

20 Bartender stops filling the beer, stares at the half-full glass for a moment, then drinks the beer.

21 Azul is staring at the three mean dudes. They stare back.

22 The bartender slaps the unopened bottle down onto the counter.

23   BARTENDER
        Ready.

24 Azul doesn't pay any attention to him.

                        AZUL
25   I'm looking for an old friend of mine. His name is . . . Moco. Do you know where I can find him?

                    MAIN MEAN DUDE
26   You can sometimes find him here. He owns this place.

                        AZUL
27   So you know him?

                    MAIN MEAN DUDE
28   We work for him.

                        AZUL
29   That's too bad.

30 Azul turns to the mean dude sitting to his left, and places the guitar case in his hands. The mean dude is confused.

31   AZUL
        Hold this, please.

32   Azul opens the case and pulls out the MAC-10. The
      other two mean dudes are already reaching for their pis-
      tols.

33   The bartender ducks beneath the counter.

34   Azul fires a million bullets into two of the mean dudes,
35   (the other is holding the case in shock). Their chests ex-
36   plode, causing neat little dollops of flesh and blood to fly
37   everywhere. The mean dude holding the guitar case is
38   frozen with fear. He manages to look up at Azul, who is
39   watching the mean dudes die a slow, bloody death. The
40   barrel of his MAC-10 is smoking. Azul turns slowly to
      the mean dude holding his case. Azul aims his MAC-10
      in the dude's face. Still frozen holding the case, he
      spends his last moments looking down the gun's barrel.

BATHROOM INT DAY

41   The shots caused old mean dude to peer out from his
42   stall as the toilet paper fell to the ground and started to
43   roll across the floor. He now watches it roll as more
44   shots ring out. He pulls up his pants and walks towards
45   the door slowly. He is sweating profusely. He slowly
      picks up the toilet paper, plotting his next move. It
      grows silent. . . . He takes a deep breath and rushes out
      the door.

CORONA CLUB MAIN ROOM INT DAY

46   The old dude bursts into the room with a roll of toilet
      paper in his hand, and a sheet of sweat sliding down his
      face.

47   The bartenders rise up from behind the counter.

48   The camera dollies slowly by the dead dudes. Their
      blood-bathed faces twisted into odd shapes and expres-
      sions. The camera continues to dolly to the one dead
49   dude still holding the case. His face is a bloody pulp. The

camera stops dollying on the old dude's mixed drink. A hand is stirring it with a straw. The camera pans up the arm to reveal Azul, standing expressionless with his gun slung over his shoulder.

Shot at 16fps the old dude quickly drops the toilet paper and runs back inside the bathroom.

16fps means fast or sped-up motion. I had intended it for the shot of the old man running back into the bathroom to hide, but used it on the keyboard player instead.

50
51
52
Azul turns to his guitar case and carefully chooses another weapon. He grabs the drink and tosses a napkin over his arm like a waiter, then casually follows the old dude into the bathroom.

53
54
55
The bartenders glance at each other. One pours a shot glass full of tequila and raises it to his lips to drink it. Shots ring out and the bartender spills the drink over himself.

56
57
58
59
Without warning Azul bursts from the bathroom and walks calmly to his case. He replaces the weapon, picks up his case and leaves.

A few seconds pass before the bartender grabs the phone and furiously dials.

> BARTENDER
> *(into phone)* Get me Moco!!

60
The door bursts open as Azul reenters, storming to the bar.

61
The bartender is so petrified he doesn't think to drop the phone.

62
Azul walks right up to the bartender.

63
64
The bartender shuts his eyes. The sound of the beer bottle popping open can be heard, along with the sound

65   of thirsty guzzling. The bartender opens his eyes to Azul. Close-up of the empty bottle slamming to the counter.

66   The bartender glances down at the bottle.

67   Close-up of Azul tossing a few coins near the bottle as payment. Azul leaves.

68   A few seconds pass as bartender is standing there. You hear Moco yelling into the receiver asking what's going on.

MOCO AT RANCH EXT DAY

Moco is on the porch trying to get the bartender to answer him.

69   MOCO
      WHAT'S GOING ON OVER THERE, ANSWER
      ME!!!

70   BARTENDER IN CORONA CLUB DAY INT

You hear Moco's voice through the phone. The camera dollies into the bartender as he screams into the receiver.

71   The camera dollies in to the corpses . . .

I dollied in on the corpses in handheld mode with the wide-angle lens by running at and then away from them very fast, and I shot in slow motion to smooth out the shakes. That worked on my wheelchair dollies as well. When the Mariachi first entered the bar and his POV is a dolly through the bar. That's a wheelchair shot in slow motion to smooth it out, as well as the push-in shot to Azul as he stirs the drink.

AZUL CORONA CLUB EXT DAY

72   . . . and finally a low outdoor frontal tracking shot of Azul walking away smiling as the image fades out.

SCENE FIVE ACT ONE
<u>OUTSIDE HOTEL COAHUILA EXT DAY</u>

Low angle of Hotel Coahuila sign. Mean Dude #5 enters the frame as his beeper goes off. He runs into the Hotel Coahuila.

<u>HOTEL COAHUILA LOBBY INT DAY</u>

#5 enters the lobby where an old clerk is sitting at the counter reading a yellowed newspaper. There is a pit bull on the floor beside him.

Our tame, lazy pit bull was supposed to play in this scene as a companion to the tame, lazy Hotel Clerk. But we liked him so much we decided to give him to Domino as if he was a gift from Moco.

> MEAN DUDE #5
> Da me telefono.

> VIEJO CLERK
> *(without looking)* Take it.

MEAN DUDE grabs the phone and dials Moco's number. He glances down at the pit bull lying on the floor.

> MEAN DUDE #5
> Pit bull?

> VIEJO CLERK
> Yeah, pit bull.

The line is picked up and Mean Dude talks into the phone. He pulls out a piece of paper from his coat pocket and places it on the counter. He begins jotting down four names. He then slowly crosses their names out.

> MEAN DUDE #5
> Dead?

The viejo clerk glances up from his paper. The pit bull also glances up.

MEAN DUDE #5
All of them? How long ago? OK, what does this
guy look like?

Clerk goes back to reading his paper. (Pit bull is still
paying attention, though.)

MARIACHI OUTSIDE HOTEL COAHUILA EXT DAY

Same low-angle shot of the outdoor sign displaying the
name Hotel Coahuila. Mariachi walks into frame, and
pulls out his wallet. Mariachi pulls out a few measly
bucks then seems to be considering what to do next.

LOBBY HOTEL COAHUILA INT DAY

An inside shot looking out the front glass reveals Mariachi looking at his wallet as Mean Dude talks on the
phone. No one notices him.

MEAN DUDE #5
. . . carries a guitar case . . . And what was he
wearing? . . . all black . . .

The pit bull turns and looks out the window. Seeing Mariachi, he gets up and walks to it.

MARIACHI OUTSIDE HOTEL COAHUILA EXT DAY

Mariachi is putting his last few dollars back into his wallet. As he is walking away he notices the pit bull and he
bends down for a closer look.

MEAN DUDE #5
Don't worry, Moco. We'll find him, and we'll
mess him up real good. *(ad lib)*

MARIACHI OUTSIDE HOTEL COAHUILA EXT DAY

Low shot with long lens at full zoom of Mariachi tapping

on glass. Close-up of dog responding. Close-up of Mariachi tapping.

<u>LOBBY HOTEL COAHUILA INT DAY</u>

Mean dude hangs up phone. He writes a few more things. He turns to leave.

> MEAN DUDE #5
> Gracias señor . . .

As he passes the camera you can see Mariachi still playing with the dog. Inside view close-up of Mariachi tapping on glass.

> VIEJO CLERK
> Callate, hombre!!!

Slow Motion Sequence?: Mariachi looks up at clerk, then stands.

The mean dude turns around and looks at the clerk. Clerk turns to look at Mean Dude, who is walking back to the counter.

Mariachi picks his guitar up from the ground. He is in full view, but no one is looking at him.

> MEAN DUDE #5
> Viejo, if you see anyone new in town, carrying
> a guitar case, dressed in black . . . you call this
> number, OK?

Mean Dude writes down a phone number and the description of Azul on a little card.

> VIEJO CLERK
> *(nodding sarcastically)* And if I don't call, you'll
> *kill* me . . .

> MEAN DUDE #5
(handing him the card) No. I won't kill you . . .
he will . . .

The sarcastic smile fades from the old man. Mean Dude walks away. The old man reads the card, then glances out the window. Mariachi is gone.

MARIACHI/MEAN DUDE #5 OUTSIDE HOTEL COAHUILA EXT DAY

Mariachi is turning a corner just as mean dude #5 exits the hotel. The mean dude walks off in the other direction.

This was supposed to be one of those cool, complex "just missed him" kind of sequences that was simplified on the day because of the availability of our cast to all be there at the same time. Also our hotel clerk only had an hour and a half to spend with us so we had to shoot him out very fast.

SCENE SIX ACT ONE BOYSTOWN SALOON DOMINGO'S EXT DAY

Mariachi enters Domino's bar. DOMINO is waiting on a few bar bums that are nursing their jaws. Mariachi sits with them, asks for a refresco. He gets looks again. Domino serves him and he asks to see the owner. She says he's looking at the owner. He then asks her for work as a mariachi. She says she has no money to pay him. He looks around the classy joint and knows she's lying. (It turns out to be true, she has no money.) When he asks how a girl can take care of herself in a town like this she stuffs a gun barrel in his mouth. He nurses his jaw, pays and leaves, as the others laugh.

We rewrote these scenes on location. I kept Domino's bar empty so that I wouldn't have to find extras to make the place look occupied.

SCENE SEVEN ACT ONE
<u>MARIACHI CHECKS IN TO HOTEL INT DAY</u>

Mariachi enters the run-down lobby of the motel. The viejo clerk at the counter is reading a yellowed newspaper. Mariachi sees the pit bull laying by the counter.

MARIACHI

Pit bull.

VIEJO CLERK

Yeah, pit bull.

MARIACHI

I need a cheap room for the week, and I'd prefer to pay you in a few days, after I've found some work.

VIEJO CLERK

Sí, later . . .

MARIACHI

Thank you.

The old man hands Mariachi a key for the second floor.

MARIACHI

Thank you, friend.

As Mariachi walks away, the clerk notices the guitar case and black clothes and he rereads the card Mean Dude left him.

VIEJO CLERK

(different tone of voice) Uh, excuse me señor? I forgot, I need a small deposit. . . .

Mariachi stops in his tracks. He turns back to clerk slowly . . . thinking.

MARIACHI
(walking back slowly) You can trust me.

VIEJO CLERK
I am very sorry, señor. But . . . how much can
you spare?

The dog is watching the event.

MARIACHI
(disappointed) I've only got a few pesos . . . I
plan on finding work in town. . . .

VIEJO CLERK
(grabbing money) Oh, that's enough for now,
sir, thank you and . . . enjoy your stay.

The clerk deposits the money, slams the register shut,
and continues reading his yellow paper. Confused, Mariachi pockets his empty wallet and turns to find his room.
The clerk peeks over his paper, eyeing the guitar case
as Mariachi goes. He hears the sound of Mariachi's footsteps trailing off. The old man drops the paper and bolts
silently to the phone as he dials El Moco's phone
number . . .

SCENE EIGHT ACT ONE
MARIACHI'S ROOM HOTEL INT DAY

Mariachi opens his room, tosses his guitar onto the bed
and hangs his jacket in the closet. He has only his white
T-shirt underneath. He glances above the bed to a
plaque bearing a mace and two crossed swords. He
checks out the shower and washes his face in the sink.
He sits down on his bed. A few seconds later he drops
back and lays there a minute before kicking the door
shut. He tries to sleep.

CLERK IN HOTEL COAHUILA LOBBY INT DAY

The old clerk is talking on the phone to the bad guys. He hangs up the phone, then reaches into the back of his counter for a gun. He places it on the counter and covers it with his newspaper and continues reading.

MARIACHI'S ROOM HOTEL INT DAY

Top shot of Mariachi sleeping. A shot of the mace on the wall.

CUT TO:

DREAM IN BOYSTOWN EXT DAY (5.7 KINOPIC LENS)

Mariachi is suddenly sleeping in the dirt. Same top shot as in the hotel. He opens his eyes, then groggily he sits up.

ESTABLISHING SHOT of Mariachi sitting in the middle of a ghost town. He stands up.

VARIOUS SHOTS of the empty town with nothing and nobody.

Medium shot dolly into Mariachi as he stands, turns and sees a boy bouncing a ball in slow motion. The boy stops short, holding the ball tight against his chest. Mariachi glances around to maybe spot more people, before concentrating on the boy.

The boy places the ball carefully on the ground, then gently rolls it to Mariachi.

Tracking shot of the ball rolling to Mariachi. The ball sounds like a speeding truck. Mariachi smiles at the boy.

CLOSE-UP of the ball rolling. CLOSE-UP of the boy smiling.

Mariachi bends to get the ball which makes the sound

of a screeching truck as it hits Mariachi's foot. Mariachi notices that it's a man's severed head.

MARIACHI'S ROOM HOTEL INT DAY

Mariachi bolts up in bed.

MEAN DUDES #5, 6, 7, 8, and 9 HOTEL COAHUILA EXT DAY

The Mean Dudes jump out of their truck and rush into the hotel, guns drawn. (Mean Dudes #5, 6, 7, 8 and 9.)

I kept track of who's who in the bad guys by giving them numbers. Since they'll never be called by name, there was no sense in me racking my brain trying to come up with cool bad guy names we'll never hear. So for script purposes they all had numbers. Which started a bad habit that I haven't been able to break. Too often now in my movies if you look at the end title sequence you realize no one has a real character name, just description names. Here are just a few examples from my other movies: In _Roadracers_ the bad guys are Crony#1 and #2. In _Desperado_ Cheech Marin plays Short Bartender and Quentin Tarantino plays Pick-Up Guy. Steve Buscemi has the most creative name in the movie: Buscemi. In _Four Rooms_ Antonio Banderas is MAN and his wife is named WIFE. Can't seem to shake that habit.

HOTEL COAHUILA LOBBY INT DAY

The men burst into the lobby and the old man tells them the room number. They run out into the courtyard with the old man following. The pit bull is uninterested in the action.

COURTYARD IN HOTEL COAHUILA EXT DAY

The Mean Dudes run up the courtyard stairs and kick open the first door they come to and start blasting into the room. Screams are heard. The men stand back, and finally look down the steps at the viejo clerk who is waving his arms frantically.

> VIEJO CLERK
> 127!! Cuarto 127, pendejos!!!

They turn to the room numbered 127 and cautiously stalk towards it as they reload their guns.

MARIACHI'S ROOM HOTEL INT DAY

Mariachi is sitting on his bed listening to all this. He bolts to the restroom and turns on the shower.

HOTEL COURTYARD EXT DAY

Shot of men still stalking, cocking pistols.
> POV shot of what men see, as camera nears the door.

MARIACHI'S ROOM HOTEL INT DAY

Mariachi rushes out of the bathroom towards the door.

Mariachi POV, as camera nears the door, doorknob starts to move. Remembering that he never locked the door, he jumps to the side of the door as . . .

HOTEL COURTYARD EXT DAY

Men kick open the door and burst into room.

MARIACHI'S ROOM HOTEL INT DAY

Low-angle shot as men burst in. There is no one in the room. Mean Dude #5 hears the shower and motions to the others to keep it down and stalk quietly. . . . They rush into the bathroom and start blasting.

Mariachi slips out from behind the door and runs out.

HOTEL COURTYARD EXT DAY

Mariachi runs out of room and jumps off the stairwell onto the courtyard in front of the clerk.

MARIACHI
(pointing to his room) Cuidado, viejo!

Mariachi darts out into the lobby. The old man watches him go then turns his attention back to Mariachi's room.

VIEJO CLERK
(pointing in Mariachi's direction) Pendejos!!!!

HOTEL COAHUILA LOBBY INT DAY

The dog watches as Mariachi tosses his keys into the cubby hole where they belong. Mariachi then jumps over the counter, banging keys on the register to get it to open.

COURTYARD COAHUILA EXT DAY

The mean dudes run out of Mariachi's room, dart down the stairs, passing the old man who is telling them where to go.

HOTEL COAHUILA LOBBY INT DAY

Mariachi, unable to open the register, jumps over the counter. CLOSE-UP of his feet as he lands, causing the register to burst open. *(also in closeup)* Mariachi turns for a second to ponder getting his money or risking dying, but then he checks to turn and run. Two seconds later the mean dudes run in, one jumping over the counter to see if he's there.

HOTEL COAHUILA EXT DAY

Mariachi runs atop the mean dudes' parked truck then jumps into the bed of a passing truck. (Used a long lens for this, also sped up top shot from mean dudes' car as he lands and car speeds away.) Mean Dudes run outside. The dudes have their hands up as if they don't know what to look for.

MEAN DUDE #5
He wears black!!!

Shot of lots of people walking around, wearing black items.

DOWN THE BLOCK EXT DAY

The truck turns a corner and the driver halts, comes out with a gun and tells Mariachi to get the hell out of his truck. Mariachi leaps out. He is about to continue running, but he stops, clenches his fists, and turns slowly as the camera dollies into his face.

MARIACHI'S HOTEL ROOM INT DAY

Camera dollies into the guitar case on Mariachi's bed.

DOWN THE BLOCK EXT DAY

Mariachi runs back in the direction of the hotel, but as he turns the corner he has to slow down for the mean dudes are everywhere. Each one has his gun out and is looking around for the man in black. Mariachi walks slowly, whistling and nodding to everyone as they pass. A few look suspiciously at him but continue searching. Mariachi ducks inside the hotel.

HOTEL COAHUILA LOBBY INT DAY

Mariachi enters the lobby and winks at the old clerk who is standing over his open register in shock. His eyes widen when he sees Mariachi. He runs outside the hotel.

VIEJO CLERK
(screaming, pointing inside) PENDEJOS!!!

MARIACHI'S HOTEL ROOM INT DAY

Mariachi rushes in, grabs his jacket and puts it on. He grabs his guitar case and squeezes it tight, his eyes shut. Slow dolly into him as his eyes open.

Close-up of plaque on wall with mace and swords. He grabs the mace, swinging it around a few times. He feels secure, now. He turns to leave.

COURTYARD COAHUILA EXT DAY

Mariachi rushes out the door, he looks down and sees the Mean Dudes entering the courtyard. He ducks his head back just as they look up to see him. Mariachi runs up a small flight of steps, where he then tosses his guitar onto a balcony, which he then jumps over to himself.

The men rush up the steps shooting at the balcony. Bullets narrowly miss Mariachi as he climbs over the balcony to safety.

HALLWAY HOTEL INT DAY

Mariachi dashes down the hallway out onto a balcony. He sees no way down.

COURTYARD BALCONY EXT DAY

The Mean Dudes are climbing over the balcony like spiders. Mariachi runs back and slams his guitar into the first guy to make it over the balcony. His dummy falls down the stairs and over the narrow railing. The dude splats on the ground in gruesome close-up.

The old man looks over at him as he dies, then he turns back as if nothing happened. Mariachi bolts back down the hill.

FRONT BALCONY HOTEL COAHUILA EXT DAY

Mariachi is looking down the balcony trying to find a way to escape. Mariachi looks behind him.

HALLWAY HOTEL INT DAY

Mean Dudes barrel down the hallway reloading their guns.

FRONT BALCONY HOTEL COAHUILA EXT DAY

Mariachi flings his mace over an electrical cable, then stands on the balcony lip, placing his guitar between his legs.

STREET SHOT OUTSIDE HOTEL EXT DAY

Mariachi is sliding down the cable as a blue school bus races down the street towards the camera. He has guitar between his legs.

Top shot of Mariachi racing down the line.

BUS TOP EXT DAY

Mariachi lands on bus and turns back to see mean dudes firing guns at him. Bus stops in traffic and Mariachi grabs his guitar and jumps onto the hood of the bus.

STREET EXT DAY

Mariachi jumps onto another car and then down into street.

Mean dudes exit hotel and chase him on foot while a few get in the truck and chase him. The truck takes a short cut.

Mariachi is running through the sidewalks and streets in front of curioso shops, jumping small carts and children and cars to escape the two men behind him. He enters a small cutoff where the truck tries to stop him by heading him off. The bad guys stick their heads and guns out of their windows and laugh as they ready to shoot him. Mariachi, though, already having built momentum runs right up the front of the truck as the guys try to shot him but succeed in only shooting each other as he runs up and over the cab, into the bed and onto the street. He swings his guitar case into another guy's groin and grabs his gun, reaiming it to shoot MEAN DUDE #5. Mariachi shoots him in the arm, and #5 drops his gun and cowers away in pain. Mariachi then turns the guy's gun on him and shoots him in the chest. Mariachi grabs his case and as #5 turns to get a look at him, all he sees is the case coming into his face. Mariachi heads back for Domino's.

The idea here was to make the movie look more expensive than regular straight-to-Spanish-video action movies by having these scenes where the actors run through the streets. We shot it on the fly out of the back of a truck but people in the business would think we closed off streets, hired security, paid for locations and extras and all that, but we just put up a sign that said if you walked through the block while filming you were giving us permission to use you in the film. Of course, we put the sign up in English so no one could read it.

SCENE ELEVEN   ACT ONE
BOYSTOWN SALOON DOMINO'S NEXT DAY
Mariachi stumbles through city streets, pausing against a telephone pole as he gazes at Domino's saloon across the street.
Mariachi stumbles across, almost getting hit by a few cars, and drags himself into the saloon.

AMADEUS INT DAY
Mariachi staggers into Amadeus and washes his face in a fountain by the door. He makes his way to the bar as a patron pays and leaves.

> DOMINO
> What happened to you, Mariachi? Too much refresco?

> MARIACHI
> I just killed four guys.

Domino turns around and looks at Mariachi, wondering hard if he's joking. He lifts up a bloody hand, grabs a napkin, and then seems to ask permission with his eyes before wiping his hands clean.

                         DOMINO
    Is it true?

Mariachi nods an ashamed yes.
Domino reaches for her gun under the counter.
The camera is on Mariachi when she brings it out and
points it at him.

                        MARIACHI
    (exhausted) Wait a minute . . . what's your
    name?

                         DOMINO
    Domino.

                        MARIACHI
    Wait a minute, Domino! It was self-defense . . .

She cocks the pistol.

                        MARIACHI
    (frantic) I'm new in town! I don't know every-
    one!! I have *no* friends here . . . and no ene-
    mies.

                         DOMINO
    (lowering the gun a bit) Thieves?

                        MARIACHI
    (nodding) No way. They were four *well-
    dressed* men. I checked into the cheapest hotel
    in town, no money, nothing of value, except
    this guitar and maybe this coat, which they
    could have taken when I left it in my room, but
    they didn't. They were only interested in *kill-
    ing me.*

                         DOMINO
    (lifting the gun back up) So why do you come
    here? You want to get *me* killed?

MARIACHI

I need a place to stay until I figure this out.
They've got me mixed up with someone else.

DOMINO

And you've never seen them before? Not even
in another town?

MARIACHI

(long pause) Are you saying they followed me,
a mariachi, here? What for?

DOMINO

Maybe they hate your music.

Mariachi stares at her expressionless. She stares back at
him.

DOMINO

Maybe you were singing in another town, they
hated your voice, and now they're trying to kill
you.

MARIACHI

Are you serious?

DOMINO

(nodding yes) No.

She laughs.

MARIACHI

Are you going to help me, or am I gonna have
to die on your porch?

DOMINO

I have a room upstairs. *My room.* Don't touch
anything. I'll be up after awhile and we can call
a friend of mine.

Mariachi shakes her hand.

MARIACHI
Thank you. I'll never forget this.

He tries to kiss her hand. She slides it away and effort-lessly slaps him.

DOMINO
This way.

He follows her to a doorway revealing an unlit staircase. When he enters, the darkness swallows him as she shuts the door behind him.

The dialogue referred to "well-dressed" bad guys. If you notice in the opening scene our bad guys were all in suits. After that our actors started showing up in T-shirts and jeans because that's all they had, and they were all we could find. The quality of our bad guys went down as the movie went on. By the end of the movie all we had were these little kids standing around Moco. It was because we had already killed off all the bigger guys in town.

SCENE TWELVE ACT ONE
UPSTAIRS DOMINO'S LOFT INT DAY

Mariachi enters a roomy, luxurious apartment above the main bar. There is a free-standing porcelain tub in the center of the room. Mariachi places his guitar halfway between the entrance and the tub. The camera is track-ing backwards with him as he walks, making the room look endless. He removes his jacket as he makes his way to the tub. He drops his jacket onto the floor and gently climbs into the tub. The camera faces him as he settles back. The camera slowly dollies into him as he lays back, crosses his fingers, and gives a relaxed smile.

SCENE THIRTEEN ACT ONE
AMADEUS INT DAY

Domino is washing a glass. She then remembers she has the gun in her waist belt so she removes it and sticks it back under the counter. Wounded Mean Dude #5 comes in limping. She takes out a towel and drops it on the counter.

> MEAN DUDE #5
>
> Good morning, Domino.

> DOMINO
>
> What happened?

> MEAN DUDE #5
>
> Give me the phone. I have to call Moco.

She brings up the phone and sets it down where the cloth was. He picks up the cloth and wraps his arm with it.

> MEAN DUDE
>
> It's not as bad as it looks. Domino, has anyone come through here? A stranger, maybe?

> DOMINO
>
> This is a border town. I get strangers all the time.

> MEAN DUDE
>
> Dressed all in black, carrying a guitar case?

> DOMINO
>
> No.

> MEAN DUDE
>
> Well, *he* shot me . . . and has killed ten of Moco's men . . . all in one day.

Domino looks a little upset. She slides the phone towards him a bit.

> DOMINO
>
> Aren't you gonna call your boss?

> MEAN DUDE
>
> *(nodding)* I have to tell Moco that he got away again . . . So, you better give me a drink first.

Domino smiles and pours him half a beer mug with tequila. He laughs and drinks. As he's dialing the camera
is on Domino as she cleans up a few things, every once
in a while glancing upstairs.

MEAN DUDE

Moco, he got away. Shot me in the arm. Killed
La Palma. Pepino, Suday. This guy is one slick
maricon. Yeah. Also, I didn't get a good look at
him. So, unless he's still carrying that guitar
around and hasn't changed clothes, I won't
even spot him, and I don't think he'll be that
obvious . . .

MOCO

Don't worry. If there's one thing I know, it's
that he'll always wear black and he'll always
carry that guitar with him. It's his signature.
Besides, that's not a guitar he's carrying. It's a
guitar case full of weapons. Find him.

Mean Dude hangs up and puts his head in his hands.

DOMINO

Que paso?

MEAN DUDE

I screwed up. This guy left his guitar case in
his hotel room. We chased him out, but he
came back for the case.

DOMINO

Maybe he loves his guitar. It's probably an antique.

MEAN DUDE

It wasn't a guitar. It was a guitar case full of
weapons that he uses on his victims. Adios,
I'm gonna take a nap. And thanks for the drink.

Mean Dude stumbles as he tries to stand.

> MEAN DUDE
> If you see this guy, call us.

He is about to walk off with the bloody towel and he turns back pointing at it. She waves her hand at him, as if granting him permission to take it. She cleans his glass, and when he is gone she slams the glass down and runs for the stairs. A few seconds later she comes back into the bar, grabs the gun from under the counter and calls her assistant to watch the bar. He sees the gun and wonders what she's up to. She storms upstairs.

Originally, this bad guy was supposed to be shot. But to keep up with that kind of continuity by keeping him bloody throughout the shoot was going to be a nightmare so we kept him normal.

SCENE FOURTEEN ACT ONE
DOMINO'S LOFT INT DAY

Domino opens the door abruptly and finds Mariachi taking a bath. He bolts upright, pulls a towel up from the floor and sits frozen waiting for Domino's next move. She laughs and walks to the counter.

> DOMINO
> *(friendly)* I thought I told you not to touch anything.

> MARIACHI
> Sorry. I needed to relax. I can . . .

> DOMINO
> *(smiling)* No, it's alright. Finish up. Do you want shampoo?

> MARIACHI
> *(laying back, closed eyes)* Yes, please.

Domino turns to a counter and her smile fades. She

looks like she wants to rip Mariachi's throat out with her teeth. She puts the gun down on the counter. She finds an ominous-looking knife and then grabs a bottle of shampoo. She walks over to him, hands him the shampoo, walks behind him, then pulls the knife up to his throat with one hand while grabbing his hair with the other. He opens his eyes wide. The shampoo hits the floor and begins to roll.

DOMINO
Who are you!

MARIACHI
(choking) I'm a musician!

The shampoo bottle rolls into the guitar case and stops. Domino sees this, and with her foot reaches out and pulls the case towards her.

DOMINO
What do you have in here? GUNS? KNIVES?

Mariachi tries to catch his breath, pausing before answering her as if wondering if all this is really happening.

MARIACHI
No! My guitar!

Domino slides her foot out of her shoe, and unsnaps one of the latches with her toes.

DOMINO
We'll see . . .

She unsnaps another. The latches snap loud and echo in the quiet room. Mariachi gasps as she tightens her grip.

DOMINO
You're very modest, Mariachi . . .

She squeezes his hair and unsnaps another latch.

> DOMINO
> *(through gritted teeth)* You told me you killed four men, when you really killed seven. Or were they still breathing even after you shot out their hearts?

Another latch snaps.

> MARIACHI
> *(growing dizzy)* I'm a mariachi . . .

SNAP!

> MARIACHI
> . . . not a murderer . . .

SNAP!

> DOMINO
> Aren't you going to watch?

She lifts the lid with her foot. It seems an eternity before the case is fully open. Domino is looking into the case, but Mariachi is not. He knows what's in there.

> MARIACHI
> I told you . . . I am a musician.

Slow dolly into the case, which contains a white, well-kept classical guitar. Domino is seeing it, and for a moment she almost believes he is telling the truth.
She rushes to it, grabs the guitar and tosses it to Mariachi. He catches it, choking after she releases the blade. She is on the other side of the tub, now. She jams the knife down between his legs. Mariachi's eyes bug.

> DOMINO
> Play it.

MARIACHI
(still choking) W . . . W . . . what?

Domino shoves the knife in deeper and Mariachi grimaces horribly.

DOMINO
Play it, dammit, play something sweet!!!

Mariachi is sweating and his face is extremely red. He pauses for a long time before plucking an odd note. She squints as if she's caught him. But he eventually starts picking out a sweet little melody.

DOMINO
(growing impatient) SING!!

Mariachi starts to sing but chokes on the words. He starts over, playing a "Rancho Grande" sounding song with his own made up words.

MARIACHI
(in a high sweet voice) What is this place? That treats me like a murderer? They've all got their heads up their butts . . . Even this beautiful girl, with a knife to my balls, should I kiss her or hit her . . . or both?

He finishes his song, bowing and thanking his imaginary audience. Domino is smiling. She pulls the knife slowly out of the water and wipes it off on her apron.

DOMINO
You're a mariachi, all right. And a good one.

Mariachi bows a solemn thank you.

MARIACHI
I think this is the best I've ever played. You . . . inspired me.

Close-up of the knife. She laughs.

> MARIACHI
> Hire me.

Domino looks at him with a silent 'what?'

> MARIACHI
> I'm good. Hire me to play in your bar. I'll work
> mostly from tips. But, I need steady work.

> DOMINO
> I couldn't pay you. I have no money.

> MARIACHI
> This fancy place and you have no money?

> DOMINO
> It's the truth.

> MARIACHI
> I'll work for room and board, then. Please, I'm
> desperate.

> DOMINO
> *(thinking)* Will I have to keep a knife at your
> balls to get you to play like that?

> MARIACHI
> *(smiling)* Not if you're paying me room and
> board. Please . . . until I find a permanent job.

> DOMINO
> *(thinking)* You won't find a permanent job in
> this town . . . but OK.

She gets up slowly, and turns to leave. Mariachi settles
back, smiling triumphantly. Suddenly she darts around
and slams the knife between his legs again with a furi-
ous look on her face. He bolts up out of his triumphant

daze with a look of complete shock. She loosens up and laughs.

DOMINO

You're going need a better sense of humor than that, if you're gonna work for me, kid.

She flings the knife aside. It sticks into a wall. She shrugs, smiles a beautiful smile, turns, and goes downstairs. Mariachi settles back down, closing his eyes. The knife slips out of the wall and clangs to the ground. Mariachi jumps again, rolls his eyes, and sinks underwater as the picture fades.

END OF ACT ONE

SCENE SEVENTEEN ACT TWO

Mariachi plays in Amadeus.

SCENE EIGHTEEN ACT TWO
AZUL'S HIDEOUT INT DAY

Camera tracks past a pool table where Azul's two rats are playing nine ball. They make a few shots, then the phone rings. The camera continues to track past a small table where Azul's guitar case lies open. Weapons adorn it, with each knife, each gun in its own pocket, in its own place. The camera continues tracking to a dresser on which sits Azul's cellular phone. A delicate female hand lifts the receiver. The camera is now positioned above the bed as the girl answers the phone.

GIRL ONE

Yes? One moment . . .

She rolls over and wakes a girl sleeping beside her. Girl #2 takes the phone and passes it to a third girl as girl #2 tries to wake Azul. *(he is sleeping between girls #2 and #3)*

#3 has the phone to her ear as if listening for background conversation.

The two rats playing pool are staring longingly at the three girls in Azul's bed. They look hungry and deprived. One hits the other, signaling it's his shot. While one shoots, the other watches.

Azul awakens and grabs the phone.

> AZUL
>
> Yeah.

MOCO'S RANCH EXT DAY

Moco is sitting in his pool. A swimming waiter is bringing him his drinks.

> MOCO
>
> Amigo!! I'm glad I've reached you! You've not answered all day. Killing ten of my men must have been very time consuming!

> AZUL
>
> Six.

> MOCO
>
> What?

> AZUL
>
> I've only killed six! You were always bad at math, Moco. I guess that's why you never paid me my half of the money. You thought it all belonged to you.

> MOCO
>
> I knew half was yours . . . I got greedy, my friend. It's my nature. But *you*!!! You are modest! You've killed *ten* of my men!! I know, be-

cause I'm having them buried in my yard right now. With my dogs and cats.

AZUL

(counting on his fingers) I killed six. But don't bother counting so soon. The number will triple by tomorrow.

MOCO

I'm sorry things turned out this way, my friend. I got greedy. I should never have tried to kill you. It would have been cheaper for me to pay you. Now I've got to find ten new men.

AZUL

Six.

MOCO

Ten.

AZUL

I tell you what. You give me my money, and I won't kill any more of your men . . . And I won't kill you.

MOCO

(takes a sip) No, it's too late for that. We're going to have to see this through.

AZUL

Just like the Moco I used to know. Still wearing white?

MOCO

(looking down at his clothes) What do you think?

AZUL

I think you should change clothes. I'd hate to ruin a white suit with your stupid blood.

Azul hangs up. He gets dressed and leaves. The little rats are about to follow, but one rat walks over to get one last look at the girls. The girls tease him, and when he tries to advance to them, they pull guns and laugh as the rat runs away.

The actor who played Azul said he'd only be in the movie if we let him have a scene with at least three girls in bed with him. I told him we weren't making that kind of movie, but that I'd write in three female bodyguards. He was happy.

SCENE NINETEEN ACT TWO
AMADEUS INT DAY

Domino walks by with a trash can. Mariachi is sitting on a barstool.

> MARIACHI
> I need to get my money back from that hotel. I'll be right back.

> DOMINO
> Are you crazy? If you go anywhere with that jacket and that case you could be killed. Leave that stuff here.

Mariachi gets up and is about to get his guitar case from under the stool.

Mariachi leaves it under the stool. And takes off the jacket.

> MARIACHI
> I never go anywhere without it. Take care of it.

Mariachi leaves. Domino drops the trash can and tells her assistant to watch the bar. She heads for the staircase.

This was a script screw-up I dealt with in the editing. Domino tells him not to go out dressed in black, yet she hasn't made the phone call yet that lets her in on the confusion of Mariachi with Azul. That's the next scene. So in editing

I simply cut out her line, and Mariachi seems to decide to take his jacket off and leave his case behind for no reason.

DOMINO'S LOFT INT DAY

Domino walks out onto her balcony, peering down into the street.
POV shot of Mariachi walking through the street.
Domino turns and walks to the phone. She dials a number by heart and sits in a plush chair.

MOCO'S RANCH EXT DAY

Moco answers the phone. Towel around his neck, wet hair.

DOMINO'S LOFT INT DAY

> DOMINO
> *(dolly in slow)* Hi. It's Domino.

> MOCO
> I know who it is . . .

Dolly into Moco.

SCENE TWENTY ACT TWO
HOTEL COAHUILA LOBBY INT DAY

The clerk is reading a paper. He hears a noise and pulls it aside. Mariachi is standing at the counter smiling. The clerk jumps in his seat, then after a few frozen seconds he sets down his paper and reaches for Mariachi's old room key.

Mariachi shakes his head 'no,' points to the register, and makes the money sign with his hand. The clerk slowly moves over to the register. He depresses a few keys to open it. It won't open. He makes a gesture like it's stuck or something (he is not very convincing). He tries again and again; each time pretending to get more impatient.

Mariachi glances down at the pit bull. The pit bull is eyeing Mariachi. Mariachi points to the clerk as if he has an inside joke with the dog ("this guy . . ."). Mariachi climbs over the counter and stands next to the clerk. The clerk thinks Mariachi is a lunatic. Mariachi holds up a finger as if cueing the clerk for a demonstration. Mariachi then leaps over the counter landing firmly back on the other side of the counter. (close-up of his feet landing hard, just as before) The register opens. Mariachi shrugs, smiles, and reaches into the register, taking his money out himself. He counts it. After a brief consideration, he decides to leave the old man a tip. Mariachi waves a 'good-bye' wave and dances out. The old man, still standing there with his arms outstretched as if he was robbed, dashes to the phone and calls Moco's men.

SCENE TWENTY-ONE ACT TWO
AMADEUS INT DAY

The bar assistant is cleaning the bar. He walks over to grab a few glasses and when he returns AZUL is sitting at the barstool Mariachi was on earlier. The assistant looks around, wondering where Azul appeared from.

> ASSISTANT
> Can I get you something to drink or eat?

> AZUL
> One beer.

The assistant grabs a mug and starts to fill it at the tap. The assistant fills it halfway when . . .

> AZUL
> In a bottle, wey.

> ASSISTANT
> *(laughs)* Sorry.

He grabs a bottle and hands it to Azul, then lifts the mug, toasts Azul and drinks it straight down.
Azul drinks his straight down, too.

> AZUL
> *(looking around)* Isn't there a girl that works here?

> ASSISTANT
> Yeah, she owns the place. She'll be back later.

> AZUL
> *(handing a few bills to assistant)* She *owns* it, now? Then she is Moco's girl?

> ASSISTANT
> *(looking around)* So-so. She's onto this new musician.

Azul takes out a few more bills and hands them to the assistant, and begins to stand up.

> AZUL
> Thank you.

SCENE TWENTY-TWO ACT TWO
STREET EXT DAY

Mariachi is out on the streets, returning to Domino's.

BOYSTOWN SALOON EXT DAY

As he crosses the street he notices Azul leaving the saloon with a guitar case. Mariachi runs into the saloon.

AMADEUS INT DAY

Mariachi runs inside and checks to see if his case is still there. Domino comes downstairs.

> MARIACHI
>
> I just saw a guy with a guitar case like mine.
> It's him they want.

> DOMINO
>
> *(to assistant)* Did he say anything?

> ASSISTANT
>
> *(nodding)* No, he just ordered a drink.

> MARIACHI
>
> I don't look anything like him . . .

There are a lot of low-budget movies that shoot without scripts. They kind of make up the story as they go. That's certainly one way to do it, but for me there's nothing that can compare to a well-laid plan. With scenes written out and ready to shoot, in a scene like this I was able to film all three characters on different days, without any of them in the same room together. Since I already knew what their lines and actions were I could cut them seamlessly together later in the editing room. Which made it a lot easier, or I'd have never been able to shoot the movie as quickly and cheaply as we did.

SCENE TWENTY-THREE ACT TWO
STREET EXT DAY

Azul is walking to his truck when he turns a corner and Mean Dude #4 sticks a gun in his face. Two more guns appear, pointed at the back of his head.

> MEAN DUDE #10
>
> Is this the guy?

> MEAN #5
>
> I'm not sure . . .

DOWN THE STREET EXT DAY

The two rats are in the blue truck half a block away. One hits the other to look at what's happening to Azul.
POV of rats seeing Azul with three guys around him with guns. They look at each other, start the truck and speed away.

STREET EXT DAY

> MEAN #5

What's in the case?

> AZUL

My guitar.

> MEAN #5

Yeah? You're one of those old-time mariachis huh?

> AZUL

(pause) Yes.

> MEAN #5

OK, let's take a look.

MEAN #4 takes the case and lays it flat in Azul's palms.

> MEAN #5

If it's a guitar like you say it is, we'll never bother you again . . .

Mean #4 unsnaps two of the latches, snap snap.

> MEAN #5

If it's not . . .

He unsnaps three more . . . SNAP . . . SNAP . . . SNAP!

> MEAN #5

. . . then we'll spray paint this street with your brains . . .

He points the gun deep into Azul's face and cocks it. Azul closes his eyes. Mean #5 lifts the lid. Azul hears a faint strumming sound, followed by the sound of Mean slamming the case shut. Azul opens his eyes. Mean re-

snaps the latches. SNAP . . . SNAP . . . SNAPSNAP-
SNAP!!!

> MEAN #5
>
> *(walking away)* Sorry . . .

They walk away leaving Azul wondering what happened.

SCENE TWENTY-FOUR ACT TWO
AMADEUS INT DAY

Domino, Mariachi, and assistant are standing at the bar.

> DOMINO
>
> Look, as long as you don't carry that case
> around, they'll leave you alone. It's that guy
> they're after.

> MARIACHI
>
> *(putting on his coat)* I better put this
> upstairs . . .

He grabs his case and begins to take it to the stairs, but
he pauses for it feels different to him. He slowly looks
down at it.

STREET EXT DAY

Azul watches the mean dudes go and when they turn
the corner he puts the case on the ground to open it.

AROUND THE CORNER EXT DAY

The mean dudes are rounding the corner, but #5, who
is last, snaps his fingers and motions to the others to
keep quiet and to watch Azul.

AMADEUS INT DAY

Mariachi shakes the case, and puts it on the counter as

if to open it . . . but he doesn't need to check it. He knows it's not his guitar.

                    DOMINO
  What's wrong?

Mariachi looks at her startled, then runs out of the bar with the case.

AROUND THE CORNER EXT DAY

Mean dudes are watching Azul unsnap his case.

STREET EXT DAY

Azul opens the lid, revealing Mariachi's guitar.

AROUND THE CORNER EXT DAY

                    MEAN DUDE #5
  That's him . . .

The mean dudes start walking towards Azul as the camera tracks back with them. Azul slams the case shut, wondering what the hell is going on. He looks up and notices the mean dudes walking towards him. He stands up and slowly walks in the other direction.

A BLOCK AWAY EXT DAY

Mariachi is running through the streets and onto the sidewalk.

STREET EXT DAY

The bad guys are pulling out their weapons.

Mariachi bolts around the corner. Now everyone is on the same sidewalk. Mariachi and Azul are on each end of the street with the mean dudes in between them.

Azul turns and sees Mariachi with his guitar. Mean Dude #5 turns and sees Mariachi, too.

                    MEAN DUDE #5
    That's him . . .

The two other mean dudes exchange glances. Mean Dude #5 stalks after Mariachi, so the other two follow. Mariachi looks to Azul for help. Azul tips the imaginary hat to Mariachi and walks away.

ANOTHER STREET EXT DAY

Mariachi runs through the street almost getting hit. Bullets are flying as the mean dudes are firing at him as they run.

DEAD END EXT DAY

Mariachi leaps over a few cars and ends up in a dead end. He turns around, drops the case on the ground and opens it. A million weapons seem to stare back at him when he opens it. He is frantic. He grabs a small gun, shakes it in his hand, doesn't like the feel so he tosses it back in.

STREET EXT DAY

The mean dudes are barreling down the street. One turns towards the dead end.

DEAD END EXT DAY

Mariachi pulls out the MAC-10 and blasts the first mean dude he sees. He grabs the case and runs out into the street, jumping onto a truck and blasting the other mean dude from up there. He sees #5 run away.
Mariachi comes off the truck and walks through the streets in slo mo. People are staring at him as if he were

Azul the killer. Mariachi walks straight to the bar. A boy is bouncing a ball on one of the sidewalks.

SCENE TWENTY-FIVE ACT TWO
AZUL'S HIDEOUT INT DAY

The camera dollies past the vacant pool table, and over to a rat sitting in a chair, drinking a beer. The other rat is pacing back and forth in front of the sitting rat. Azul enters the room. Throwing his guitar case onto the pool table as a grand entrance gesture. The sitting rat stands beside pacing rat.

> RAT #1
> I'm sorry we left . . .

> RAT #2
> . . . We didn't know what to do . . .

> RAT #1
> . . . We figured you could defend yourself!!!

Rat #2 nods in agreement. Azul unsnaps one of the latches. SNAP!

> AZUL
> You thought I could defend myself . . .

SNAP! SNAP!

> AZUL
> . . . against three *armed* men . . .

SNAP!

> AZUL
> . . . using *this*?

He opens the case and the guitar sparkles out at them. The rats exchange glances. They look at the guitar then back at Azul.

> AZUL
>
> My case got switched with some maricon mari-
> achi!

> RAT #1
>
> Where is this mariachi?

> AZUL
>
> He's dead by now . . . So, I want you to go look
> for my case.

The two rats are about to leave.

> AZUL
>
> Leave me a weapon.

Both rats take out their guns. Azul takes #2's gun.

> AZUL
>
> That was disloyal of you to leave me out there.
> You should be as loyal to me as you are to each
> other.

The rats exchange glances, then aim their eyes back to
the floor. Azul turns to #2.

> AZUL
>
> Are you loyal?

> RAT #2
>
> *(after glancing at #1)* Yes.

> AZUL
>
> *(to #1)* Are *you* loyal?

> RAT #1
>
> Yes.

Azul gestures to #2.

> AZUL
>
> Then shoot *him.*

Rat #1 turns to #2 who is in shock.

> AZUL
>
> You are loyal, are you not? SHOOT HIM. Or I shoot you.

Azul aims his gun at Rat #1, who immediately aims his gun at #2. Rat #2 is sweating bullets. Rat #1 puts his gun down.

> RAT #1
>
> I can't.

> AZUL
>
> Why not?

> RAT #1
>
> You said we should be as loyal to you as we are to each other. I couldn't shoot him, for that would be as disloyal as shooting you.

Rat #2 glances back and forth between #1 and Azul.

> AZUL
>
> Very good. Now go find my case.

Azul puts his gun down and motions the rats to leave. They leave. When they exit, Rat #1 turns to Rat #2 and snaps his fingers. Rat #2 shakes his hand. They leave.

SCENE TWENTY-SIX ACT TWO
DOMINO'S LOFT INT NIGHT

Domino is dabbing hydrogen peroxide onto a cotton swab. She applies it to Mariachi's body scars on his back. Mariachi has his eyes closed. He washes the blood from his face.

> MARIACHI
>
> Where were you when he came into the bar?

DOMINO

I was on the phone, talking to a friend that knows what's going on.

MARIACHI

Did you mention me?

DOMINO

No . . . He told me the man in black is Azul.

MARIACHI

If his name is Azul why doesn't he wear blue?

DOMINO

I don't know . . . Anyway, he's killing the men of the town drug dealer. The dealer's name is Mauricio. But he's known as Moco.

MARIACHI

And Moco is sending these men to find Azul. So, why do they chase me?

DOMINO

They have never seen Azul . . . only Moco knows him. My friend says the description Moco gave his men was that he wears black, and carries a guitar case. Sounds like you, no?

MARIACHI

Couldn't your friend tell Moco that there are two people like that in this town? One is a killer, and one is a mariachi.

DOMINO

Only special people can talk to Moco. Besides, you've killed a few of his men, now. Your best option is to keep out of sight, stop wearing black, and to hide that stupid case until this is all over.

SCENE TWENTY-SEVEN ACT TWO
MOCO RANCH EXT DAY

Mean Dude #5 comes in and approaches Moco.

> MEAN DUDE #5
> He got away . . . but I got a good look at him.

Moco takes out a cigarette and puts it in his mouth.

> MEAN DUDE #5
> Coca, Caca, and Beto were killed.

Moco takes out a match.

> MEAN DUDE #5
> He won't get away again, Moco. I promise . . .

Moco lights his match across Mean #5's face and lights his cigarette. Mean walks away, as Moco flicks his match at him in slo mo.

Here's where I was applying my three-time rule. Anything like Azul asking for the drink, or Mariachi jumping in a truck was repeated three times. The third time there would be a twist to the action. Azul finally gets his drink, Mariachi jumps in the wrong truck, and Moco gets the match lit on his own dead face. The kindergarten school of screenwriting.

SCENE TWENTY-EIGHT ACT TWO
DOMINO'S LOFT INT NIGHT

Mariachi is about to lay on floor. She tosses him a blanket.

> MARIACHI
> Are you always closed Monday nights, or did you close since I can't play my guitar tonight?

> DOMINO
> Mondays are my day off. Want to play a game?

> MARIACHI
> Sure.

The phone rings. Domino gets up to answer it. Mariachi

reaches under his blanket for a small mirror and combs his hair, putting spit in his hair to slick it down. He quickly stashes the mirror.

> DOMINO
>
> Hello?

> MOCO
>
> Come see me.

> DOMINO
>
> I can't.

> MOCO
>
> Please.

Moco is sitting at a table playing cards.

> DOMINO
>
> I don't feel well. I've got to go.

> MOCO
>
> Have you ridden the bike?

> DOMINO
>
> No . . . I've got to go . . .

She hangs up.

> MARIACHI
>
> Boyfriend.

> DOMINO
>
> *(quiet as if thinking)* No . . .

> MARIACHI
>
> I can't figure something out. You tell me you're poor. Poor family. Yet you've got this place.

> DOMINO
>
> *(sighing)* This place is a gift.

MARIACHI

From who?

DOMINO

From Mauricio.

MARIACHI

From El MOCO? The man trying to kill me?

DOMINO

He's *not* trying to kill you, his men had you confused with Azul.

MARIACHI

Same thing.

DOMINO

Look, you know how if you want to impress a girl, you send her flowers, candy, jewelry until you win her love?

MARIACHI

Yes.

DOMINO

If one present doesn't work, you keep sending bigger and better things until you win her or you're broke?

MARIACHI

Correct . . .

Well, Mauricio sent me flowers, then jewelry, then he gave me a job at his saloon, then he gave me the *whole* saloon . . . etc.

MARIACHI

He's still giving you things?

DOMINO

He'll never run out of money.

MARIACHI

And you accept it all? What's the last thing he
sent you?

Domino walks over to the counter and picks up a key.

DOMINO

A motorcycle.

Mariachi laughs.

DOMINO

He wants me to ride out to his ranch when I've
decided to be his. He thinks he's close to having me.

MARIACHI

Is he?

DOMINO

(pause) He was.

She sits next to Mariachi.

DOMINO

Not anymore.

They kiss. She gets up and is about to turn off the lights.

MARIACHI

So, you really are from a poor family?

Click!

DOMINO

(in the dark) I remember when I was growing
up, we were so poor, that my brothers and sisters and I all slept on the same blanket

stretched out across the floor. We had to sleep in a circle, with our fingers in each other's ears, to keep the bugs from crawling into them.

> MARIACHI
> *(after a pause)* Ay, wey . . .

Domino laughs . . .

This joke was conceived as a way to stretch the movie out a little in postproduction if the running time came in under ninety minutes. It would play over black because the lights were out so I wouldn't have to shoot additional footage, simply add black to the movie. Then I could record the actress telling this story or a longer one depending on how much time I needed to make the movie a sellable length. As it turned out, the movie was long enough and I didn't have to do it. But it was a good idea.

SCENE THIRTY ACT TWO
AMADEUS INT DAY

Domino hands Mariachi a wad of money.

Mariachi sees the money and looks up at her bewildered.

> DOMINO
> Here's a little bit I've saved. I want you to go get a new guitar.

Mariachi starts to put up his hand as if to refuse . . .

> DOMINO
> Take it, stupid. I'm not saying go by the best one, just a temporary one so you can play again tonight.

Mariachi stops and thinks . . . He looks up at her questioningly, then he shrugs an "OK" and grabs the money and jogs out excitedly. Domino is smiling.

SCENE THIRTY-ONE ACT TWO
MARIACHI ON STREET EXT DAY

Mariachi walks down the sidewalk, passing curioso shops. The camera is low and zoomed in all the way. Mariachi stops by one window that has a guitar in the glass. He pulls out his money and counts it. He stops after he notices someone's reflection in the window. He turns around and sees it is Mean Dude #5 right across the street. He puts his money away. Mean Dude #5 is crossing the street. He meets up with another mean dude. They are standing right behind Mariachi. Mariachi is pretending to still look at the window. The mean dudes walk past Mariachi so Mariachi walks in the opposite direction. Mean Dude #5 stops and then turns around slowly. Far zoomed shot of Mariachi walking down street with guys behind him. They start after him.

MEAN DUDE #5
That's him . . .

Tracking shot following Mariachi. Tracking shot in front of mean dudes walking at Mariachi. (wheelchair)

Mean dude #5 pulls out a small walkie-talkie and calls his buddy in the truck a block away.

MEAN DUDE #5
Loco, he's headed your way . . . black pants, white shirt.

IN A TRUCK DOWN THE STREET

Loco starts the truck and starts driving slowly across the street. As he turns on the corner, Mariachi sees the truck and casually climbs inside and hides in the back. Mean dude #5 turns the corner then whispers into walkie-talkie.

MEAN DUDE #5
Where did he go, Loco?

LOCO
(in truck) He got in my truck.

Mean dude laughs.

MEAN DUDE #5
Take him around the block.

Mean dude #5 taps his buddy and they start running down the block.

Mariachi is in back of truck searching for a weapon. The trucks stops. Mariachi rolls to the side and gently lifts his head.

POV Mariachi sees the two Mean Dudes walking at him. Mariachi turns and Loco is there to knock him in the face with the rifle butt. Mariachi falls into truck, blood trickling from his dizzying head. He tries to get up a bit but Loco is in the truck now, and slams the rifle down into his face hard . . . Blackout.

Again, here's another place to add a dream sequence made up of miscellaneous weird shots we would shoot on location to stretch out the movie. Since my script was forty-five pages I was constantly worried I'd end up with only half a movie.

SCENE THIRTY-TWO ACT THREE
DUSTY ROAD TO MOCO'S

Mariachi is unconscious in the back of Loco's truck. Mean Dude #5 and other mean dude are riding in back with Mariachi.

ROAD TO MOCO'S EXT DAY

The above scene intercuts back and forth with the arrival of Loco. Loco arrives at the gate, Mean #5 opens the gate, they drive through. The truck is facing Moco so he can't see Mariachi yet. Mean #5 closes the gate and walks over to the truck, opens the back door, and calls Moco over. Moco walks over to the truck and looks inside.

TRUCK EXT DAY

Mariachi is laying there unconscious. Moco puts his arm around Mean #5, who is looking very proud, and Moco pulls out a cigarette and a match.

> MOCO
>
> That's not him.

Moco strikes the match behind Mean dude's head. Mean dude stops smiling.

SCENE THIRTY-THREE ACT THREE
AMADEUS INT DAY

Domino is waiting on customers. She glances at her watch. A few seconds later she glances at it again. She looks very worried.

SCENE THIRTY-FOUR ACT THREE
AZUL'S HIDEOUT INT DAY

Azul's rats burst into the hideout. Four girls pop up over the partition with guns. The rats stop in their tracks. The girls sigh a "oh, it's them" sigh and slink back to bed. Top shot of them trying to wake Azul. Azul wakes up and looks over the partition.

> AZUL
>
> Where's my case?

> RAT #1
>
> We couldn't find it.

> RAT #2
>
> We heard they caught you and were taking you
> to Moco's ranch.

> RAT #1
> . . . so we came to see if it was true.

Azul thinks a moment. He stands up.

> AZUL
> They caught the mariachi.

Azul dresses, smiling . . .

SCENE THIRTY-FIVE ACT THREE
MOCO'S RANCH INT DAY

Mariachi is in a holding cell at the ranch. He twitches, finally waking up.

He sees a guard outside and finds a way to escape.

He grabs the guard's assault rifle and turns a corner. Two men grab him. He slams the butt of the rifle, knocking the wind and the teeth out of Bad Guy #1, then he kicks down and breaks the shin bone of Bad Guy #2 who screams out in agony. Mariachi silences him by karate punching his throat. The bad guy gurgles and hits the ground. Angle from the ground as Mariachi smashes the guy with his gun.

He crawls up a wall, trying to escape as quietly as he can. He sees two more men running towards him since they heard some noise. Mariachi aims his assault rifle at the blue Chevy parked behind them. He fires and it explodes. (develop later)

Mariachi jumps Loco, gets him to drive him to the saloon. He also takes Loco's money. (develop later)

This was an action scene we ended up not shooting. It was something we had a lot of ideas for and we needed a big action scene near the end since the final showdown with Azul and Moco was to be anticlimactic. But the people we borrowed our camera from needed it back sooner than we had expected, so we had to not shoot this. Instead, what happens is they dump the Mariachi in the street back in town after they realize they got the wrong guy. We were looking forward to it, especially the part where the Chevy blows up. A friend of Carlos's owned a junkyard and was donating a gutted Chevy to the movie that our special effects friend Falomir was going to blow up for us. That would have added some great production value that we could have included in our promo trailer.

SCENE THIRTY-SIX ACT THREE
<u>SALOON BOYSTOWN EXT DAY</u>

Azul walks into frame, looks around then proceeds into the bar.

<u>AMADEUS INT DAY</u>

Azul goes inside and finds Domino tending the bar.

DOMINO
What can I get you?

AZUL
One beer.

She grabs a bottle and slams it down on the counter unopened. He eyes her admirably and then pops the top with one hand.
He guzzles the drink, slamming it down empty.

DOMINO
Anything else?

AZUL
(nodding) My guitar case.

DOMINO
Where's Mariachi?

AZUL
Where's my case?

DOMINO
Upstairs.

                              AZUL
    Get it.

Domino grabs another beer for him and runs to get the
case.
(in between this time, Mariachi escapes with Loco)
She returns, slamming it to the floor.

                              AZUL
    If you want your mariachi back, come with me.

                            DOMINO
    Why will you help me?

                              AZUL
    Because you know where Moco's ranch is . . . I
    don't.

Domino calls her assistant.

                              AZUL
    You help me, I'll help you.

                            DOMINO
    Let's go.

They leave. The assistant tends to the bar.

SCENE THIRTY-SEVEN ACT THREE
<u>ROAD TO MOCO'S</u>

They drive out to Moco's ranch in Azul's truck. Little
do they know, they passed Loco's truck with Mariachi
crouched in the passenger seat. He gets up after the
truck passes. Mariachi didn't know it was Domino in
Azul's truck or he could have turned around and kept
her from going to Moco's ranch.

They arrive at the gate and get out of the truck.

DOMINO
(over the gate) Mauricio!!

Azul grabs Domino and puts a gun to her head. He whispers to her . . .

AZUL
Play along . . .

He kicks at the gate.

AZUL
Open the gate or she's dead!

The gate opens and we see Moco standing at a three-quarter stance, flanked with his men on both sides. Azul drags Domino in and faces her at Moco with a gun to her head.

MOCO
(to Domino) I'm sorry he used you to get to me, Domino.

Azul cocks the pistol.

MOCO
Azul, let her go and you'll get your money.

AZUL
Moco, give me my money or I ruin your clothes with *her* blood.

Moco signals his men to get the money.

DOMINO
What have you done with Mariachi?

MOCO
Who?

DOMINO
The musician your men confused with Azul.

MOCO

(staring at her) So that's why you were *busy* that night . . .

Azul is glancing between Domino and Azul.

MOCO

. . . you had that little monkey climbing all over you.

AZUL

Give me my money or I kill her NOW!!!

MOCO

After all I've done for you, this is how you treat me?

DOMINO

I never asked you for anything until now. Let Mariachi go.

Azul is anxious now.

AZUL

I swear I'll kill her!

MOCO

No you won't. I will.

Moco pulls out his gun and shoots her in the heart. She falls limp in Azul's arms. Azul tries to hold her up, but she's dead. Azul rests her on the ground, looking down at her, wondering why it's all come to this.

AZUL

All I wanted was my rightful share. But you've got to kill everybody.

MOCO

You feel sorry for her, don't you? See, that's why you can't ever be as big as me.

Azul slowly looks up at Moco.

> MOCO
>
> *(aiming gun)* Because you have too much heart.

Moco shoots Azul in the heart. Azul had his hands to his side, and now he falls to his knees. Moco shoots him again, and Azul dies next to Domino.

Mean Dude #5 is exchanging glances with the others. No one seems to be on Moco's side.

SCENE THIRTY-EIGHT ACT THREE
<u>NEAR SALOON EXT DAY</u>

Mariachi is still in Loco's truck.

> MARIACHI
>
> Stop here.

Loco stops the truck and Mariachi gets out. Loco drives back when Mariachi motions for him to leave. Mariachi watches him go then dashes around the corner to the saloon.

<u>AMADEUS INT DAY</u>

Mariachi runs into the bar . . .

> MARIACHI
>
> Domino!!! We're leaving!!!! Right now!!!

The assistant rushes over to Mariachi.

> ASSISTANT
>
> She's gone.

> MARIACHI
>
> Where is she?

> ASSISTANT
>
> Looking for you.

Mariachi is about to race upstairs.

> ASSISTANT
>
> She gave the case back to that guy. She left with him to find you.

Mariachi tries to make sense of it all for a minute before grabbing the gun from under the counter and rushing upstairs.

DOMINO'S LOFT INT DAY

Mariachi grabs the key to the motorcycle and runs out. The motorcycle burns down the road.

SCENE THIRTY-NINE ACT THREE
MARIACHI ON ROAD TO MOCO'S

Mariachi barrels down the road on the motorcycle.

MOCO'S RANCH EXT DAY

Moco is walking away from the bodies.

> MOCO
>
> Bring that musician out here so he can be re-united with my Domino.

Some men go to check. (cut back and forth with Mariachi coming)

> MEN
>
> He's gone, sir.

> MOCO
>
> Find him!!

Mariachi rides through the semi-open gate . . . stopping at the bodies. He dismounts the bike and holds Domino.

He has the gun in the back of his pants. You can see it while his back is to the camera and men are approaching him. Moco comes out for the show.

> MOCO
> *(good shot)* So you're the little Mariachi that came to town, killed my men, and stole my girl . . .

Mariachi slowly lifts his eyes to Moco.

> MOCO
> You are very talented.

Mariachi stands, his hands up.

> MOCO
> · I bet you play the guitarra real well, huh?

Mariachi says nothing.

> MOCO
> *(raising gun)* Not anymore.

Moco fires into Mariachi's left hand. Mariachi grimaces, crumbling to the floor. He keeps a tight grip on his hand. When he opens his hand to see the damage, the camera can see right through his hand for a reverse shot of his face through the hole.

> MOCO
> Now get the hell off my property and take your hand with you!!!

Moco is laughing and looking at his men for support, but no one else laughs. Mariachi tries to stand but he falls back. When he rises again he has the gun in his hand. He shoots Moco in the chest. Moco falls back and hits the ground hard. He gasps for air . . .

Moco's men gather around him. Mean Dude #5 crouches down to check Moco's throat pulse. Moco's dead. Mean Dude #5 strikes a match across Moco's face and lights up a cigarette. He turns and walks away. The others follow.

Mariachi wraps a tourniquet on his arm, kisses Domino, opens Azul's case, sees the weapons, and rides off with it.

SCENE FORTY ACT THREE

Mariachi on the road. He looks back at the town behind him, then places his hand on the motorcycle to drive off. We notice the metal brace on his hand.

Mariachi rides into the sunset road. He speeds off past a sign:
ACUÑA 18 MILES

Coming Soon
EL MARIACHI 2

The original version of EL Mariachi has the "Coming Soon" tag right as the movie fades out, because originally we intended to shoot a second part right away. While shooting, we switched the pit bull to play in the scenes with the girl, so at the end it made sense that we had Mariachi drive away with the motorcycle and the dog. We also added the turtle which Azul had found before shooting began. I knew I wanted some kind of voice-over here, to be written and recorded during postproduction, and in the final movie we have Mariachi's voice-over setting up the character for the next adventure, with the line "now, I'm prepared for the future."